The Minimum Means of Reprisal

The American Academy Studies in Global Security book series is edited at the American Academy of Arts and Sciences and published by The MIT Press. Please direct any inquiries about the series to:

American Academy of Arts and Sciences

136 Irving Street
Cambridge, MA 02138-1996
Telephone: (617) 576-5000
Fax: (617) 576-5050
email: ciss@amacad.org
Visit our website at www.amacad.org

The Minimum Means of Reprisal
China's Search for Security in the Nuclear Age

Jeffrey G. Lewis

American Academy of Arts and Sciences
Cambridge, Massachusetts

The MIT Press
Cambridge, Massachusetts
London, England

This book was set in ITC Galliard by Anne Read.
Printed and bound in the United States of America.

Library of Congress Cataloging-in-Publication Data

Lewis, Jeffrey G.
  The minimum means of reprisal: China's search for security in the nuclear age /
Jeffrey G. Lewis
    p. cm. — (American academy studies in global security)
  Includes bibliographical references and index.
  ISBN 978-0-262-12284-9 (hardcover : alk. paper) — ISBN 978-0-262-62202-8 (pbk. :
alk. paper)
    1. China—Military policy. 2. Strategic forces—China. 3. Nuclear weapons—China. 4.
Nuclear arms control—China I. Title.
UA835.L427 2007
355.02'170951—dc22
                            2006038615

The views expressed in this volume are those held by the author. They do not
necessarily represent the position of the Officers and Fellows of the American
Academy of Arts and Sciences.

Contents

Foreword

For more than two decades China has maintained nuclear forces that are smaller and more restrained than those of any of the five major nuclear powers. Based on an extensive review of available evidence, Jeffrey Lewis suggests that this minimal deterrent posture reflects an enduring strategic rationale that says, in essence: Nuclear weapons are only useful for deterring a nuclear attack, and sufficient deterrence can be achieved with a small number of weapons. The expansion of China's nuclear forces—a move predicted, as Lewis documents, by nearly all U.S. intelligence estimates since the 1980s—has yet to occur.

Lewis provides an overview of China's current nuclear force, including its size, delivery vehicles, deployment, command and control arrangements, and operational doctrine. He estimates that the number of nuclear weapons currently in China's arsenal is around eighty. (The current number of nuclear weapons in the U.S. arsenal is approximately 10,000.) China's forces are not launch-ready; warheads are stored separately from their delivery vehicles. The force is controlled by a highly centralized and unified command. Since its initial nuclear test in 1964, China has consistently declared that it would not initiate a nuclear war. Lewis traces the evolution of China's strategic thinking and force posture, and he finds that current choices about force modernization are rooted in an intellectual and organizational context that has continuously emphasized the sufficiency of a limited retaliatory capability.

China's nuclear policies have also been shaped by their international context. Lewis examines in detail the history of China's arms control positions as well as China's perspectives on proposed changes in U.S. capabilities as outlined in the 2001 *Nuclear Posture Review* and other documents. He attributes China's behavior in arms control negotiations to its confidence, on the one hand, in its small deterrent force, and to its concern, on the other, that its deterrent capability be preserved. Evidence of China's confidence can be found in its negotiation of and agreement to the Comprehensive Test Ban Treaty (CTBT). China's concern has been expressed in persistent advocacy for negotiations to prevent the weaponization of space. Lewis provides a comprehensive examination of China's efforts in the Conference on Disarmament in Geneva to advance new rules governing weapons deployments in space. The United States' refusal to enter into negotiations on space weapons and China's insistence on such negotiations have paralyzed the consensus-bound Conference on Disarmament for the past decade.

China's concern with outer space is understandable. As Lewis explains, advanced satellite communications, observation, and navigation enable the United States to bring decisive military force to bear almost anywhere on Earth with little or no warning. This rapid strike capability is a central element of the U.S. post-9/11 national security strategy. The United States has not achieved with any confidence the ability to wipe out China's deterrent force in a single preemptive strike. But, as Lewis documents, the U.S. aspiration to such a capability—evident in U.S. strategy statements, missile defense deployments, and military planning documents—is alarming to China.

As Lewis points out, the United States reaps considerable benefits from China's continuing embrace of a minimum means of reprisal as the principle behind its strategic posture. These benefits include greater crisis stability, lower proliferation incentives in Asia, and fewer constraints on U.S.-Russian force reductions. Whether China's nuclear posture remains stable will depend on Beijing's continuing confidence in its deterrent force. Lewis suggests that, "China is not likely to ignore indefinitely substantial U.S. preparations to conduct preventive interference against Chinese strategic forces." He notes that although a major buildup of strategic forces in China is possible, it is unlikely. More likely is the acquisition of asymmetric means of hampering U.S. preemptive capabilities. These means may include countermeasures to defeat U.S. missile defenses and, possibly, anti-satellite capabilities placing U.S. space assets at risk.

Yet, China has appeared to prefer an alternative future. For the tenth year running, in May 2006, China advanced proposals at the Conference on Disarmament for new legal instruments to prevent outer space from being weaponized. In October 2006, the United States released a new National Space Policy. The policy asserts that the United States will deny access to space to those "hostile to U.S. national interests" and "will oppose the development of new legal regimes or other restrictions that seek to prohibit or limit U.S. access to or use of space." To preserve the benefits conferred by China's current force posture, the United States would do well to heed Lewis's recommendations: China's confidence in its small deterrent force should not be undermined by the U.S. pursuit of preemptive dominance. The new U.S. space policy offers no reassurance on this score.

This book is part of the American Academy's "Reconsidering the Rules of Space" project. The project is examining the implications of U.S. policy in space from a variety of perspectives, and considering the international rules and principles needed for protecting a long-term balance of commercial, military, and scientific activities in space. The project has also produced a series of papers and monographs intended to help inform public discussion of legitimate uses of space, and induce a further examination of U.S. official plans and policies in space. The papers and monographs are available on the American Academy's website (www.amacad.org).

We join Jeffrey Lewis in thanking two anonymous reviewers for their comments on an earlier draft of this book. We also thank John Grennan, Jennifer Gray, Anne Read, and Kathy Garcia for their respective contributions to preparing the book for publication. The Rules of Space project is carried out under the auspices of the American Academy of Arts and Sciences and its Committee on International Security Studies. It is supported by a generous grant from the Carnegie Corporation of New York. We thank the Carnegie Corporation for its support and Patricia Nicholas for her assistance.

John Steinbruner	Carl Kaysen	Martin Malin
University of Maryland	*Massachusetts Institute of Technology*	*American Academy of Arts and Sciences*

Acknowledgments

This book is based on my doctoral dissertation, which celebrates at some length the many people to whom I am indebted for insight, encouragement, and kindness. I cannot better express my appreciation for those souls, so, as my affection and admiration remain unchanged, I simply refer readers to the original expression of gratitude to: John Steinbruner, I.M. "Mac" Destler, Steve Fetter, Tom Schelling, George Quester, Wade Boese, Kris Bergerson, Jeremy Bratt, Jonah Czerwinski, Jonathan Dean, Nancy Gallagher, Lisbeth Gronlund, Laura Grego, Adam Grissom, Theresa Hitchens, Mike Horowitz, Iain Johnston, Paul Kerr, Michael Krepon, Gregory Kulacki, Li Bin, Joseph Logan & Ronya Anna, Clay Moltz, Götz Neuneck, Stacy Okutani, Dan Pittman, Todd Sechser, Rob Sprinkle, Nina Tannewald, Chuck Thornton, David Wright, Logan Wright, Zhao Wuwen, Jennifer Ober, and my parents.

After completing my dissertation, I was fortunate to spend the better part of the 2004–2005 and 2005–2006 academic years continuing my research as a postdoctoral fellow with the Advanced Methods of Cooperative Security Program with the Center for International and Security Studies at Maryland (CISSM). I placed the final, sometimes agonizing, touches on the manuscript shortly after becoming Executive Director of the Project on Managing the Atom, at the Belfer Center for Science and International Affairs, John F. Kennedy School of Government, Harvard University.

Maryland and Harvard have provided wonderful academic settings for reflection. Both the Advanced Methods program and the Project on Managing the Atom are generously supported by the John D. and Catherine T. MacArthur Foundation.

In addition to the long list of people thanked in the dissertation, I must also thank the American Academy of Arts and Sciences, including the series editors: John Steinbruner, Carl Kaysen, and Martin Malin; Jennifer Gray; John Grennan; and two anonymous reviewers.

Although the suggestions of my colleagues have tremendously improved the manuscript from its initial form, even the most generous assistance, as I have enjoyed, cannot probe all the unexamined premises, correct all the infelicities of language, and mend all the errors. That responsibility lies with the author alone.

Figures and Tables

Acronyms

ABM – Antiballistic Missile

ASW – Anti-submarine Warfare

AWE – Atomic Weapons Establishment

BMD – Ballistic Missile Defense

BMDO – Ballistic Missile Defense Organization

BMDS – Ballistic Missile Defense System

C2 – Command and Control

C2I – Command, Control, and Intelligence

C4ISR – Command, Control, Communications, Computers, Intelligence,
    Surveillance, and Reconnaissance

CAV – Common Aero Vehicle

CCCPC – Central Committee of the Chinese Communist Party

CCP – Chinese Communist Party

CD – Conference on Disarmament

CIA – Central Intelligence Agency

CMC – Central Military Commission

CSC – Special Commission of the CCCPC

CTBT – Comprehensive Nuclear Test Ban Treaty

CWC – Chemical Weapons Convention

DARPA – Defense Advanced Research Projects Agency

DEFCON – Defense Condition

DF – Dong Feng

DIA – Defense Intelligence Agency

DoD – Department of Defense

DoE – Department of Energy

DSB – Defense Science Board

DSTC – Defense Science and Technology Commission

EHF – Extremely High Frequency

EIF – Entry-into-force

ESD – Environmental Sensing Device

FMCT – Fissile Material Cut-off Treaty

GBI – Ground Based Interceptors

GMD – Ground-based Midcourse Defense

GPALS – Global Protection Against Limited Strikes

HDBT – Hard and Deeply Buried Target

HEU – Highly Enriched Uranium

IADS – Integrated Air Defense System

IAEA – International Atomic Energy Agency

IAPCM – Institute of Applied Physics and Computational Mathematics

ICBM – Intercontinental Ballistic Missile

IFICS – In Flight Interceptor Communication System

INF – Intermediate-range Nuclear Forces

IOC – Initial Operating Capability

IRBM – Intermediate-range Ballistic Missile

ISC – International Seismological Centre

JL – Julang

LPAR – Large Phased Array Radar

LTBT – Limited Test Ban Treaty

MEO – Medium-Earth Orbits

MIRV – Multiple Independently Targetable Reentry Vehicle

MOU – Memorandum On Understanding

MRBM – Medium-range Ballistic Missile

MRV – Multiple Reentry Vehicle

MSX – Midcourse Space Experiment

NASIC – National Air and Space Intelligence Center

NIC – National Intelligence Council

NIE – National Intelligence Estimate

NMD – National Missile Defense

NPT – Nuclear Nonproliferation Treaty

NRDC – National Resource Defense Council

NTM – National Technical Means

ODA – Overseas Development Assistance

OSI – On-site Inspections

PAL – Permissive Action Link

PAROS – Preventing An Arms Race In Outer Space

PBV – Post-boost Vehicle

PDD – Presidential Decision Directive

PLA – People's Liberation Army

PNE – Peaceful Nuclear Explosion

PRC – People's Republic of China

QRA – Quick Reaction Alert Airplane

RV – Reentry Vehicle

SBIRS – Space-based Infra Red System

SDI – Strategic Defense Initiative

SLBM – Submarine-launched Ballistic Missile

SOI – Space Object Identification

SR – Space Radar

SRBM — Short-range Ballistic Missile

SSBN — Nuclear Ballistic Missile Submarine

SSM — Surface-to-surface Ballistic Missile

SSTL — Surrey Satellite Technology Ltd.

START — Strategic Arms Reduction Treaty

STSS — Space Tracking and Surveillance System

TMD — Theater Missile Defense

TSAT — Transformational Communication Satellite

UEWR — Upgraded Early Warning Radar

UNIDIR — United Nations Institute for Disarmament Research

WMD — Weapons of Mass Destruction

XSS — Experimental Spacecraft System

The Minimum Means of Reprisal

CHAPTER 1

The Minimum Means of Reprisal

My attitude was clear throughout. For more than a century, imperialists had frequently bullied, humiliated and oppressed China. To put an end to this situation, we had to develop sophisticated weapons such as the guided missile and the atomic bomb, so that we would have the minimum means of reprisal if attacked by the imperialist with nuclear weapons.

—Marshal Nie Rongzhen, *Memoirs*[1]

Among the five states authorized under the Nuclear Nonproliferation Treaty to possess nuclear weapons, China has the most restrained pattern of deployment: the People's Republic of China (PRC) deploys just eighty or so operational warheads exclusively for use with land-based ballistic missiles. China's declared nuclear doctrine rejects the initiation of nuclear war under any circumstances. The PRC does not maintain tactical nuclear forces of any kind, and its strategic forces are kept off alert, with warheads in storage.

The stability of this posture over time and through changes in threat perception suggests that restraint is the result of choice and not expediency. China has long had the economic and technical capacity to build larger forces. Chinese deployment patterns have clearly been subjected to review, alteration, and modification. The apparent implication of the sustained pattern of Chinese restraint is a distinctly different strategic assessment from that developed by Russia and the United States to justify and direct their larger and more actively deployed forces.

Overall, the agreement appears to have chosen nuclear deployment and arms control patterns that reflect the belief that deterrence is relatively

---

[1] Nie Rongzhen, *Inside the Red Star: The Memoirs of Marshal Nie Rongzhen*, trans. Zhong Rongyi (Beijing: New World Press, 1988), p. 702.

insensitive to changes in the size, configuration, and readiness of nuclear forces. As a result, Chinese policy has tended to sacrifice offensive capability in exchange for greater political control and lower economic costs.

This choice, evident in Chinese declaratory policy and consistent with China's deployment history, contradicts the typical strategic assessments of outside observers, especially those that have been most prominently advanced within the United States. These observers have often projected larger forces, the imminent deployment of tactical nuclear weapons (or other forces that would be more actively deployed), and the adoption of operational patterns that reflect commonly held U.S. deterrent conceptions.

The evident problem with Beijing's choice is that China's nuclear forces will be subjected to increasing pressure by the evolving capability and declaratory doctrine of U.S. strategic forces. As articulated in the *2001 Nuclear Posture Review*, the United States, in an effort to maximize the influence of its strategic forces, seeks credible options to undermine Chinese leaders' confidence that a small strategic force provides adequate deterrence against a U.S. attack.

If China were subjected to a level of preemptive threat that Beijing judged intolerable, Chinese leaders would likely reject, at least initially, the systematic emulation of U.S. deployment patterns. Although the inner deliberations of China's leadership are only barely perceptible, patterns in Chinese defense investments, strategic force deployments, and arms control behavior suggest China would consider asymmetric responses that targeted the vulnerable command, control, and intelligence (C2I) systems essential to preventive operations.

There is no evidence yet of a fundamental revision in the traditional deployment pattern of Chinese strategic forces. Instead, the Chinese response has been limited to diplomatic initiatives within the Conference on Disarmament (CD). China is less likely to fundamentally revise its nuclear weapons and arms control policies in response to changes in the objective balance of capabilities—prompted for example by the deployment of a missile defense system to intercept Chinese ballistic missiles—than as a result of Chinese internal politics and bureaucratic interests.

Yet, the *2001 Nuclear Posture Review* presents the United States with an opportunity cost. If Chinese leaders begin to lose confidence in their deterrent, there are many things Washington might do, in the interest of stability, to reassure China's leadership that its nuclear forces are sufficient for deterrence. The United States will not, of course, take these actions if a collapse in confidence among China's leaders is a policy goal.

In this book, I examine Chinese policy statements and diplomatic actions for two purposes:

- To test the plausibility of China's apparent strategic logic against the conflicting expectations of prevailing U.S. assessments
- To provide guidance for shaping both the specific U.S. security relationship with China and global security arrangements in general.

HOW MUCH IS 'ENOUGH' IN THEORY?

This difference between Chinese deployments and those of the other declared nuclear powers centers on the fundamental questions of nuclear sufficiency: How much is enough? What are the requirements for deterrence? How difficult is it to achieve and maintain deterrence? How important are technical details such as the size, configuration, and readiness of nuclear forces to the goal of maintaining deterrence?

"Enough" describes not just the number of warheads and delivery vehicles, but also their sophistication and operational readiness to conduct nuclear operations.[2] As a nuclear force becomes increasingly capable of conducting operations, it acquires the characteristics of a highly complex organization.[3] In general, investments in operational readiness are

---

[2] The capability to conduct active operations is not merely a function of the number of delivery vehicles and warheads, but also other forms of capability. For example, a National Academy of Sciences report notes, "In assessing the risks associated with nuclear arsenals, the operational and technical readiness of nuclear weapons for use is at least as important as the number of delivery vehicles or warheads." National Academy of Sciences, Committee on International Security and Arms Control, *The Future of U.S. Nuclear Weapons Policy* (Washington, DC: National Academy Press, 1997), p. 62.

[3] Two such characteristics are "interactive complexity" and "tight coupling." "Interactive complexity," Scott Sagan writes, "is a measure, not of a system's overall size or the number of subunits that exist in it, but rather of the way in which parts are connected and interact." Tightly coupled systems have two characteristics: "First, tightly coupled systems have more time dependent processes: planned and unplanned interactions occur quickly ... Second, in tightly coupled systems, the sequences and coordinated activities needed to produce the product are invariant: there is only one way to make the item and each step must be taken in sequence." Some nuclear weapons organizations, Sagan argues, are characterized by "interactive complexity" and "tight coupling" and, therefore, are prone to accident. Scott D. Sagan, *The Limits of*

undertaken because policymakers presume they will enhance the credibility of deterrence. Nuclear missions can range from the relatively simple mission of deterring a nuclear attack on one's own territory to more difficult operations such as protecting allies from attack (extended deterrence), providing superior capabilities at every conceivable level of conflict (escalation dominance), and war-fighting and termination. Even though bureaucratic or organizational imperatives pressing for increasingly capable forces may be decisive, these imperatives—as a policy matter—will usually be expressed in terms of enhancing deterrence.

Investing in the deterrent effect, beyond a minimum retaliatory capability, is subject to declining marginal returns. "Our twenty thousandth bomb," Robert Oppenheimer predicted, "will not in any deep strategic sense offset their two-thousandth."[4] Policymakers, as McGeorge Bundy would later note, are unlikely to "double-check the detailed consequences of an exchange, or to review how such a war might be fought." Leaders are likely to have "a healthy disrespect for such exercises," recognizing that the avoidance of a nuclear war is imperative.[5] Such arguments are typically made by those who emphasize the importance of custodial competence over readiness to conduct operations, but proponents of extensive preparations for the full spectrum of deterrent operations (including Herman Kahn and Keith Payne) have also observed the "healthy disrespect" for such calculations. During the Cold War, Payne and Colin Gray argued that the extreme caution introduced by nuclear weapons—the so-called Armageddon Syndrome—was a purely American phenomenon that undermined rational defense planning and was subject to technical remedies such as the deployment of confidence-inspiring ballistic missile defenses.[6]

Safety: Organizations, Accidents, and Nuclear Weapons (Princeton, NJ: Princeton University Press, 1995), p. 32–34.

[4] J. Robert Oppenheimer, "Atomic Weapons and American Policy," *Foreign Affairs*, vol. 31, no. 4 (July 1953), pp. 525–535.

[5] McGeorge Bundy, *Danger and Survival: Choices about the Bomb in the First Fifty Years* (New York: Random House, 1988), p. 461.

[6] One crude method of measuring the operational capability of a nuclear posture, beyond counting warheads or throw weight, is to estimate the number of casualties that a given posture might produce. U.S. nuclear war-fighting proponents, for reasons not entirely clear, seem to have fixated on the figure of twenty million U.S. persons killed to define "victory" in a nuclear conflict, i.e., they believed that U.S. deterrent threats would only be credible if American dead could be kept to that level or below. The corollary to this statement is that

In the process of increasing its ability to conduct a wide variety of nuclear missions, the state incurs certain costs, from the economic burden of large, alert forces to the dangers of an accidental or inadvertent war. In his careful study of nuclear accidents, false alarms, and other safety related concerns, Scott Sagan found compelling empirical evidence that "nuclear weapons may well have made *deliberate* war less likely, but, the complex and tightly coupled nuclear arsenal [the United States has] constructed has simultaneously made *accidental* war more likely."[7] At some theoretical point, the risk of accidental war—or the costs associated with more active deployments—will exceed the security benefit from the reduction in the danger of deliberate war. That is the point at which we have "enough"—more would be worse.

Figure 1-1: How Much Is Enough?

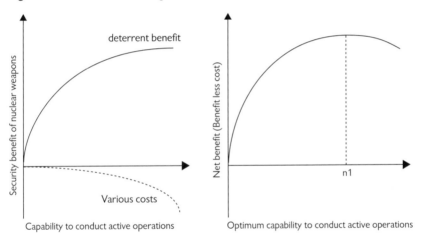

Moscow would have received little deterrent benefit from the ability to inflict substantially more than 20 million casualties. Put another way, proponents of nuclear war-fighting believed that Soviet postures capable of inflicting 50 or 100 million casualties would have been equally successful at deterring the United States.

[7] Sagan, *The Limits of Safety: Organizations, Accidents, and Nuclear Weapons*, p. 264. Emphasis in original. See also John D. Steinbruner, *The Cybernetic Theory of Decision: New Dimensions of Political Analysis* (Princeton, NJ: Princeton University Press, 1974); Kurt Gottfried et al., *Crisis Stability and Nuclear War* (Ithaca, NY: Cornell University Press, January 1987); and Bruce G. Blair, *The Logic of Accidental Nuclear War* (Washington, DC: Brookings Institution, 1993).

Figure 1-1 expresses this trade-off. In the graph on the left, the solid line represents the security benefit from increasingly capable forces, subject to diminishing returns. The dotted line represents various costs such as the inadvertent risk of war, economic burdens, and possible costs to the state's image. The net benefit to security comprises the sum of these two curves, shown by the graph on the right. Once the security benefit levels off, even small costs bend the curve downward. The apex of the curve, or "enough," represents the optimum capability to conduct active operations.

Of course, we do not know the shape of these curves or the current position of any nuclear weapon state. We can, however, say something about the rationales that determine whether an analyst will believe a country should alter the mix of factors that determine its overall risk.

Policy debates about nuclear weapons typically turn on the slope of the curve representing danger from deliberate attack, with judgments about costs playing a subordinate role.[8] The idea of "enough," expressed as the need to meet deterrent requirements at the minimum level of capability, is captured by a 1983 NATO Nuclear Planning Group decision declaring that the "policy of the Alliance is to preserve the peace through the maintenance of forces at the lowest level capable of deterring the Warsaw Pact threat."[9]

Those who favor using nuclear forces for a wide variety of missions typically express concern that deterrence will be very difficult to maintain and will depend very much on the details of the technical balance. Influential early expressions of this argument emphasized uncertainty about future technological developments that might open the theoretical possibility of dramatic changes in the deterrent balance—possibilities that created a "delicate balance of terror."[10] More recent expressions of the idea, couched in

---

[8] If one believes that deterrence is very difficult, it is not surprising that an analyst would believe the risk of accident is comparatively low. Nina Tannenwald notes this kind of cognitive consistency in nuclear war planning for North Korea, where opinions about the objective utility of using nuclear weapons in North Korea (expressed as a statement about the presence of suitable targets for nuclear weapons in North Korea and the PRC) was usually consistent with an analyst's moral or political judgments. Nina Tannenwald, "The Nuclear Taboo: The United States and the Normative Basis of Nuclear Non-Use," *International Organization,* vol. 53, no. 3 (Summer 1999), pp. 446–448.

[9] "The Montebello Decision on Reductions of Nuclear Forces Announced by the Nuclear Planning Group in Ministerial Session," Montebello, Canada, October 27, 1983.

[10] Albert Wohlstetter, *The Delicate Balance of Terror,* P-1472 (Santa Monica, CA: RAND, 1958).

the language of capabilities-based planning, focus on uncertainty regarding future threats rather than technological change.[11] In both cases, deterrence is elusive and presumably requires increasingly capable forces.

Skeptics of preparing for multiple kinds of nuclear operations, in contrast, have emphasized the destructiveness of nuclear weapons to suggest that the risks of even modest retaliation overwhelm any potential gains from the use of nuclear weapons in any plausible scenario. Deterrence is achieved with the very first deployments of nuclear weapons, with sharply declining marginal benefits from adding complexity to the arsenal after initial deployments. Reflecting on the Cuban Missile Crisis, for example, six of President John F. Kennedy's advisors wrote:

> American nuclear superiority was not in our view a critical factor [during the Cuban Missile Crisis], for the fundamental and controlling reason that nuclear war, already in 1962, would have been an unexampled catastrophe for both sides; the balance of terror so eloquently described by Winston Churchill seven years earlier was in full operation. No one of us ever reviewed the nuclear balance for comfort in those hard weeks.[12]

As Bundy would later explain, the critical factor compelling both sides to a political solution was "a parity of mortal danger that is not sensitive to this or that specific difference in numbers of warheads or megatons."[13] Looking back at the Cuban Missile Crisis, former Secretary of Defense Robert McNamara concluded that "In 1962 it would have made no difference in our behavior whether the ratio had been seventeen to one, five to one, or two to one in our favor—or even two to one against us."[14]

The difference between these two schools of thought on deterrence can be characterized as a statement about the sensitivity of the deterrent effect to changes in the size, configuration, and readiness of nuclear forces. If increasing the capability of strategic forces has a large effect on reducing the danger of deliberate attack, then a state will prefer larger, more diverse forces kept on higher rates of alert and will eschew arms

---

[11] Keith Payne, *Strategic Force Requirements and the Nuclear Posture Review's New Triad* (Arlington, VA: National Institute for Public Policy, 2003).

[12] Dean Rusk, Robert McNamara, George Ball, Roswell Gilpatric, Theodore Sorenson, and McGeorge Bundy, "The Lessons of the Cuban Missile Crisis," *Time,* September 27, 1982.

[13] Bundy, *Danger and Survival,* p. 606.

[14] Robert S. McNamara, *Blundering into Disaster: The First Century of the Nuclear Age* (New York: Pantheon Books, 1986), p. 45.

control (unless political costs compel it to do otherwise). Conversely, if larger or more capable forces add more risk of inadvertent forms of nuclear danger, such as an accident, then some form of restraint, formal or otherwise, will be preferable.

Fundamentally different assessments of the relative nuclear danger from deliberate and inadvertent routes to war produce fundamentally different views about nuclear weapons and arms control policies. Compare two contemporary statements from the National Academy of Sciences and the Defense Science Board concerning proposals for de-alerting U.S. nuclear forces:

> During the Cold War, reducing the risk of a surprise attack appeared to be more important than the risks generated by maintaining nuclear forces in a continuous state of alert. With the end of that era, the opposite view is now more credible [to the National Academy of Sciences]. This has important implications for U.S. nuclear policy and calls for dramatically reduced alert levels.[15]

> The [Defense Science Board] Task Force found the current set of arguments for further de-alerting difficult to understand. The arguments stress potential weakness in the Russian command and control system as a source of danger of unauthorized or accidental use…. The central issue must be stability. This was the central issue guiding START II goals and the principal driver of the outcome. Hence, to do violence to the stability of the force over a perceived danger not addressed by de-alerting US systems seems unwise in the extreme.[16]

The tension between secure deterrence and accidental war prevention has been noted by several analysts. The trade-off—whether we describe it as a "usability" paradox in Scott Sagan's phrase or the "always/never dilemma" as Peter Stein and Peter Feaver did—is a fundamental tension in nuclear weapons policy: the ability to use nuclear weapons whenever necessary works at cross purposes with the desire never to use them accidentally.[17]

---

[15] National Academy of Sciences, *The Future of U.S. Nuclear Weapons Policy*, p. 6.

[16] Report of the Defense Science Board Task Force on Nuclear Deterrence (Washington, DC: Defense Science Board, 1998), p. 15.

[17] Scott D. Sagan, *Moving Targets: Nuclear Strategy and National Security*, (Princeton, NJ: Princeton University Press, 1989), pp. 176–186, and Peter

Choices about balancing these risks will depend, in part, on beliefs about how other states view the importance of relative force levels. Extensive preparations for deterrent operations have been justified, in the United States, on the grounds that the Soviet Union was said to be undertaking similar preparations. These preparations allegedly revealed a high Soviet tolerance for nuclear danger and keen sensitivity to the balance of forces. In a crisis, U.S. inattention to the technical balance might have created a situation that could have led the Soviets to attempt a limited strike, either to signal resolve or to create a more favorable balance of forces. The latter case, the so-called window of vulnerability scenario, in particular, depended on Soviet perceptions of nuclear superiority. Where American participants in the Cuban Missile Crisis emphasized the irrelevance of nuclear superiority, Paul Nitze suggested the Soviets drew a different lesson:

> Harking back to the Soviet penchant for actually visualizing what would happen in the event of nuclear war, it seems highly likely that the Soviet leaders, in those hectic October days in 1962, did something that U.S. leaders, as I know from my participation, did only in more general terms—that is, ask their military just how a nuclear exchange would come out. They must have been told that the United States would be able to achieve what they construed as victory, that the U.S. nuclear posture was such as to be able to destroy a major portion of Soviet striking power and still itself survive in a greatly superior condition for further strikes if needed. And they must have concluded that such a capability provided a unique and vital tool for pressure in a confrontation situation. It was a reading markedly different from the American internal one, which laid much less stress on American nuclear superiority....[18]

Archival evidence suggests that the Soviet leaders drew much more circumspect conclusions than Nitze imagines, but the logic of his argument is clear: "Ultimately the quality of that deterrence depends importantly on the character and strength of the US nuclear posture versus that

---

Stein and Peter Feaver, *Assuring Control of Nuclear Weapons: The Evolution of Permissive Action Links*, CSIA Occasional Paper no. 2 (Cambridge, MA: Center for Science and International Affairs, Harvard University, 1987).

[18] Paul H. Nitze, "Assuring Strategic Stability in an Era of Détente," *Foreign Affairs*, vol. 54, no. 2 (January 1976), p. 216.

of the Soviet Union."[19] The idea that one's own beliefs about the sensitivity of deterrence might be dangerous could be taken to an extreme—some proponents suggested suppressing research into the climactic effects of a nuclear exchange because of the danger that might result from an asymmetry in beliefs about the environmental consequences of nuclear war.[20] If other countries, however, are easily deterred, then a very different set of policies is appropriate. One's own preparations will be wasteful and may incur an unnecessary risk of inadvertent nuclear danger. Moreover, such preparations might lead other states to doubt the credibility of their deterrent with respect to one's own forces.

Alleged Soviet preparations to fight and win a nuclear war were sometimes invoked to justify similar preparations on the part of the United States. For example, Nitze argued that even if Soviet leaders abhorred the prospect of nuclear war, they would "consider themselves duty bound by Soviet doctrine to exploit fully that strategic advantage [conferred by preparations for fighting and winning a nuclear war] through political or limited military means."[21] Of course, U.S. preparations would provide the same dilemma for the Soviet Union or other parties.

FACTS AND IMPLICATIONS OF THE CHINESE CASE

The attitudes of Chinese policymakers toward nuclear weapons and arms control are not directly available for examination, nor would one expect to find a monolithic set of beliefs among a variety of political, scientific, and military elites. However, some conclusions about the inherent biases within the Chinese planning system may be inferred from the historic and current deployment of China's strategic forces, as well as Chinese behavior in arms control negotiations.

Figure 1-2 suggests that relative to other states, Chinese deployments are consistent with the belief that the security benefit from nuclear weapons increases much more quickly after a state acquires a small nuclear capability, and that additional capability confers little benefit.

---

[19] Nitze, p. 223. On Soviet views of the Cuban Missile Crisis, see Aleksandr Fursenko and Timothy J. Naftali, *One Hell of a Gamble: Khrushchev, Castro, and Kennedy, 1958–1964* (New York: W.W. Norton & Company, 1998).

[20] *Nuclear Winter: Uncertainties Surround the Long-term Effects of Nuclear War* GAO/NSIAD-86-92 (Washington, DC: Government Accounting Office, March 1986), pp. 30–35.

[21] Nitze, p. 223.

This view is roughly comparable to the skepticism expressed by U.S. participants in the Cuban Missile Crisis regarding nuclear superiority. In fact, a very similar formulation to the one offered by President Kennedy's six advisors is found in a text used to train Chinese Communist Party cadres at the Chinese National Defense University:

> Though the United States was superior to the Soviet Union in nuclear weapons at that time, if a nuclear war broke out, no country could avoid the destiny of destruction. There is sharp conflict between the super destructive power of the means of war and the thinking of the war launcher who wants to get his interest on one hand, but fears destruction on the other.[22]

Figure 1-2: Comparative View of the Security Benefit of Nuclear Weapons

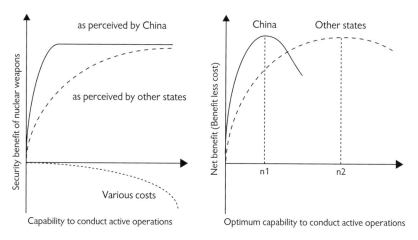

Chinese force deployments and arms control behavior both suggest that the Chinese leadership has decisively chosen a small nuclear force based on the principle that a more capable arsenal would not substantially enhance deterrence. In other words, "enough" is, in the phrase of Marshal Nie Rongzhen, "the minimum means of reprisal."[23] In a 2000 interview with a newspaper reporter, the PRC's then-Ambassador for Disarmament Affairs Sha Zukang articulated confidence in the PRC's nuclear deterrent in terms that Bundy and McNamara would immediately recog-

---

[22] *Strategic Studies* (Zhanlue xue) (Beijing: Academy of Military Sciences, 2000) ch. 20, p. 7.

[23] Nie, *Inside the Red Star*, p. 702. See also Nie Rongzhen, "How China Develops Its Nuclear Weapons," *Beijing Review*, 17 (April 29, 1985), pp. 15–18.

nize. Sha argued that even a very small, unsophisticated force maintained a measure of deterrence against larger, more sophisticated nuclear forces:

> I must emphasize that "strategic balance" and "strategic parity" are two different concepts. [A] nuclear weapon is [a] kind of special weapon. Due to its gigantic destructive force, to achieve strategic balance among nuclear countries [China] does not need to posses the same amount of nuclear weapons. As far as the medium and small nuclear countries are concerned, after being hit by the first nuclear strike, as long as they still possess the capability of launching the second nuclear strike to inflict unbearable losses to the attacking side, they can still reach a certain kind of strategic balance with major nuclear countries which possess quantitative and qualitative superiority of nuclear weapons. [sic][24]

Much as Bundy and McNamara, facing the prospect of nuclear war over Cuba, concluded that even small, unsophisticated nuclear arsenals achieved a large measure of deterrence, recent historical scholarship suggests Chinese leaders drew similar conclusions after facing nuclear threats during the Korean War.

Historical scholarship is, of course, only suggestive. In the succeeding chapters, I will attempt to document the effect of this view of deterrence on various decisions related to Chinese force deployments and arms control policies. Here I note only two anecdotes.

In his study of the formation of Chinese attitudes about nuclear weapons during the Korean War, Mark Ryan concludes the first generation of Chinese Communist leaders formed highly accurate assessments about the physical limitations of nuclear weapons and the political constraints on the U.S. use of nuclear weapons.[25] Despite caricatures of Chinese attitudes toward nuclear weapons during the Korean War as ignorant or facile, Ryan finds Chinese assessments from the period are consistent with those found in declassified U.S. documents from the same time. Ryan notes that one particular Western text translated for the

---

[24] Interview with Sha Zukang, director-general of the Department of Arms Control and Disarmament of Ministry of Foreign Affairs, in Tseng Shu-wan, "U.S. Nuclear Proliferation Threatens Global Security—Sha Zukang on Ways China Should Handle It, Stressing Needs to Ensure the Effectiveness of Retaliatory Capacity," *Wen Wei Po* (June 11, 2000), FBIS-CPP-2000-0711-000024.

[25] Mark A. Ryan, *Chinese Attitudes toward Nuclear Weapons: China and the United States during the Korean War* (New York: ME Sharpe, 1989), p. 179.

Chinese leadership—P.M.S. Blackett's *Military and Political Consequences of Atomic Energy*—was particularly influential in the formation of
Chinese attitudes toward U.S. nuclear threats.[26] Interestingly, Blackett's
"optimism on the stability of the balance of terror" that influenced the
Chinese is criticized by Albert Wohlstetter in *The Delicate Balance of Terror* on the grounds that a technological innovation—the introduction of
ballistic missiles—threatened to undermine the stability of the deterrent
balance.[27] Whether Blackett or Wohlstetter better assessed the impact of
the ballistic missiles and other technical developments of the period in
question is less important than the direct way in which Chinese attitudes
map to the model in the preceding section and provide a candidate
rationale for arms limitations.

Ryan concludes that by the end of the Korean War, Chinese leaders
had developed a "genuine self-confidence derived from the successful
endurance of risk and from the experience gained in implementing defensive measures against nuclear attack during the war."[28] This confidence in
the robust character of the deterrent balance continues to determine Chinese force deployments through the current period; the next chapter suggests that this confidence remains in evidence based on U.S. intelligence
assessments.

The integrated realism suggested by Ryan is evident in a remarkable
assessment produced by four senior Chinese military officials (including
Marshal Nie Rongzhen) during the 1969 fighting between China and
the Soviet Union over the Zhenbao (Damansky) Islands. Although Mao
had told a visiting dignitary that China "in a sense, is still a non-nuclear
power," Nie and his colleagues expressed confidence in the deterrent
quality of China's small force:

> Will the U.S. imperialists and the Soviet revisionists launch a
> surprise nuclear attack on us? We must be fully prepared for this.
> However, it is not an easy matter to use a nuclear weapon.
> When a country uses nuclear weapons to threaten another
> country, it places itself under the threat of [the] other country's

---

[26] P.M.S Blackett, *Military and Political Consequences of Atomic Energy* (London:
Turnstile Press, 1948).

[27] "It is now widely known that intercontinental ballistic missiles will have hydrogen warheads, and this fact, a secret at the time, invalidates Mr. Blackett's calculations and, I might say, much of his optimism on the stability of the balance
of terror." Wohlstetter, *The Delicate Balance of Terror*, np.

[28] Ryan, p. 10.

nuclear weapons, and will thus inevitably face the strong opposition of its own people. Even the use of nuclear weapons cannot conquer an unbending people.[29]

This statement is a remarkable expression of confidence in the deterrent effect of an extremely small arsenal—China had tested its first warhead deliverable by a missile less than two years before Mao's statement and could not have produced more than a handful of warheads and gravity bombs.

Given Chinese confidence in the insensitivity of deterrence, one would expect the Chinese leadership to be sensitive to costs associated with larger, more capable forces. Chinese leaders probably also considered the maximization of political control over national nuclear forces to be a goal equal in importance to the minimization of economic burdens. This is evident in the complex relationship between the Chinese Communist Party and the People's Liberation Army—captured in the oft-quoted Maoist aphorism: "Our principle is that the Party commands the gun, and the gun must never be allowed to command the Party."[30] To this day, Chinese leaders emphasize the need to maintain control over nuclear weapons.[31]

---

[29] Mao made his remark to Australian Communist Party leader E. F. Hill in November 1968. The passage quoted at length is from Chen Yi, Ye Jianying, Xu Xiangqian, and Nie Rongzhen, "Report to the Central Committee: A Preliminary Evaluation of the War Situation ," July 11, 1969. Both documents are translated in Chen Jian and David L. Wilson, "All under the Heaven is Great Chaos: Beijing, the Sino-Soviet Border Clashes, and the Turn toward Sino-American Rapprochement, 1968–69," *Cold War International History Project Bulletin,* vol. 11 (1996), pp. 159, 167.

[30] The literature related to civil-military relations in China is vast. Excellent introductions can be found in chapter two of David Shambaugh, *Modernizing China's Military: Progress, Problems, and Prospects* (Berkeley: University of California Press, 2003) and the conference papers published in James C. Mulvenon and Andrew N.D. Yang (eds.), *Seeking Truth from Facts: A Retrospective on Chinese Military Studies in the Post-Mao Era* (Washington, DC: RAND, 1999). The aphorism from Mao is taken from "Problems of War and Strategy (1938)" in *Selected Military Writings of Mao Tse-tung* (Beijing: Foreign Language Press, 1967), p. 274.

[31] During a March 2002 inspection of China's strategic rocket forces—known as the Second Artillery (*di er pao*)—China's paramount leader, Jiang Zemin, reportedly said the "special nature" of the Second Artillery's mission "requires that the Second Artillery unit politically must be absolutely reliable" and added that the political reliability of the Second Artillery unit ought to exceed that of other units. See "Forging the Republic's Shield of Peace," *People's Daily*, March 21, 2002, FBIS-CPP-2002-0321-000103. Zhang Wannian, vice chairman of

There is no evidence that China has ever placed its strategic forces on alert. The 1969 border clashes with the Soviet Union are widely regarded as the most serious foreign policy crisis during China's period as a nuclear power.[32] Although Soviet aircraft practiced bombing runs in preparation for a strike on Chinese nuclear facilities, the Chinese leadership did not order the Second Artillery to prepare for nuclear use. During a talk to senior Chinese leaders, Mao emphasized defensive preparations, stating that China's "nuclear bases should be prepared, be prepared for the enemy's air bombardment."[33] Mao made no corresponding comment about preparations for the use of nuclear weapons in retaliation.[34] No preparations to use Chinese nuclear weapons were detected by U.S. intelligence, which noted only defensive preparations consistent with the "war preparations" campaign that was underway.[35]

---

the Central Military Commission, suggested that the Second Artillery, relative to other military units, must "set higher standards, impose stricter requirements on itself and do a better job in this connection and strive to be an exemplary model in assigning importance to politics." See "Chinese Military Leader Outlines Goals for Army Missile Unit," Xinhua News Agency, June 7, 2002.

[32] For discussions of the crisis, see William Burr, "Sino-American Relations, 1969: The Sino-Soviet Border War and Steps towards Rapprochement," *Cold War History,* vol. 1, no. 3 (April 2001), pp. 73–112.

[33] Mao Zedong, "Talk at a Meeting of the Central Cultural Revolution Group," March 15, 1969, in Chen and Wilson, p. 162.

[34] The Chinese Communist Party (CCP) Central Committee's order for a nationwide mobilization in August 1969 also makes no mention of nuclear weapons. The order emphasizes ending the factional struggle that characterized the Cultural Revolution in order to unite against a common external threat. Presumably, the active deployment of nuclear weapons during factional infighting and tenuous political control would have given the Chinese leadership pause. The CCP Central Committee, "Order for General Mobilization in Border Provinces and Regions," August 28, 1969, in Chen and Wilson, pp. 168–169.

[35] At the time, the U.S. intelligence community assessed that China had no operationally deployed nuclear weapons. See "The National Intelligence Estimate: The USSR and China NIE 11/13–69," August 12, 1968, p. 6 and John K. Allen, Jr., John Carver, and Tom Elmore, eds., *Tracking the Dragon: National Intelligence Estimates on China during the Era of Mao, 1948–1976* (Washington, DC: Government Printing Office, 2004), p. 549. In 1974, however, the Defense Intelligence Agency (DIA) revised this assessment, noting "There is good evidence now that a limited number of nuclear-equipped CSS-1 MRBMs and some Soviet SS-2-type short-range ballistic missiles (SRBMs) were deployed by the end of 1966." See "National Intelligence Estimate: China's Strategic Attack Programs, NIE-13-8-74," June 13, 1974, p. 9, in *Tracking the Dragon,* p. 642.

Chinese emphasis on maintaining control, even at the expense of readiness, is in stark contrast to U.S. operational practices during much of the Cold War. For example, a U.S. team inspecting American nuclear weapons based overseas once discovered an extreme instance of the kind of bias toward readiness at the expense of operational control that marked early assessments of the relative risks of deliberate and inadvertent routes to nuclear war. The inspection team reportedly found a German quick-reaction alert airplane (QRA), loaded with fully operational nuclear weapons, sitting on a runway with a German pilot in the cockpit. "The only evidence of US control was a lonely 18-year-old sentry armed with a carbine and standing on the tarmac." He was operating with conflicting advice about whether to shoot the pilot or the bomb in the event of an unauthorized take-off.[36] This admittedly extreme example has no analogue in the Chinese case.

The PRC's strategic forces lack capability even in comparison with the other "second tier" nuclear powers. Chinese officials themselves claim that "the nuclear policy of China is to a large extent different from that of the [United Kingdom] and France in terms of what nuclear weapons deter against, the amount of nuclear weapons required for a retaliatory strike that is sufficient to inflict unacceptable damage on the enemy, and other aspects."[37] The PRC relies on an operationally deployed force of about 80 land-based ballistic missiles, with the warheads stored separately and the missiles kept unfueled. In contrast, both Britain and France maintain fleets of nuclear ballistic missile submarines (SSBNs) that continue operational patrols, although Britain's 1998 *Strategic Defence Review* announced reductions in the nuclear stockpile to 192 operationally available warheads available exclusively for use by Trident SSBNs "at several days 'notice to fire.'"[38] France continues to maintain 348 operationally deployed nuclear warheads, available for use by strategic submarines, carrier-based strike aircraft, and land-based bombers. Neither Britain nor France have indicated whether they have installed permissive action links, environmental sensing devices, or other positive control mechanisms on their nuclear weapons.

---

[36] The story is recounted in Stein and Feaver, pp. 30–31.

[37] Document is not for attribution; citation available from author.

[38] *Strategic Defence Review* (London: Secretary of State for Defence, July 1998), available at http://www.mod.uk/issues/sdr/wp_contents.htm.

The evident problem with the rationale that underpins Chinese restraint is the evolving capability and declaratory doctrine of U.S. strategic forces. The United States has in recent years sought credible options for the preemptive use of strategic forces for what two analysts, writing during the Cold War, described as "coercive, yet politically defensive, purposes."[39] The condition that Sha Zukang describes as balance in his interview looks quite different to the authors of the *2001 Nuclear Posture Review*. Keith Payne, for instance, noted the "obvious fact" that a U.S. intervention in a dispute over Taiwan might "risk escalation to a large-scale theater war and Chinese ICBM [intercontinental ballistic missile] threats against the U.S. homeland." Payne explained:

> Preserving the credibility of U.S. deterrence commitments in such circumstances would require Chinese leaders to believe that Washington would persevere despite their nuclear threats and possible regional nuclear use. Washington would have to deny Chinese leaders confidence that such threats could deter U.S. intervention, a hope to which they would likely cling. Consequently, U.S. deterrence policy in this case could require that the United States be able to limit its own prospective losses to a level compatible with the stakes involved.[40]

The modernization outlined in the *2001 Nuclear Posture Review* would transform fundamentally the way that the Chinese leaders view the efficacy of their own deterrent. Whereas Wohlstetter warned about a technological breakthrough that might disrupt the delicate balance of terror, the *2001 Nuclear Posture Review* deliberately seeks such a breakthrough through conventional precision-strike systems to neutralize or undermine Chinese deterrent capabilities, missile defenses to reduce homeland vulnerability, and a responsive defense infrastructure to indefinitely maintain the advantage.[41] In short, the modernization outlined in the *2001 Nuclear Posture*

---

[39] Colin S. Gray and Keith B. Payne, "Victory is Possible," *Foreign Policy*, vol. 39 (Summer 1980), p. 20.

[40] Keith B. Payne, "Post-Cold War Deterrence and a Taiwan Crisis," *China Brief*, vol. 1, no. 5 (September 12, 2001), available at: http://www.jamestown.org. See also Keith B Payne, *The Fallacies of Cold War Deterrence and a New Direction* (Lexington, KY: University Press of Kentucky, 2001), pp. 115–168.

[41] Stephen A. Cambone, principal deputy undersecretary of defense for policy during the drafting of the 2001 *Nuclear Posture Review*, told the 36th Annual IPFA-Fletcher Conference on National Security and Policy that the original

Review is designed to enable coercion by demonstrating that the United States is no longer deterred by Chinese strategic forces. This modernization will substantially increase the apparent willingness of the United States to subject China to a disarming first strike and will presumably complicate the efforts of those seeking to sustain Chinese restraint.

There is no evidence, yet, of a fundamental revision in the traditional deployment pattern of Chinese strategic forces, or even in the underlying strategic logic. For the foreseeable future, a U.S. force with the capability outlined in the *2001 Nuclear Posture Review* remains an aspiration. China will continue to preserve a modest level of capability sufficient for its minimalist conception of the role of nuclear weapons despite U.S. investments in missile defenses and in other aspects of strategic modernization. More importantly, the bureaucratic structure that sustains China's unique view of deterrence appears to remain intact.

SCOPE AND PURPOSE

Although the inner deliberations of China's leadership are only barely perceptible, additional evidence can be derived from patterns in Chinese defense investments, strategic force deployments, and arms control behavior. In particular, the recent history of Chinese engagement in multilateral arms control negotiations reflects the logic of restraint, which is evident both in Chinese statements and in strategic force deployments.

This book attempts a systematic examination of Chinese policy statements and diplomatic actions, examining the plausibility of alternative strategic rationales for China's nuclear forces. In so doing, the book provides policy guidance for those interested in the U.S.-Chinese security relationship and in global security arrangements more generally.

Chapter two sketches current Chinese nuclear force deployments based on admittedly scant Chinese statements and on U.S. intelligence assessments that have appeared in open source literature. Detailed information about the status of Chinese nuclear testing program is contained in chapter four.

---

draft of the *Nuclear Posture Review* identified a robust command, control, and intelligence capability as the third leg of the "New Triad." This more closely reflects the suite of capabilities that Payne identifies in *The Fallacies of Cold War Deterrence* to enhance U.S. nuclear capabilities in a conflict with China. See *Nuclear and Non-Nuclear Forces in 21st-Century Deterrence: Implementing the New Triad,* Final Report of the 36th Annual IFPA-Fletcher Conference on National Security and Policy, January 25, 2006.

The book shows that the majority, if not all, of unclassified estimates of the Chinese nuclear arsenal were badly in need of revision. Most estimates derive from research done in the mid-1980s, before a flood of new information became publicly available. These estimates were necessarily based on informed speculation, but that speculation was often incorrect—particularly with regard to the first generation of solid-fueled ballistic missiles in China's inventory. Overall, the new picture of the Chinese strategic force that emerges is one that is smaller, less diverse, and less ready to conduct actual operations than most analyses suggest. Overall, I estimate that the Chinese have around eighty operationally deployed nuclear warheads, which are stored separately from and assigned exclusively to ballistic missiles that are kept unfueled. The exclusive purpose of these weapons, along with any warheads or gravity bombs maintained in storage, is to retaliate in the event of a nuclear attack against the PRC.

Since the 1980s, two major developments have made a significant portion of U.S. intelligence community judgments available to open source analysts. First, the natural progress of declassification has released a large number of intelligence estimates from the 1960–1990 period, including a collection of seventy-one declassified National Intelligence Estimates (NIEs) related to China between 1948 and 1976. These documents reveal a tremendous amount about the development of the Chinese arsenal and its present configuration. Second, the partisan U.S. politics of the 1990s played out over a number of issues that created pressure to either declassify or provide unclassified summaries of intelligence judgments relating to alleged nuclear espionage, the need for continued nuclear testing, the ballistic missile threat to the United States, and the need for arms sales to Taiwan. In some cases, dissatisfied parties leaked entire classified documents to the public. In arguments over the ballistic missile threat and the pace of Chinese defense modernization, the intelligence community itself became a subject of debate, resulting in the disclosure of substantial information about the community's methodology and diversity of opinions. These documents contain a wealth of information about the Chinese nuclear and ballistic missile programs. Although the decision to declassify, summarize in unclassified form, or leak was quite often partisan, the motives were no more subtle than the judgments of the intelligence community.

Though U.S. intelligence analyses are not perfect, they are the proper place to begin an analysis for three reasons. First, the U.S. intelligence community has unparalleled access to national technical means of data collection. For example, the intelligence community uses a variety of means to monitor ballistic missile tests. Such monitoring, for example, revealed Chinese development of penetration aids and other measures to defeat ballistic missile defenses. There is no comparable unclassified source of such data, unless it is released by the government that conducted the test.

Second, secondary sources are often difficult to assess. Citing a *Jane's* publication or the International Institute of Strategic Studies' *Military Balance* tells very little about the provenance of the information, unless the secondary source cites an intelligence report itself. In that case, scholars should refer to the primary source directly.

Third, the intelligence community employs well-known methods that can be considered for gaps or bias. Although intelligence estimates are sometimes politicized or agenda driven, systematic bias is often evident and can be observed by comparing estimates over time. For example, the intelligence community has tended to exaggerate Chinese ballistic missile deployments, in part because Chinese industrial capacity has exceeded production. This is useful information when considering estimates of future Chinese deployments. After establishing the official estimates, scholars can, of course, debate the implications of the estimates or inquire about whether intelligence community estimates are consistent with other sources of information.

Chapter three reviews the history of Chinese nuclear deployments, with an effort to reconstruct the decision-making that has produced the visible features of China's strategic posture. Based on this history, I conclude that the limited posture is substantially the result of deliberate choices by the Chinese leadership that reflect a belief that deterrence is relatively insensitive to changes in the size, configuration, and readiness of nuclear forces. I have attempted to use U.S. intelligence analyses to track Chinese deployments and budgetary allocations, but such information is difficult to obtain and often very speculative. Moreover, intelligence sources offer little information about the internal decision-making that determines Chinese force structure. A handful of Chinese sources exist but few are unquestionably official.

Chapter three draws on the ground-breaking work of John Wilson Lewis and his Chinese collaborators Xue Litai and Hua Di, as well as a number of Chinese documents translated into English, including *China*

Today: Nuclear Industry, *China Today: Defense, Science and Technology*, the *Memoirs of Marshal Nie Rongzhen*; and a pair of textbooks from the Chinese National Defense University, *Strategic Studies* and *Operational Studies*.[42] One Chinese language source deserves special attention: a collection of twenty-three biographical essays about the most important figures in China's nuclear, missile, and space programs entitled *Biographies of the Founders of the Nuclear, Missile, and Satellite Program* (Liangdan Yixing Yuanxunzhuan), Tsinghua University Press, 2001. This document contains a number of revelations about the Chinese nuclear weapons program, particularly in the 1980s.[43]

Chapter four sketches a history of China's participation in the Conference on Disarmament (CD) during the negotiations of two treaties: the Comprehensive Nuclear Test Ban Treaty (CTBT) and the Fissile Material Cut-off Treaty. The significance of the Chinese decision to negotiate and sign the CTBT has been overlooked, particularly in the deadlock that has afflicted the CD since 1996. The actual positions of the participants in the CD, particularly the United States and China, have been poorly understood and sometimes misrepresented. I have attempted to reconstruct the broad outline of a decade of negotiations from several sources, including documentary records of the CD; published accounts of the participants (including the U.S. Congressional testimony during the CTBT ratification debate); a small number of subsequently declassified documents; and a series of interviews and conversations in Washington, New York, Beijing, and Geneva with American and Chinese CD participants. The status of the Chinese nuclear testing program is an important

---

[42] John W. Lewis and Xue Litai, *China Builds the Bomb* (Stanford, CA: Stanford University Press, 1988); John W. Lewis and Hua Di, "China's Ballistic Missile Programs: Technologies, Strategies, Goals," *International Security*, vol. 17, no. 2 (Autumn 1992), pp. 23–24; John W. Lewis and Xue Litai, *China's Strategic Seapower: The Politics of Force Modernization in the Nuclear Age* (Stanford, CA: Stanford University Press, 1994; Nie Rongzhen, *Inside the Red Star*; *China Today: Defense Science and Technology* (Beijing, China: National Defense Industry Press, 1993); *China Today: Nuclear Industry* JPRS-CST-88-002 and JPRS-CST-88-008 (Foreign Broadcast Information Service, U.S. Department of Commerce Joint Publications Research Service, 15 January 1988) 43–44; *Operational Studies (Zhanyi xue)* (Beijing: National Defense University, 2000); *Strategic Studies (Zhanlue xue)* (Beijing: Academy of Military Sciences, 2000).

[43] My own Chinese language skills were quite inadequate to make thorough use of this collection. I would like to thank Dr. Gregory Kulacki for generous assistance in finding and helping me use this collection of biographies.

piece of the story of CTBT negotiations. Therefore, I try to present a more detailed account of its status in chapter four than I do here, relying as much as possible on official judgments that have appeared as declassified documents, unclassified summaries, or leaked documents.

Chapter five compares two explanations of Chinese participation in these negotiations with the revised historical record presented in chapter four. Chapter five also examines the current academic literature that documents Chinese arms control behavior. The relevant literature includes the prevailing judgments that China signed the CTBT under duress and that future Chinese arms control concessions are unlikely. Comparing this literature to the principles of design suggested in the first three chapters and to the actual conduct of negotiations in the CD, I conclude that China's support for the CTBT is a natural result of the view that deterrence is insensitive to changes in the size, configuration, and readiness of nuclear forces. As a result, the United States may be missing an opportunity for further arms control negotiations with China.

Chapter six and chapter seven examine current Chinese perspectives on the modernization of U.S. strategic forces. These chapters also explore possible arms control solutions that would manage the vulnerability of the Chinese arsenal created by both the future U.S. deployment of capable antiballistic missile systems and the expansion of military activities in outer space. This information is largely based on official Chinese government documents and papers, reports by Chinese officials and well-connected academics, and interviews and conversations conducted during several trips to Beijing and Geneva. Official statements and speeches are obvious, but often overlooked, sources of information about Chinese government policy. As John Lewis wrote forty years ago in *Major Doctrines of Communist China*, "Although many Communist statements are idealized versions of events and social conditions in China, it is in such statements that Party leaders regularly communicate the ideas and policies which obedient cadres—the Chinese leaders at all levels of Party, government, and social organizations—are expected to apply to a wide inventory of routine tasks." Lewis concludes, "On most domestic and international questions, the Communists leave no doubt about their general positions … In the main, their statements and reports have been prepared for internal consumption."[44] This tendency is evident in other

---

[44] John W. Lewis, *Major Doctrines of Communist China* (New York: W.W. Norton, 1964), pp. 3–4.

countries, including the United States, and remains relevant for China today.[45]

An essential, but often implicit, source of context against which to interpret Chinese statements is the set of judgments derived from the historical account of the evolution of China's nuclear forces and its arms control behavior. In combination, China's past behavior and statements suggest a very different account of Chinese attitudes toward nuclear weapons and arms control than is commonly presented by U.S. analysts. On the whole, Chinese policies reflect a more skeptical view of the role of nuclear weapons and a greater interest in arms control than the U.S. foreign policy community has generally recognized.

---

[45] On the role of public statements in setting internal bureaucratic priorities within the United States, see Warren Christopher, *In the Stream of History: Shaping Foreign Policy for a New Era* (Stanford, CA: Stanford University Press, 1998), p. 9 and Henry Kissinger, *American Foreign Policy: Three Essays* (New York: W.W. Norton, 1969), pp. 22–23.

CHAPTER 2

Chinese Strategic Forces, 2006

China possesses a small number of nuclear weapons entirely for self-defense. China undertakes not to be the first to use nuclear weapons, and not to use or threaten to use nuclear weapons against non-nuclear-weapon states. China does not participate in any nuclear arms race, and never deploys any nuclear weapons beyond its borders.

China maintains a small but effective nuclear counterattacking force in order to deter possible nuclear attacks by other countries. Any such attack will inevitably result in a retaliatory nuclear counter-strike by China. China has always kept the number of its nuclear weapons at a low level. The scale, composition and development of China's nuclear force are in line with China's military strategy of active defense.

China's nuclear force is under the direct command of the Central Military Commission (CMC). China is extremely cautious and responsible in the management of its nuclear weapons, and has established strict rules and regulations and taken effective measures to ensure the safety and security of its nuclear weapons.

—China's National Defense, 2000[1]

China probably has eighty operationally deployed nuclear warheads, assigned exclusively to ballistic missiles that are kept unfueled and that are stored separately from the warheads. China's strategic forces are significantly smaller, less diverse, and less ready to conduct actual operations than those of the other four nuclear powers recognized under the Nuclear Nonproliferation Treaty (NPT). The exclu-

---

[1] Information Office of the State Council, "China's National Defense in 2000," in *White Papers of the Chinese Government* (Beijing: Foreign Language Press, 2002), p. 236.

sive purpose of these weapons, along with any warheads or gravity bombs maintained in storage, is to discourage states from using nuclear weapons against the PRC and to retaliate against any state that does.

This conclusion is based on the limited number of official Chinese documents available for examination and U.S. intelligence assessments that have appeared in open source literature. Official Chinese statements regarding the size, readiness, and configuration of Chinese nuclear forces are limited—but not as limited as one might believe. The most detailed public statement appears in *China's National Defense* (2000), which describes China's "small but effective nuclear counterattacking force" in very general terms. The passage quoted at the beginning of this chapter implies that China's nuclear forces are (1) small in number and based largely on land-based ballistic missiles, (2) kept under tight central control and off-alert, and (3) limited in their operational missions to retaliatory strikes.

These statements are consistent with two internal Chinese government publications, *Strategic Studies* (2000) and *Operational Studies* (2000) that are used to train Chinese Communist Party cadres, as well as with the available U.S. intelligence estimates.[2] This chapter reviews the status of Chinese nuclear delivery vehicles, command and control arrangements, and operational doctrine. It concludes with a discussion of China's anticipated modernization.

CHINA'S STRATEGIC DELIVERY VEHICLES

China probably deploys the smallest force among the five nuclear weapons states recognized by the Nuclear Nonproliferation Treaty (See Table 2-1).

The Chinese government does not provide estimates of the number of nuclear weapons it possesses or deploys, but the official, unclassified U.S. estimate of the number of Chinese nuclear weapons states that China "currently has more than 100 nuclear warheads."[3] For many years,

---

[2] *Operational Studies* (*Zhanyi xue*) (Beijing: National Defense University, 2000) and *Strategic Studies* (*Zhanlue xue*) (Beijing: Academy of Military Sciences, 2000). My copies are Defense Intelligence Agency (DIA) translations, generously made available by Alistair Iain Johnston.

[3] Lieutenant General Michael Maples, Director, Defense Intelligence Agency, *Current and Projected National Security Threats to the United States*, Statement for the Record, Hearing Before the Senate Armed Services Committee (Febru-

Table 2-1: Operationally Deployed Strategic Warheads

USA	5,966
Russia	4,380
France	Approximately 350
UK	Less than 200
China	Approximately 80

Sources: U.S. and Russian estimates are based on the START Memorandum of Understanding (MOU) submitted on July 1, 2005 and do not necessarily reflect those weapons
systems that are operationally deployed. The French estimate of "approximately 350" is
from The Arms Control Association, "Nuclear Weapons: Who Has What at a Glance"
(April 2005). The UK estimate of "less than 200 operationally available warheads" is
from *Strategic Defence Review* (London: Secretary of State for Defence, July 1998), p.
31 and the testimony of the Rt Hon John Reid, MP, Secretary of State for Defence, *Oral
Evidence Taken before the Defence Committee,* November 1, 2005. The Chinese estimate is based on author's assessment of available sources.

estimates provided by nongovernmental organizations (e.g., the Council
on Foreign Relations, the National Resources Defense Council, and the
International Institute for Strategic Studies) were much higher, generally
describing the People's Republic of China as the world's third largest
nuclear power, ahead of the British and the French, with four hundred or
so warheads.[4] The differences among these estimates largely reflect
accounting methodologies.[5] Most likely, the U.S. intelligence commu-

---

ary 28, 2006). See also *Proliferation: Threat and Response,* (Washington, DC:
Department of Defense, 2001), p. 14.

[4] Such estimates are often based on two comments in the open literature: In
1979, a senior Defense Department official described the nuclear forces
deployed by China, France, and the United Kingdom as "more or less comparable with China perhaps being the leader of the three. So it is possible that China
might be the third nuclear power in the world." See *Department of Defense
Authorization for Appropriations for FY80. Part 1: Defense Posture; Budget Priorities and Management Issues; Strategic Nuclear Posture* (Washington, DC:
Government Printing Office, 1979), p. 357. A "senior Chinese military officer"
purportedly told John Lewis and Xue Litai that China maintained "a nuclear
weapons inventory greater than that of the French and British strategic forces
combined." See John W. Lewis and Xue Litai, *China Builds the Bomb* (Stanford,
CA: Stanford University Press, 1988), p. 253.

[5] The Council on Foreign Relations, the National Resources Defense Council,
and the International Institute for Strategic Studies estimate that China has
between 130 and 140 ballistic missiles with nuclear deterrent roles. See Harold

nity does not have direct evidence regarding the number of Chinese nuclear weapons. Instead, U.S. analysts are counting a proxy: delivery vehicles that are believed to have operationally deployed warheads assigned to them.[6]

The U.S. intelligence community used this methodology for Chinese and Soviet estimates at least through the mid-1980s.[7] Deployed weapons are those that would actually be used in a conflict and, as a result, define the balance of forces. Deployed weapons are the most relevant for examining the choices made by the Chinese planning system and for understanding what those choices indicate about how Chinese policymakers view deterrence.

The Department of Defense (DoD) assesses that China's nuclear warheads are deployed operationally only for use with its inventory of about one hundred land-based ballistic missiles: China "has over 100 warheads deployed operationally on ballistic missiles. Additional warheads are in storage."[8] Although the DoD does not define "deployed operationally," basic information about the readiness of China's land-based ballistic missile force strongly suggests that other methods of delivery (including aircraft-delivered gravity bombs and submarine-launched ballistic missiles) do not factor into Chinese assessments of their national retaliatory capability. As early as 1984, the Defense Intelligence Agency argued that "land-based surface-to-surface ballistic missile (SSM) systems are currently China's only credible means of strategic nuclear delivery."[9] This is consis-

---

Brown et. al., *Chinese Military Power* (New York: Council on Foreign Relations, 2003), pp. 51–53; Hans M. Kristensen and Joshua M. Handler, "Tables of Nuclear Forces," in *SIPRI Yearbook: Armaments Disarmament and International Security* (Oxford, UK Oxford University Press, 2001), pp. 475–478; and *Military Balance 2000-2001* (Oxford, UK: International Institute for Strategic Studies, 2000).

[6] This was also the practice with the Soviet Union during the Cold War. See for example, William Arkin and Jeffrey I. Sands, "The Soviet Nuclear Stockpile: Defense Department Sees 'Warhead Gap,'" *Arms Control Today,* vol. 14, no. 5 (June 1984), pp. 1, 4–8.

[7] See, for example, Arkin and Sands, "The Soviet Nuclear Stockpile," p. 1.

[8] *Proliferation: Threat and Response*, (Washington, DC: Department of Defense, 1997). Available on-line at: http://www.defenselink.mil/pubs/prolif97/ne_asia.html#china.

[9] *Handbook of the Chinese People's Liberation Army*, DDB-2680-32-84 (Washington, DC: Defense Intelligence Agency, 1984), p. 70.

tent with official Chinese descriptions. For example, *China's National Defense* notes that China's "strategic nuclear missile force, under the direct command of the [Central Military Commission], constitutes the *main part* of China's limited nuclear counterattack capability."[10] *Operational Studies* suggests "The nuclear retaliation campaign of the Second Artillery [China's strategic rocket force] *mainly uses* ground-to-ground nuclear missiles."[11]

Basic estimates on the size and quality of China's ballistic missile force are available from the National Air and Space Intelligence Center (NASIC), which publishes *Ballistic and Cruise Missile Threat* and the Department of Defense's *Annual Report on the Military Power of the People's Republic of China* (See Table 2-2).[12]

National Air and Space Intelligence Center (NASIC) estimates and analyses occasionally appear in the conservative press, often in response to Central Intelligence Agency (CIA) estimates that some conservatives claim are "biased in favor of a benign view" of China.[13] Past NAIC estimates of the size of Chinese ballistic missile deployments do, in fact, appear larger than estimates that appear in unclassified NIEs. For example, the 2006 edition of *Ballistic and Cruise Missile Threat* lists China as having deployed "less than 25" CSS-3 (DF-4) ballistic missile launchers,

---

[10] "China's National Defense in 2000."

[11] *Operational Studies*, ch. 14, p.3. Emphasis added.

[12] National Air Intelligence Center, *Ballistic and Cruise Missile Threat*, revised, NAIC-1031-0985-06 (Washington, DC: National Air Intelligence Center, March 2006). See also National Air Intelligence Center, *Ballistic and Cruise Missile Threat*, NAIC-1031-0985-00 (Washington, DC: National Air Intelligence Center, September 2000); National Air Intelligence Center, *Ballistic and Cruise Missile Threat*, revised, NAIC-1031-0985-03 (Washington, DC: National Air Intelligence Center, August 2003); *Annual Report on The Military Power of the People's Republic of China*, Report to Congress Pursuant to The FY2000 National Defense Authorization Act (Washington, DC: Department of Defense, May 2006), p. 50; and *Annual Report on The Military Power of the People's Republic of China*, Report to Congress Pursuant to The FY2000 National Defense Authorization Act (Washington, DC: Department of Defense, July 2005), p. 45.

[13] See Bill Gertz and Rowan Scarborough, "Target: CIA China Shop," *Washington Times,* October 27, 2000, and George J. Tenet, "CIA Analysts are Not Pro-China Apologists," letter to the editor, *Washington Times,* November 1, 2000.

Table 2-2: Estimated PRC Missile Deployments

U.S. Desig.	PRC Desig.	Class	Range (miles)	National Air and Space Intelligence Center, 2006	DoD, 2006 (Missiles / Launchers)
CSS-4	DF-5	ICBM	8,000	~ 20	20 / 20
CSS-3	DF-4	IRBM	3,400	< 25	10-14 / 20-24
CSS-2	DF-3	MRBM	1,750	< 50	44 / 37*
CSS-5	DF-21	MRBM	1,100		
CSS-X-10	DF-31	ICBM	4,500	Not Deployed	Not Deployed
DF-31A		ICBM	7,000		
JL-2		SLBM	4,500		
CSS-NX-3	JL-1	SLBM	>1000	Not Deployed	10 / 14
Total				**< 95**	**74-78 / 77-85****

Sources: *National Air and Space Intelligence Center, Ballistic and Cruise Missile Threat,*
March 2006 and Department of Defense, *Annual Report on the Military Power of the*
People's Republic of China, May 2006.
* Chinese Military Power lists between 19 and "50" missiles for the CSS-5; 50 is almost
certainly an error given the estimate in Ballistic and Cruise missile threat and the previ-
ous year's DoD estimate of 19-23 CSS-5 ballistic missiles.
** Excludes JL-1.
ICBM = Intercontinental Ballistic Missile; IRBM = Intermediate-range Ballistic Missile;
MRBM = Medium-range Ballistic Missile; SLBM = Submarine-launched Ballistic Missile

while other estimates credit China with "about a dozen."[14] When a more
specific, official estimate is available from a source other than *Ballistic*
and Cruise Missile Threat, I present that specific estimate—although the
overall difference is always relatively small.[15]

---

[14] *CIA National Intelligence Estimate of Foreign Missile Developments and The*
Ballistic Missile Threat through 2015, Hearing before the International Security,
Proliferation, and Federal Services Subcommittee of the Committee on Governmental Affairs, United States Senate, S. Hrg. 107–467 (March 11, 2002),
p. 32. Similar estimates are provided in National Air Intelligence Center, *Bal-*
listic and Cruise Missile Threat (March 2006) and the 2005 and 2006 editions
of *Chinese Military Power*.

[15] A note on terminology: Chinese ballistic missiles are generally numbered
sequentially. The Chinese use the prefixes DF or JL, from the Pinyin system of
transliteration, to identify their ballistic missiles. Land-based ballistic missiles
are part of the Dong Feng (DF), or "East Wind" series, while sea-based ballis-

The best guess, derived from official sources, estimates the size of the Chinese strategic arsenal at around eighty operationally deployed nuclear warheads. Only a handful of China's ballistic missiles are ICBMs: probably eighteen CSS-4 (DF-5) missiles and about twelve CSS-3 (DF-4) missiles. The remainder of the nuclear force, numbering about forty-four launchers, comprises what one member of the intelligence community called "theater" forces: medium-range ballistic missiles MRBMs like the liquid-fueled CSS-2 and its replacement, the solid-fueled CSS-5.[16] These launchers may have a re-fire capability.

The liquid-fueled CSS-4 (DF-5) intercontinental ballistic missile, with a range of 8,000 kilometers, is the only Chinese missile capable of striking targets throughout the entire United States. First deployed in 1981, this missile underwent flight testing that suggests it was principally designed to penetrate the air defense system around Moscow.[17] In Congressional testimony, General Eugene Habiger revealed that China had eighteen CSS-4 (DF-5) ICBMs, all of which are reportedly based in silos.[18] The U.S. intelligence community assesses that the Chinese leadership "almost certainly believes its silos to be vulnerable"; there were

---

tic missiles are part of the Julang (JL) or "Great Wave" series. U.S. designations for all "Chinese surface to surface" ballistic missiles, both land- and sea-based, use the prefix CSS. An N indicates "naval;" while an X indicates that the missile is under development or experimental. I use the Western designation, with the Chinese designation in parentheses.

[16] *Foreign Missile Developments and the Ballistic Missile Threat through 2015* (Washington, DC: National Intelligence Council, December 2001), p. 8.

[17] *Special Defense Intelligence Estimate: China's Evolving Nuclear Strategies* DDE-2200-321-85 (Washington, DC: Defense Intelligence Agency, May 1985), p. 8. A CIA report suggested that five of the eighteen CSS-4 ICBMs were targeted at Moscow. See Bill Gertz, "China Targets Nukes at U.S.: CIA Missile Report Contradicts Clinton," *Washington Times*, May 1, 1998.

[18] *Ballistic Missiles: Threat and Response*, Hearings before the Committee on Foreign Relations United States Senate, S. Hrg. 106-339 (April 15 and 20, May 4, 5, 13, 25, 26, and September 16, 1999), p. 165. The 2000 edition of "Chinese Military Power" notes that "China reportedly has built 18 CSS-4 silos." See the Department of Defense, "Chinese Military Power," *Annual Report on The Military Power of the People's Republic of China*, Report to Congress Pursuant to The FY2000 National Defense Authorization Act (Washington, DC: Department of Defense, June 2000) np. Available at: http://www.defenselink.mil/news/Jun2000/china06222000.htm.

unofficial reports that the Chinese engineers responsible for CSS-3 and CSS-4 missile silos referred to the installations as "missile tombs."[19] China has reportedly built many dummy silos as part of a camouflage and concealment effort.

Although *Chinese Military Power* and other intelligence assessments note that the Chinese are replacing CSS-4 Mod 1 ICBMs with longer range CSS-4 Mod 2 ICBMs, the significance of the upgrade program appears to be minimal. In 1998, after intelligence reports of the upgrades first became public, General Habiger, who was then the STRATCOM Commander, said, "the CSS-4 ICBM that the Chinese have deployed today has been deployed since 1981. And there have been some modifications, but nothing significant."[20] The CSS-4 is probably equipped with China's largest nuclear warhead, which has a 4 to 5 megaton estimated yield, and it is the only Chinese ballistic missile sufficiently powerful to accommodate multiple reentry vehicles (RVs).[21] To place multiple RVs on the CSS-4, China could use technology from its commercial "Smart Dispenser" upper stage as a "technology bridge" to a post-boost vehicle (PBV) that could accommodate three or four 470 kilogram CSS-X-10-type RVs on the CSS-4.[22] The U.S. intelligence community disagrees about whether China intends to do so.

---

[19] China's current force of about twenty CSS-4 ICBMs can reach targets in all of the United States, although Beijing almost certainly considers its silos to be vulnerable. *National Intelligence Estimate on the Ballistic Missile Threat to the United States*, Hearing before the International Security, Proliferation, And Federal Services Subcommittee of The Committee on Governmental Affairs, United States Senate, S. Hrg. 106–671 (February 9, 2000), p. 8. The description of silos as "missile tombs" is found in Lewis and Hua, *International Security*, p. 24.

[20] General Eugene Habiger, Commander of U.S. Strategic Command, "DoD News Briefing," June 16, 1998, http://www.defenselink.mil/transcripts/1998/t06231998_t616hab2.html.

[21] The NIE defines multiple reentry vehicle payload systems to "include those that independently target each RV and those that do not provide independent targeting for each RV (MRV)." See *Foreign Missile Developments and the Ballistic Missile Threat through 2015*, p. 8.

[22] "China could use a DF-31-type RV for a multiple-RV payload for the CSS-4 in a few years." See *Ballistic Missiles: Threat and Response*, S. Hrg. 106–339, 358. On the ability of the "smart dispenser"—an upper rocket stage developed to deploy satellites into different orbits from single launch—to use a modified

China also maintains "about a dozen CSS-3 [DF-4] ICBMs that are almost certainly intended as a retaliatory deterrent against targets in Russia and Asia."[23] Although these missiles are listed as intercontinental ballistic missiles by the intelligence community, they would be characterized as intermediate range ballistic missiles under the 1987 Intermediate-range Nuclear Forces (INF) treaty due to their 3,400 kilometer-range.[24] The CSS-3 can be launched either by rolling it out to a launch site or from an elevate-to-launch silo.[25] In 1993, the U.S. intelligence community estimated that two of China's approximately ten CSS-3 ICBMs "are based in silos but most are stored in caves and must be rolled out to adjacent launch pads for firing."[26] In August 1995, the Second Artillery completed a major construction project that apparently created a network of interconnected caves and tunnels to enhance survivability under conditions of a nuclear attack. The CSS-3 reportedly has the same 2,000 kilogram/3 megaton RV as the CSS-2.[27]

The intelligence community has offered less detailed information about China's nuclear-capable, theater ballistic missile force, which comprises CSS-2 (DF-3) and CSS-5 (DF-21) ballistic missiles. The CSS-5 Mod 1 is a land-based derivative of the CSS-NX-3 (JL-1) SLBM that was devel-

---

CSS-X-10 (DF-31)-type RV, estimated at 470 kilograms, see [No Title] NAIC 1442-0629-97 (National Air Intelligence Center, December 10, 1996) in Bill Gertz, *Betrayal: How the Clinton Administration Undermined American Security*, (Washington, DC: Regency Publishing, 1999) pp. 21–252.

23 *CIA National Intelligence Estimate Of Foreign Missile Development …*, S. Hrg. 107–467, p. 32

24 *The Treaty between the United States and the Union of Soviet Socialist Republics on the Elimination of their Intermediate-Range and Shorter-Range Missiles.* Treaty text available at: http://www.state.gov/www/global/arms/treaties/inf1.html.

25 "Chinese Military Power," (June 2000) np. Available at: http://www.defenselink.mil/news/Jun2000/china06222000.htm.

26 *Report to Congress on Status of China, India and Pakistan Nuclear and Ballistic Missile Programs*, (July 28, 1993), Available at: http://www.fas.org/irp/threat/930728-wmd.htm.

27 *Soviet and People's Republic of China Nuclear Weapons Employment Strategy* (Washington, DC: Defense Intelligence Agency, 1972). See Tables 5 and 6; page number redacted in declassification. See also John W. Lewis and Xue Litai, *China's Strategic Seapower: The Politics of Force Modernization in the Nuclear Age* (Stanford, CA: Stanford University Press, 1994) p. 177.

oped for deployment on China's Xia-class SSBN. China is currently deploying an upgraded CSS-5 Mod 2 to replace the much older CSS-2, although an unspecified number of CSS-5 ballistic missiles will be deployed to conduct conventional missions. During normal peacetime operations, CSS-2 and CSS-5 launchers remain in their garrisons, where the principle method of protecting deployments is extensive tunneling.[28] These missiles may be dispersed in a crisis. The Chinese have apparently tested endoatmospheric reentry decoys on R&D flight tests for the CSS-5 Mod 2 (November 1995) and CSS-5 Mod 1 (January 1996). In 1972, U.S. intelligence assessed that the CSS-2 was equipped with China's earliest 3 megaton thermonuclear warhead.[29] Unofficial reports indicate that China planned a 600-kilogram warhead for the CSS-5 with a yield of 400 or more kilotons, although the relatively late deployment of the CSS-5 may have allowed the missile to be outfitted with CSS-X-10-type warheads tested between 1992 and 1996.[30]

Ballistic and Cruise Missile Threat estimates the number of launchers for the CSS-2, CSS-5 Mod 1, and CSS-5 Mod 2 MRBMs as less than fifty for each missile, implying that there may be up to 150 total MRBM launchers in China. U.S. intelligence documents leaked to the press suggest that there are fewer than fifty total MRBM launchers *of all types,* with the CSS-5 replacing the CSS-2 on a one-to-one basis.[31] The 2005 edition of *Chinese Military Power* estimates six to ten CSS-2 and thirty-four to thirty-eight CSS-5 launchers—for a total of forty-four MRBM launchers.

---

[28] On peacetime CSS-2 operations, including tunneling efforts, see the Defense Intelligence Agency *Intelligence Appraisal China: Nuclear Missile Strategy,* DIAIAPPR 34–81 (March 13, 1981), pp. 4–5.

[29] *Soviet and People's Republic of China Nuclear Weapons Employment Strategy,* tables 5 and 6; page number redacted in declassification.

[30] Lewis and Xue, *China's Strategic Seapower,* p. 177.

[31] A 1997 NAIC report on the program to replace the CSS-2 with the CSS-5 suggested there were approximately forty-five CSS-2 launchers. See the National Air Intelligence Center, *China Incrementally Downsizing CSS-2 IRBM Force,* NAIC-1030-098B-96 (November 1996) in Bill Gertz, *The China Threat: How the People's Republic Targets America* (Washington, DC: Regency Publishing, 2000), pp. 233–234. Presidential Review 31 (1993): *U.S. Policy on Ballistic Missile Defenses and the Future of the ABM Treaty,* summarized a CIA assessment that "China's medium and intermediate range missile force currently is composed of some 50 launchers."

This suggests the intelligence community remains uncertain about the pace at which the CSS-5 is replacing the CSS-2.[32]

China currently has a single Xia-class SSBN, which is not operational.[33] The submarine that carried the Xia-class SSBN "went on one cruise and has been essentially in dry dock ever since," according to General Habiger.[34] The Xia was designed to carry twelve CSS-NX-3 (JL-1) missiles, but these missiles have not been deployed despite successful flight tests in 1988.[35] The U.S. Office of Naval Intelligence reports that the submarine "fell short of expectations" due to a noisy and unreliable propulsion system and "was never equipped with a missile with intercontinental range."[36] One edition of *Chinese Military Power* states that the "capabilities [of the Chinese nuclear submarine fleet] would be limited against modern Western and Russian [anti-submarine warfare] ASW capabilities."[37] These factors may explain why China delayed, and then suspended, plans to build additional Xia-class SSBNs in the 1980s and 1990s.[38] Press reports indicate that the JL-2 SLBM was test fired from a

---

[32] The U.S. intelligence community uses crew training and infrastructure modernization to infer which units have been converted from CSS-2 to CSS-5 deployments. See *China Incrementally Downsizing CSS-2 IRBM Force*, in Gertz, *The China Threat*, pp. 233–234.

[33] *Current and Projected National Security Threats to The United States,* Hearing before the Select Committee on Intelligence of The United States Senate, S. Hrg. 107–597 (February 6, 2002), pp. 78–79.

[34] *Ballistic Missiles: Threat and Response*, S. Hrg. pp. 106–339, 165–166.

[35] Department of Defense, *Annual Report On The Military Power Of The People's Republic Of China*, Report To Congress Pursuant To The FY2000 National Defense Authorization Act (July 2003), p. 31.

[36] The phrase "fell short of expectations" is from *Worldwide Submarine Challenges* (Washington, DC: Office of Naval Intelligence, 1997), p. 22. The phrase "was never equipped" is from *Worldwide Maritime Challenges*, (Washington, DC: Office of Naval Intelligence, 2004), p. 36. On the limitations of the submarine, see Lewis and Xue, *China's Strategic Seapower*, pp. 120–122.

[37] "Chinese Military Power," *Selected Military Capabilities of the People's Republic of China*, Report to Congress Pursuant to Section 1305 of the FY97 National Defense Authorization Act (Washington, DC: Department of Defense, April 1997), p. 4.

[38] Lewis and Xue, *China's Strategic Seapower*, p. 121. United States intelligence was reporting the delay in construction by early 1985. See *Special Defense Intelligence Estimate: China's Evolving Nuclear Strategies*, p. 8.

retrofitted Golf-class submarine, which suggests the Xia may never be outfitted with the JL-2.[39]

COMMAND AND CONTROL ARRANGEMENTS

China maintains "a highly centralized and unified command" system for nuclear operations. Although the declaratory policy in *China's National Defense* only implies highly centralized command and control arrangements, *Operational Studies* offers a much more detailed description:

> The nuclear retaliation campaign of the Second Artillery carries out a special strategic task. Its main combat issue and operation are all related with the overall situation of war. Therefore, we have to have a highly centralized and unified command. All the important campaign issues, such as campaign guidance, campaign goal, campaign deployment, targets, and the time of nuclear retaliation, have to be decided by the supreme command. The Second Artillery has to follow the order of the supreme command very strictly and correctly to organize and conduct the nuclear retaliation campaign.... The highly centralized and unified strategic command is an outstanding characteristic of the nuclear retaliation campaign.[40]

Authority to use nuclear weapons rests with the Party Central Committee and the Central Military Commission.[41] The Central Military Commission directly controls the six base commands of the Second Artillery (each base command controls two or three missile brigades), bypassing China's military region commands.[42]

---

[39] Bill Gertz and Rowan Scarborough, "Inside the Ring: China Tests JL-2," *Washington Times*, November 2, 2001.

[40] *Operational Studies (Zhanyi xue)*, ch. 14, p. 3.

[41] See, for example, Jiang Zemin's March 2002 speech indicating that, "At any time and under any circumstance, [the Second Artillery] must absolutely obey the command of the CPC Central Committee and the Central Military Commission." See "RMRB Summarizes Report on Jiang Praise for Second Artillery Corps," March 21, 2002, FBIS-CPP-2002-0321-000103. For a general discussion of the Central Military Commission, see David Shambaugh, "The Pinnacle of the Pyramid: The Central Military Commission," in James C. Mulvenon and Andrew N. D. Yang, eds., *The People's Liberation Army as Organization: Reference v.1.0* CF-182-NSRD, (Washington: RAND, 2002), pp. 95–121.

[42] Bates Gill, et al., "The Chinese Second Artillery Corps: Transition to Credible Deterrence," in Mulvenon and Yang, eds., p. 546.

Chinese Military Power suggests that "China has an extensive network of hardened, underground shelters and command and control (C2) facilities for both its military and civilian leadership."[43] The Second Artillery headquarters is located in Qinghe, a suburb to the north of Beijing.[44] A declassified Defense Department document, however, suggests the Second Artillery Headquarters commands only routine operations: "During wartime, Chinese strategic missile forces would be controlled from the [General Staff Department] command center."[45] The General Staff Department command center is believed to be a large underground facility near Xishan, in the western hills of Beijing.[46]

Open source information about the quality of communication links between China's leadership and national nuclear forces is limited. Leadership facilities are connected to separate military and civilian telecommunications networks. *Chinese Military Power* suggests that the Second Artillery began installing a digital microwave communications system around 1995 to support its missile launches by providing all-weather and encrypted communication ability.[47] The systems are probably "at least two generations behind that of Western countries" and are based largely on commercial off-the-shelf technology.[48] *Operational Studies* suggests

---

[43] "Chinese Military Power," *Annual Report on the Military Power of the People's Republic of China*, Report to Congress Pursuant to the FY2000 National Defense Authorization Act (Washington, DC: Department of Defense, July 2003), p. 34.

[44] Secretary of Defense Donald Rumsfeld visited this facility in October 2005. See Ann Scott Tyson, "Rumsfeld to Make Official Visit to Beijing," *Washington Post*, October 15, 2005, and Paul Eckert, "China Allows Rumsfeld Peek at Secretive Military," Reuters, October 19, 2005. The facility is described in Mark A. Stokes, *China's Strategic Modernization: Implications for The United States* (Carlisle, PA: Army War College, 1999), p. 93.

[45] *Strategic Missile Tidbits* (1995), p. 3. [Declassified Department of Defense document with incomplete citation]

[46] Michael Swaine, *The Military and Political Succession in China: Leadership, Institutions Beliefs* R-4254-AF (Santa Monica, CA: RAND, 1992), pp. 122–123, and Lewis and Xue, *China's Strategic Seapower*, p. 154.

[47] "Chinese Military Power," (June 2000). See also Bates Gill et al., "The Chinese Second Artillery Corps: Transition to Credible Deterrence," in Mulvenon and Yang, eds., pp. 546–547.

[48] "Chinese Military Power," (April 1997), p. 5. "China still lags far behind western standards for controlling complex joint operations and lacks the robust

these systems may be vulnerable at the brigade level following dispersal in a crisis. Dispersal would be "good for the hiding and survival of the missile force. But at the same time, because the troops are highly scattered, under serious nuclear circumstances, their telecommunication systems are vulnerable, making the commanding and control of the campaign very complicated and difficult."[49]

Launch commands to the Second Artillery may not be automated. *Chinese Military Power* (1997) assesses that "most [People's Liberation Army] command and control systems are still manual, there are long delays in dissemination of directives"—problems that *Operational Studies* alludes to in warning commanders that "the issuance of a launching order has to be timely, accurate, and secret." *Operational Studies* even suggests that the content of a launch order should "be brief and clear" and identify "the missile troops to carry out the attacking task, the serial number of [the] card [with] missile firing data to be used, the time frame of the launch, the action of the troops after the launch, and other things to be watched."[50]

The U.S. intelligence community does not appear to believe China has developed the capacity to integrate permissive action links (PALs), environmental sensing devices (ESDs), or other safety devices into its warheads.[51] China reportedly sought technical assistance from the United States, and possibly from Russia, to develop such devices.[52] The U.S.

C4I architecture required to meet the demands of the modern battlefield." "Chinese Military Power," *Future Military Capabilities of the People's Republic of China*, Report to Congress Pursuant to Section 1226 Of The FY98 National Defense Authorization Act (Washington, DC: Department of Defense, 1998).

[49] *Operational Studies* (*Zhanyi xue*), ch. 14, p. 7.

[50] Ibid.

[51] More recent NIEs offer less detailed information on this point, although the 1999 National Intelligence Estimate assessed that "an unauthorized launch of a Chinese strategic missile is highly unlikely" omitting any reference to "technical safeguards." *National Intelligence Estimate on the Ballistic Missile Threat*..., S. Hrg. 106–671, pp. 49–50.

[52] Danny Stillman, head of the intelligence division at Los Alamos National Laboratory, was reportedly asked by Chinese scientists to provide PAL technology. "Every trip, they asked for that. I always thought the world would be a safer place if they got that," Stillman told the *Washington Post*. Kurt Campbell, former deputy assistant secretary of defense for Asia-Pacific affairs reportedly con-

intelligence community estimates that "China keeps its missiles unfueled and without warheads mated" as its primary safety measure.[53] As a consequence, Chinese missile units reportedly require many, perhaps tens of, hours of pre-launch exposure to complete the launch sequence.[54]

DEPLOYMENT

China does not deploy nuclear gravity bombs for use with its aging bomber fleet on a day-to-day basis. In 1984, the U.S. intelligence community was "unable to identify the associated airfield storage sites" for the "small number" of nuclear capable aircraft that "probably" had nuclear bombs assigned to them.[55] The Defense Intelligence Agency

---

firmed Stillman's story to the *Post*, adding "There was a big debate in the United States about how far we should go to assist them with that technology. I think they [the Chinese] truly were interested in what they called positive control." See Steve Coll, "The Man inside China's Bomb Labs: U.S. Blocks Memoir of Scientist Who Gathered Trove of Information," *The Washington Post*, May 16, 2001. The story is also recounted in Dan Stober and Ian Hoffman, *A Convenient Spy: Wen Ho Lee and the Politics of Nuclear Espionage* (New York: Simon & Schuster, 2001), pp. 93–94.

[53] Robert D. Walpole, National Intelligence Officer for Strategic and Nuclear Programs, speech at the Carnegie Endowment for International Peace, September 17, 1998. Available at: http://www.cia.gov/cia/public_affairs/ speeches/1998/walpole_speech_091798.html. *Operational Studies* implies this arrangement by defining the "missile base group" as "two or more missile bases and warhead bases." See *Operational Studies (Zhanyi xue)*, ch. 14, p. 1. For a description of Chinese operating practices, see: *Strategic Missile Tidbits* (1995), p. 3.

[54] General Habiger told a conference that Chinese ICBMs "don't sit the same kind of alert [as those in Russia and the United States]. In other words, there's several tens of hours of preparation to get a missile ready for launch as compared to the Russian and the U.S. model." Eugene Habiger, "Problems and Prospects of New Alaska Missile Interceptor Site," remarks before the Carnegie Endowment for International Peace (September 20, 2004). Available at: http://www.carnegieendowment.org/static/npp/habiger.pdf. Lewis and Hua estimate that Chinese missiles would be exposed for two to three hours before launch. John W. Lewis and Hua Di, "China's Ballistic Missile Programs: Technologies, Strategies, Goals," *International Security*, vol. 17, no. 2 (Autumn 1992), pp. 23–24.

[55] *Defense Estimative Brief: Nuclear Weapons Systems in China*, pp. 3–4.

(DIA) concluded that it was "improbable that China's air forces have a strategic nuclear delivery mission" because "it is unlikely that these obsolescent aircraft could successfully penetrate the sophisticated air defense networks of modern military powers."[56] In 1993, the U.S. intelligence community concluded that the "Chinese Air Force has no units whose primary mission is to deliver China's small stockpile of nuclear bombs."[57]

Chinese leaders have allowed the national bomber fleet to atrophy further in the intervening decade.[58] In all likelihood, Chinese leaders have made a deliberate decision to focus scarce resources on ballistic missiles rather than on strike aircraft—a decision consistent with recent Chinese efforts to supplement conventional strike aircraft with conventionally-armed ballistic missiles.[59] The lack of identifiable storage sites near airfields and the continued decline of the bomber force strongly suggest that China has held this capability in reserve.[60]

Proliferation: Threat and Response suggests that Beijing stores all warheads that are not "operationally deployed" for use on ballistic missiles— possibly in a single stockpile site. The process of moving warheads from a central stockpile site to airbases around the country probably would be

---

[56] *Handbook of the Chinese People's Liberation Army*, p. 70.

[57] *Report to Congress on Status of China, India, and Pakistan Nuclear and Ballistic Missile Programs*, np.

[58] For a study projecting trends in China's bomber forces, see Kenneth Allen et al., *China's Air Force Enters the 21st Century* (Washington, DC: RAND, 1995), pp. 165–168. For a review of recent developments, see David Shambaugh, *Modernizing China's Military: Progress, Problems, and Prospects* (Berkeley: University of California Press, 2002), p. 265.

[59] *CIA National Intelligence Estimate of Foreign Missile Development* ..., S. Hrg. 107–467, p. 33. Lewis and Hua suggest this reflects a deliberate decision by the Chinese leadership. Lewis and Hua, "China's Ballistic Missile Programs," p. 6.

[60] In 1982, a Chinese defense official reportedly told a French delegation that China had no tactical nuclear weapons deployed at "ground division or below"—the implication being that "tactical" nuclear weapons might be held at a higher echelon. Based on the fragmentary evidence available about the report, as well as the difficulty in defining tactical nuclear weapons, it seems probable to me that the official was referring to warheads for China's nuclear capable aircraft rather than atomic demolition munitions, or warheads for rockets and guided missiles. Anderson, "China Shows Confidence in Its Missiles," *Washington Post*, December 19, 1984, p. F11.

lengthy and visible. The intelligence community is probably aware of the locations of any stockpile facilities, based on its previous success in locating China's nuclear weapons stockpile site in the mid-1960s. A leaked 1984 DIA report noted that "only one national stockpile site and no regional sites have been observed in China."[61] China's central stockpile comprised three vaults in a ridge near China's Haiyan nuclear weapons production complex through the early 1970s.[62] The Haiyan complex has since been decommissioned and opened to tourists. The national stockpile site has presumably moved, along with the facilities to conduct warhead assembly and disassembly, to Mianyang in Sichuan province—although at least one unofficial assessment places the national stockpile site near the test facility at Lop Nur.[63]

OPERATIONAL DOCTRINE

China's National Defense explicitly defines the mission of Chinese nuclear weapons as retaliatory and reiterates a number of negative security assurances, such as a "no-first-use" pledge, that are consistent with a retaliation-only doctrine. Beginning with its first nuclear test in 1964, China undertook to "never at any time or under any circumstances be the first to use nuclear weapons."[64] In subsequent years, that declaration was supplemented by other security assurances not to use or threaten to use nuclear weapons against non-nuclear weapon states or nuclear-weapon-free zones.[65]

China's "no first-use" pledge continues to guide China's operational doctrine. *Operational Studies* warns commanders that launch operations

---

[61] Anderson, "China Shows Confidence in Its Missiles," F11.

[62] *Soviet and People's Republic of China Nuclear Weapons Employment Strategy*, II-E-5.

[63] Joseph Cirincione et al., *Dangerous Arsenals: Tracking Weapons of Mass Destruction* (Washington, DC: Brookings Institution Press, 2002), pp. 141–163. Robert Norris et al. place a "few" warheads in research and production facilities near Mianyang and Zitong in Sichuan province. See Robert Norris et al., *Taking Stock: Worldwide Nuclear Deployments 1998* (Washington, DC: National Resources Defense Council, March 1998).

[64] *Statement of the Government of the People's Republic of China* (October 16, 1964).

[65] For the official Chinese statement, see *China's Contribution to Nuclear Disarmament* (Beijing: Ministry of Foreign Affairs, no date).

will have to be undertaken in a nuclear environment: "According to our principle of 'no first-use of nuclear weapons,' the nuclear retaliation campaign of the Second Artillery will be conducted under the circumstances when the enemy has launched a nuclear attack on us." This description of China's operational doctrine is consistent with Second Artillery exercises reported in the press. For example, Chinese units rode out a simulated "bolt from the blue" attack in their bunkers during a 1994 exercise, waiting for nuclear decontamination units to complete their missions before launching a retaliatory strike.[66]

Operational Studies describes three tasks for China's nuclear forces, which are essentially phases of a retaliatory mission:

- Conduct anti-nuclear deterrence combat (alert operations to demonstrate willingness to retaliate);
- Guard against an enemy surprise attack (ride out a nuclear attack); and
- Conduct a nuclear missile attack (launch operations to retaliate).

This list is probably comprehensive, given the size of China's nuclear arsenal, which is too small for most counterforce missions; moreover, China's forces require several hours of pre-launch exposure that would provide substantial tactical warning to a potential adversary. Chinese operational doctrine focuses on counter-value targeting—"targets that are strategically highly valuable, influential on the overall situation, and easy to hit"—including population centers or military bases.[67] Second Artillery commanders are also likely to preserve a "strategic and campaign nuclear reserve force with suitable numbers and capabilities, according to the strategic intent of the supreme command and the actual situation of the missile force."[68]

The intent of the Chinese leadership to ride out a nuclear attack is evident from the lack of Chinese early warning assets. China reportedly

---

[66] Dong Jushan and Wu Xudong, "True Story: China's Mysterious Strategic Missile Forces on Rise," *Guangzhou Ribao* (July 1, 2001), FBIS-CPP-2001-0703-000044. The exercise is consistent with warnings in *Operational Studies* that a nuclear campaign will be conducted in "a bleak nuclear environment...under very serious nuclear circumstances. The personnel, position equipment, weapons equipment, command telecommunication system and the roads and bridges in the battlefield will be seriously hurt and damaged."

[67] *Operational Studies* (*Zhanyi xue*) Ch. 14, p. 7.

[68] Ibid.

has a single, large phased array radar (LPAR) positioned on a mountain slope at a 1,600-meter elevation near Xuanhua, manned by Second Artillery forces. This site, allegedly visible on the road from Beijing to Zhangjiakou, may be inactive.[69] Without early warning assets, Chinese forces would be unable to adopt alternative postures.[70]

Perhaps the best evidence of China's retaliatory operational doctrine is the substantial criticism the doctrine has endured in Chinese military journals since the early 1980s. Many of these articles criticize the Second Artillery for adopting an unrealistic and inflexible operational doctrine.[71] Western observers have long predicted that this dissenting school of thought will eventually come to dominate Chinese operational doctrine. For example, a 1985 DIA study noted:

> Particularly noteworthy is the concern exhibited by some writers over the dilemma that would face Chinese leaders if the Soviet Union were to limit its use of nuclear weapons in any attack. Chinese nuclear strategy, as it is now focused on the Soviet Union, is predicated upon deterring attack by maintaining a small but credible capability to retaliate against Soviet urban-industrial areas. Existing forces provide Chinese leaders little flexibility for other targeting options. Recognizing the great disparity between Chinese and Soviet capabilities, some Chinese military writers have argued

---

[69] Stokes, pp. 41–42, 67n 56.

[70] Some observers suggest that compromises made in the design of China's Bei Dou satellite navigation constellation, which provides relatively inaccurate guidance from geosynchronous orbit, appear to confirm retaliatory missions for China's Second Artillery. The constellation is optimized to guide post-boost vehicles through space to ensure the accuracy of China's ICBMs to down to about 1 kilometer circular error—probably to "facilitate MIRVing [Chinese] missiles without significantly improving their accuracy." The ability to maneuver post-boost phase would, in combination with warhead decoys, serve as countermeasure to U.S. midcourse ABM interceptors because the maneuvers would occur after U.S. space-based tracking systems determined the trajectory of an ICBM. These satellites are placed in geosynchronous orbit, which provides a substantial security against possible anti-satellite systems. See Geoffrey Forden, "Strategic Uses for China's Bei Dou Satellite System," *Jane's Intelligence Review* (October 2003), pp. 26–33.

[71] Alastair Iain Johnston, "China's New 'Old Thinking': The Concept of Limited Deterrence," *International Security*, vol. 20, no. 3 (Winter 1995/96), pp. 21–23

the need for more options—both tactical and theater—below the strategic level to respond to a limited Soviet attack.[72]

The theme of China moving toward greater operational flexibility appears in early analyses of China's nascent nuclear doctrine by RAND's Alice Langley Hsieh as well as in the work of more recent scholars.[73] For example, Iain Johnston published a 1983 article in the *Journal of Northeast Asian Studies* and an influential 1996 article in *International Security*, both of which suggested that China would adopt a more flexible operational doctrine.[74] The argument also appears in recent editions of *Chinese Military Power*. The 2003 edition noted that "despite Beijing's 'no first use' pledge, there are indications that some strategists are reconsidering the conditions under which Beijing would employ theater nuclear weapons against U.S. forces in the region."[75] The 2006 edition cited "recent high-profile Chinese statements" to "suggest that this policy may be under discussion."[76] Overall, however, Chinese proponents of such views appear to remain a minority within the Chinese leadership. Hua Hongxun, a Chinese academic, notes that the authors cited by Johnston and others "do not reflect the accepted views of the PLA and, indeed, they are criticized implicitly" in a speech by the vice chairman of the Central Military Commission.[77] In fact, one finds little evidence in either China's public declaratory statements or internal documents, such as *Operational Studies*, which suggests a doctrinal shift. Chinese proponents of a doctrinal shift toward additional operational flexibility have had more success convincing Western analysts of their case.

---

[72] *Special Defense Intelligence Estimate: China's Evolving Nuclear Strategies*, pp. 8–9.

[73] Alice Langley Hsieh, "China's Nuclear-Missile Programme: Regional or Intercontinental?" *China Quarterly*, vol. 45 (January–March 1971), pp. 85–99.

[74] Alistair Iain Johnston, "Chinese Nuclear Force Modernization: Implications for Arms Control," *Journal of Northeast Asian Studies*, vol. 2, no. 2 (June 1983), pp. 13–28 and Johnston, "China's New 'Old Thinking,'" pp. 5–42.

[75] "Chinese Military Power," (July 2003), p. 31.

[76] *Annual Report on the Military Power of the People's Republic of China*, Report To Congress Pursuant to The FY2000 National Defense Authorization Act (Washington, DC: Department of Defense, June 2006) pp. 28.

[77] Hua Hongxun, "China's Strategic Missile Programs: Limited Aims, Not 'Limited Deterrence," *The Nonproliferation Review*, vol. 5 (Winter 1998), p. 64.

Many Western analysts, working from the security concerns articulated in Chinese military journals and other circumstantial evidence, have concluded that China maintains an inventory of "tactical" nuclear warheads. Although the Defense Intelligence Agency noted "no evidence confirming production or deployment" of tactical nuclear weapons by the mid-1980s, the DIA still offered a "best estimate" of fifty atomic demolition munitions in the Chinese stockpile at that time. In addition to military writings, the evidence for Chinese tactical nuclear weapons is threefold:

- China conducted low-yield nuclear tests to develop fission bombs for delivery by aircraft and short-range ballistic missiles in the 1970s and to develop enhanced radiation warheads in the 1980s.
- China has conducted military exercises that involved the simulated offensive use of tactical nuclear weapons. The most well known exercise took place in 1982, although other exercises have been reported.[78]
- In 1982, a Chinese defense official reportedly told a French delegation that China had no tactical nuclear weapons deployed at "ground division or below," implying that tactical nuclear weapons might be held at a higher echelon.

The first two pieces of evidence are largely inferential and do not preclude the possibility that China developed the capability to produce low-yield nuclear weapons but did not actually produce more than a token number of them.[79] The last piece of evidence—the comment by a senior Chinese defense official—might have referred to simple fission devices, to be delivered by aircraft or short-range ballistic missiles. Shortly after that statement, the DIA concluded that Beijing might be considering the use

---

[78] For a review of published reports about Chinese military exercises, see Lin Chong-Pin, *China's Nuclear Strategy: Tradition within Evolution* (Lexington, MA: Lexington Books, 1988), pp. 92–95.

[79] For a skeptical view of Chinese tactical nuclear weapons production, see Charles D. Ferguson, Evan S. Medeiros, and Phillip C. Saunders, "Chinese Tactical Nuclear Weapons" in Brian Alexander and Alistair Millar, eds., *Tactical Nuclear Weapons: Emergent Threats in an Evolving Security Environment* (New York, NY: Brasseys, 2003), pp. 110–128. See also Kenneth W. Allen, "China's Perspective on Non-Strategic Nuclear Weapons and Arms Control" in Jeffrey A. Larsen and Kurt J. Klingenberger, eds., *Controlling Non-Strategic Nuclear Weapons: Obstacles and Opportunities* (Colorado Springs, CO: USAF Institute for National Security Studies, 2001), 159–196.

of aircraft-delivered bombs and short-range missiles to blunt a Soviet attack. Although that report posited fifty atomic demolition munitions, another DIA product from the same year reached the opposite conclusion: "China is not now assessed as having any stockpile of nuclear rockets, guided missiles, or atomic munitions."[80] *Operational Studies* does not include any information regarding China's tactical use of nuclear weapons delivered by either aircraft or missiles. In contrast, it makes explicit reference to the April 1998 creation of operational plans for the conventional use of ballistic missiles in support of joint operations.

The intelligence community probably does not currently believe that China has deployed tactical nuclear weapons. Unclassified assessments of China's nuclear weapons capability such as *Proliferation: Threat and Response* and *Chinese Military Power* do not mention possible Chinese tactical nuclear weapons other than theater ballistic missiles like the CSS-5.[81] To the contrary, *Chinese Military Power* specifically identifies Beijing's SRBM force as conventionally-armed—a feature that frees Beijing from "the political and practical constraints associated with the use of nuclear armed missiles."[82]

PROPOSED MODERNIZATION PLAN

The United States intelligence community expects that the "number, reliability, survivability and accuracy of Chinese strategic missiles capable of hitting the United States will increase during the next decade."[83] A basic outline of the intelligence community's judgments about China's strategic force modernization was provided in a December 2001 National Intelligence Estimate and subsequent Congressional testimony.[84] The

---

[80] *Handbook of the Chinese People's Liberation Army*, p. 36.

[81] The CSS-5 (M-9 export version) is the only Chinese system that was mentioned in the declassified sections of *A Guide to Foreign Tactical Nuclear Weapon Systems under the Control of Ground Force Commanders*, DST-1040S-541-87 (Washington, DC: Defense Intelligence Agency and Army Foreign Science and Technology Center, September 1987), p. 79.

[82] "Chinese Military Power," (July 2003), p. 29.

[83] Vice Admiral Lowell E. Jacoby, U.S. Navy, Director, Defense Intelligence Agency, *Statement for the Record*, Senate Armed Services Committee (February 26, 2004).

[84] Unless otherwise noted, this estimate is derived from *CIA National Intelligence Estimate of Foreign Missile Development* ..., S. Hrg. 107–467. *Annual*

central feature of Beijing's current modernization program is the introduction of mobile, solid-propellant ballistic missiles to address survivability concerns. The intelligence community expects that by 2015 China
will have deployed approximately seventy-five to one hundred strategic
nuclear warheads, primarily against the United States, and another two
dozen shorter-range ballistic missiles capable of reaching parts of the
United States. Most of these missiles are expected to be mobile.

Modernization of China's shorter-range ICBMs will occur first. China
is expected to retain more than a dozen CSS-3 (DF-4) ballistic missiles
through the end of the decade. The intelligence community anticipates
that China will supplement and then replace the CSS-3 (DF-4) with the
8,000-kilometer range CSS-X-10 (DF-31), a mobile, solid-fueled ballistic
missile that will be deployed primarily against targets in Russia and East
Asia.[85] China "could begin deploying the CSS-X-10 ICBM during the next
few years," although "countries are much less likely to [deploy] by the
hypothetical 'could' dates than they are by the projected 'likely' dates."[86]
In 1996, NAIC predicted CSS-X-10 (DF-31) deployment "about the turn
of the century." Since the missile remains to be deployed, the program
may be under-funded or experiencing technical problems. The CSS-X-10
(DF-31) reportedly incorporates many advanced technologies similar to
current generation Russian missiles: upgraded mobility for the transporter-erector-launcher, advanced materials for the booster and payload,
use of penetration aids such as decoys or chaff, and an improved solid pro-
pellant. These technologies were "presenting Chinese designers with substantial challenges."[87] A series of flight tests were conducted in 1999 and

---

Report on the Military Power of the People's Republic of China, Report To Congress Pursuant to The FY2000 National Defense Authorization Act (Washington, DC: Department of Defense, June 2002), p. 27.

[85] *Ballistic and Cruise Missile Threat* gives the range as "4,500+ km"—although
the 8,000-kilometer range is found in other documents, including classified
NAIC reports leaked to the press. For example, see *Chinese ICBM Capability
Steadily Increasing*, NAIC-1030-098B-96 (Washington, DC: National Air
Intelligence Center, November 1996) in Bill Gertz, *Betrayal: How the Clinton
Administration Undermined American Security* (Washington, DC: Regency
Publishing, 1999), p. 253 and *Proliferation: Threat and Response* (Washington,
DC: Department of Defense, 2001), p. 15.

[86] *CIA National Intelligence Estimate of Foreign Missile Development ...*, S. Hrg.
107–467. p. 30.

[87] *Chinese ICBM Capability Steadily Increasing*, in Gertz, *Betrayal*, p. 253.

2000.[88] Although one intelligence official in 2001 predicted imminent deployment of the CSS-X-10 based on the formation of Second Artillery units for the missile and the beginning of crew training, the U.S. intelligence community continues to describe this missile as not deployed.[89]

The intelligence community believes that China is "developing two follow-on extended range versions of the CSS-X-10 (DF-31) "to supplement the CSS-4 (DF-5): a solid-propellant, road-mobile ICBM and a solid-propellant SLBM." The CSS-X-10 (DF-31) follow-on is expected to have a range of 12,000 kilometers.[90] China could deploy the CSS-X-10 (DF-31) follow-on "in the last half of the decade,"—again, with "could" implying the last half of the decade is the *earliest* deployment date. China is designing a new SSBN that will carry the JL-2 ballistic missile, which is expected to have a range of over 8,000 kilometers. The JL-2 and a new SSBN (the Type 094) "likely will be *developed and tested* later this decade."[91] When deployed, the JL-2 will allow China to target the United States from operating areas near the Chinese coast.

The U.S. intelligence community's estimate that China will deploy seventy-five to one hundred warheads by 2015 does not reflect uncertainty, but rather two distinct modernization plans:

- "Seventy-five warheads" assumes that China will not place multiple RVs on the CSS-4 (DF-5).
- "One hundred warheads" assumes the Chinese will build fewer missiles, but place multiple CSS-X-10 (DF-31)-type RVs on the CSS-4 (DF-5).

The intelligence community does not provide disaggregated estimates of CSS-4 (DF-5), CSS-X-10 (DF-31) follow-on, or JL-2 deployments, beyond noting that half the missiles will be mobile.

---

[88] *Current and Projected National Security Threats to the United States,* S. Hrg. 107–597, p. 79.

[89] Bill Gertz, "China Ready to Deploy its First Mobile ICBMs," *Washington Times,* September 6, 2001.

[90] As in the case of the CSS-X-10 (DF-31), NAIC's *Ballistic and Cruise Missile Threat* lists a much lower range, (7,000+ kilometers) than other official documents, in this case the 1997 edition of *Chinese Military Power.*

[91] Current and Projected National Security Threats to the United States, S. Hrg. 107–597, p. 79. Emphasis Added. Bill Gertz reported that the "new 094-class submarine was launched in late July [2004]." The United States intelligence community has not confirmed this claim. See Bill Gertz, "China Tests Ballistic Missile Submarine," *Washington Times,* December 3, 2004.

The intelligence community also does not provide details on its assumptions about possible scenarios for multiple CSS-4 (DF-5) RVs, beyond noting that China would probably use a CSS-X-10 (DF-31)-type RV. One senior intelligence official, however, gave an interview to the *New York Times* describing the difference between the two options as "add new warheads to their old eighteen CSS-4s, transforming them from single-warhead missiles into four-warhead missiles" or "double the size of their projected land-based mobile missiles."[92] This is broadly consistent with Congressional testimony, where intelligence officials have predicted that the Chinese decision to place multiple reentry vehicles on the CSS-4 (DF-5) would reflect a vulnerability assessment of silo-based missiles, that is, whether the Chinese "view [multiple reentry vehicles on the CSS-4] as throwing good money after bad, on the side they are vulnerable."[93] If Chinese leaders view silo-based ICBMs as too vulnerable, they would presumably increase their production of CSS-X-10 ballistic missiles rather than silo-based CSS-4s.

Based on predictions from the intelligence community, one can infer a deployment estimate as depicted in table 2-3. This estimate would be consistent with earlier intelligence community predictions that "China will likely have tens of missiles targeted against the United States [by 2015], having added a few tens of more survivable land- and sea-based mobile missiles with smaller nuclear warheads."[94] It is also consistent with the 2002 Defense Department estimate that the number of Chinese ICBMs "will increase to around 30 by 2005 and may reach 60 by 2010."[95]

The intelligence community may have developed alternative estimates of China's modernization program in part, because of the difficulty in predicting international reaction to a U.S. missile defense system that remains ill-defined. National Intelligence Officer for Strategic and Nuclear Programs Robert Walpole has suggested that the Chinese leader-

---

[92] An earlier estimate by the National Air Intelligence Center, however, suggested that the CSS-4 (DF-5) might carry up to three 470-kilogram CSS-X-10 (DF-31) type RVs—although one assumption of this analysis was that a "minimum number of changes" was made to modify a Smart Dispenser upper stage for use as a post-boost vehicle. NAIC-1442-0629-97 in Gertz, *Betrayal*, p. 252.

[93] *Ballistic Missiles: Threat and Response*, S. Hrg. 106–339, p. 372.

[94] *National Intelligence Estimate on The Ballistic Missile Threat...*, S. Hrg. 106–671, p. 51.

[95] "Chinese Military Power," (July 2003), p. 31.

Table 2-3: Intelligence Community Estimates of Chinese ICBM Deployments

	Case 1: No MIRV	Case 2: MIRV	
CSS-4 (DF-5)	18	18 x 4	72
CSS-X-10 (DF-31, DF-31A, and JL-2)	56		28
Total	72		100

CIA National Intelligence Estimate of Foreign Missile Developments and the Ballistic Missile Threat through 2015, Hearing before the International Security, Proliferation, and Federal Services Subcommittee of the Committee on Governmental Affairs, United States Senate, S. Hrg. 107–467 (March 11, 2002).

ship will not commit to a set of countermeasures until the precise architecture of U.S. missile defense efforts becomes clear. In the end, this architecture will determine "both the numbers of weapons they would put together and the types of weapons, because they would want to carry countermeasures on these that they would use."[96]

Chinese officials have made the same point themselves. For example, Sha Zukang, China's then-Ambassador for Disarmament Affairs, noted that the United States "will need more time to design [its missile defense deployments] and to resolve technical problems. So it's too early to say what kind of countermeasures China will take."[97] Asked whether the intelligence community projections on future Chinese deployments were "baseless speculation," Walpole admitted that "One out of two is not bad. It is speculation. We are speculating, but it is far from baseless."[98] Either projection would suggest a major departure for the Chinese leadership. Past intelligence community projections have overestimated both the scope and pace of Chinese ballistic missile deployments (See Table 2-4).

One source of bias is the difficulty that the intelligence community has in interpreting Chinese intentions. Chinese industrial capacity has

---

[96] *CIA National Intelligence Estimate of Foreign Missile Development* ..., S. Hrg. 107–467, p. 27.

[97] Sha Zukang, "Transcript Briefing On Missile Defense Issue," March 23, 2001. Available at http://www.fmprc.gov.cn/eng/wjb/zzjg/jks/cjjk/2622/ t15417.htm.

[98] *Foreign Missile Developments and the Ballistic Missile Threat Through 2015: Unclassified Summary of a National Intelligence Estimate* (December 2001) in *CIA National Intelligence Estimate of Foreign Missile Development* ..., S. Hrg. 107–467, 27.

Table 2-4: Ten-Year Projections of Chinese Missile Threats (1974, 1984, and 1993)

	1984		1994		2003	
	Projected, 1974	*(Actual)*	*Projected, 1984*	*(Actual)*	*Projected, 1993*	*(Actual)*
CSS-4	50-75	(2)	16	(7)	24-28	(18)
CSS-3	15-35	(8)	32	(12)	100	(57)
CSS-2	50-75	(110)	120	(45)	–	–
SLBM	80-160	(0)	48	(0)	–	(0)
Total	195-345	(120)	216	(64)	124-128	(75)

1974 projections for 1984 are taken from *Defense Intelligence Estimate: PRC Strategic Nuclear Forces: How Much is Enough?* DIE FE 7-74 (December 3, 1974), p. 3.
1984 projections for 1994 are taken from: *Defense Estimative Brief: Nuclear Weapons Systems in China* DEB-49-84 (April 24, 1984), p. 3.
1993 projections for 2003 are taken from Presidential Review 31 (1993): *U.S. Policy on Ballistic Missile Defenses and the Future of the ABM Treaty.*
"Actual" figures for each year are drawn from the report dated that same year, i.e.
"Actual 1984" is drawn from DEB-49-84 *Nuclear Weapons Systems in China.*

long exceeded Beijing's intent to produce ballistic missiles. For example, China deliberately slowed construction of its SSBN fleet in the mid-1980s and, based on the difference between delivery vehicle production and industrial capacity (inferred from floor-space estimates derived from overhead imagery), operated its ballistic missile factories and warhead production facilities below capacity.[99] This situation persists: the 1997 edition of *Chinese Military Power* noted that China "will probably have the industrial capacity, though not necessarily the intent, to produce a large number, perhaps as many as a thousand, new missiles within the next decade."[100]

---

[99] The construction of the 093 SSBN, to follow the 092 SSBN launched in 1981, was initially delayed and then scrapped altogether. See Lewis and Xue, China's Strategic Seapower, p. 121. United States intelligence was reporting the delay in construction by early 1985. See *Defense Estimative Brief: China's ICBM Force Begins to Take Shape*, p. 2. China appears to have built redundant production facilities for missiles and nuclear warheads, see *Defense Estimative Brief: Nuclear Weapons Systems in China*, p. 3.

[100] "Chinese Military Power," (April 1997), p. 4

The intelligence community has also overestimated the speed at which new systems would enter the Chinese inventory. The history of anticipated deployment dates for the CSS-X-10 demonstrates this tendency. In 1984, the intelligence community forecast the first solid-fueled ICBM deployments in 1994; in 1996, the National Air Intelligence Center predicted CSS-X-10 deployment "about the turn of the century." If recent reports of a 2002 CSS-X-10 flight test failure prove true, China may not meet more recent predictions of CSS-X-10 deployment later this decade.

CONCLUSION

China's small but effective nuclear counterattacking force—comprising around eighty operationally deployed nuclear warheads that are stored separately from their land-based ballistic missiles and intended for retaliatory missions—is significantly smaller, less diverse, and less ready to conduct actual operations than any of the arsenals maintained by the other four nuclear powers recognized under the NPT. China's posture, which is vulnerable to preemptive interference, deviates significantly from accepted wisdom about deterrence and the posture necessary for its credibility. Current Chinese strategic forces look very little like the projections offered by the intelligence community in the past, predictions that began with the assumption that Chinese strategic forces would increasingly resemble those of other nuclear states.

The historical pattern of Chinese deployments, examined in the next chapter, suggests that the current force reflects a very different set of design principles. To the extent that Chinese forces continue to reflect a distinct logic, current projections may exaggerate the future Chinese deployments and misrepresent the unique features of Chinese posture as an ephemeral phenomenon.

CHAPTER 3

Chinese Strategic Nuclear Forces: Evolution and Design

For national security reasons, official documents elaborating on China's nuclear strategic theory have not been released to the public in the past decades. But the fact remains that China has maintained a consistent framework of nuclear policy that is based on a clear understanding of the nature of nuclear weapons.

—Sun Xiangli, Institute of Applied Physics and Computational Mathematics, 2005[1]

The idea that Chinese nuclear weapons developments and deployments reflect a consistent outlook on the "special nature" of nuclear weapons—particularly the insensitivity of the deterrent balance to changes in the technical details of forces—is the central theme of this study. This hypothesis is one explanation for why China maintains strategic forces that are significantly smaller, less diverse, and less ready to conduct actual operations than those of the other four nuclear powers recognized under the NPT.

One way to test this hypothesis is to consider the historical development of Chinese strategic forces. Figure 3-1 shows the most widely accepted estimate of the total number of Chinese nuclear weapons each year since 1965, as well as my revised estimate. My estimate suggests an entirely different history of the development of China's nuclear forces—one reflecting the natural technological evolution of China's strategic forces guided by the principle of maintaining the minimum means of reprisal.

---

[1] Sun Xiangli, "Analysis of China's Nuclear Strategy," in *China Security*, Issue No. 1 (Autumn 2005), p. 24.

Figure 3-1: China's Nuclear Forces, 1965–2005

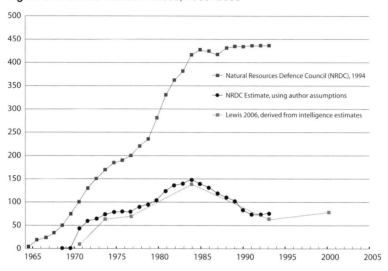

This is a comparison of the estimates provided by NRDC and the author. "NRDC 1994" includes a variety of systems that were very likely never deployed, including SLBMs, tactical nuclear weapons, and gravity bombs; "NRDC Estimate, using author assumptions" includes only CSS-1, CSS-2, CSS-3, CSS-4, and CSS-5 ballistic missiles, creating an "apples-to apples" comparison with my estimates in chapters 1 and 2.

Sources: Robert S. Norris, Andrew S. Burrows, and Richard W. Fieldhouse, *Nuclear Weapons Databook Volume 5: British, French, and Chinese Nuclear Weapons* (Boulder, CO: Westview Press, 1994), p. 359. *NIE-13-8-71 Communist China's Weapons Program For Strategic Attack*, (Washington, DC: Central Intelligence Agency, October 28, 1971) p. 31. *NIE-13-8-74 China's Strategic Attack Programs* (Washington, DC: Central Intelligence Agency, June 13, 1974) p. 35–39. *DIANM 2-77 PRC Strategic Attack Forces* (Washington, DC: Defense Intelligence Agency, June 6, 1977) pp. 7–8. *DEB-49-84 Defense Estimative Brief: Nuclear Weapons Systems in China*, (Washington, DC: Defense Intelligence Agency, April 24, 1984) p. 2.

This chapter focuses on the choices that Chinese leaders made regarding the development of their country's nuclear force.[2] It draws exten-

---

[2] The history of the Chinese nuclear weapons community is recounted in John Wilson Lewis and Xue Litai, *China Builds the Bomb* (Stanford, CA: Stanford University Press, 1988) and *China's Strategic Seapower: The Politics of Force Modernization in the Nuclear Age* (Stanford, CA: Stanford University Press, 1994); John Wilson Lewis and Hua Di, "China's Ballistic Missile Programs" and John Wilson Lewis, Hua Di, and Xue Litai, "Beijing's Defense Establishment," *International Security*, vol. 17, no. 2 (Autumn 1992), pp. 5–40. For a

sively from the work of John Lewis, including his books *China Builds the Bomb* and *China's Strategic Seapower*, a pair of official Chinese histories published by the National Defense Industry Press entitled *China Today: Nuclear Industry* and *China Today: Defense, Science, and Technology*, and a new reference work that has not appeared in English—*Biographies of the Founders of the Nuclear, Missile and Satellite Program* (2001), which is a compendium of biographies about twenty-three Chinese scientists involved in the development of these three programs.

THE EVOLUTION OF CHINA'S STRATEGIC FORCES

The development of China's strategic forces can be divided broadly into three periods. During the first period from 1955 to 1966, the Chinese defense-industrial community focused on developing atomic and thermonuclear warheads as well as long-range ballistic missiles. During the second period from 1967 to 1981, Chinese scientists struggled through the Cultural Revolution and its aftermath as they developed China's first generation of operational strategic systems—most of which remain in service today. Since 1981, China's leaders have reorganized the country's strategic programs to complete the deployment of first-generation systems and have turned to developing ballistic missiles with solid propellants and miniaturized nuclear warheads.

High-Yield Nuclear Weapons and Long-Range Missiles, 1955–1966

Chinese state media sometimes date the decision to pursue nuclear weapons and ballistic missiles to a spring 1955 meeting at Zhongnanhai that followed explicit nuclear threats from the United States.[3] The actual decision, however, seems to have been undertaken earlier at a meeting, in January 1955, that Mao Zedong convened to consider the question of

---

review of the development of the Second Artillery, see Bates Gill, James Mulvenon, Mark Stokes, "The Chinese Second Artillery Corps: Transition to Credible Deterrence," in *The People's Liberation Army as an Organization: Reference Volume v1.0.* CF-182, James C. Mulvenon, Andrew N. D. Yang, eds. (Santa Monica, CA: RAND, 2002) pp. 510–586.

[3] For example, see Xu Zuzhi, "China's Strategic Missile Unit Now Possesses Fighting Capability under High-Tech Conditions; from National Day Background News Series," *Beijing Zhongguo Xinwen She* (October 1, 1999), FBIS-FTS-1999-1002-00009.

nuclear weapons and that included presentations by several well-known Chinese scientists.[4]

China's leaders initially expected substantial Soviet assistance for their country's nuclear and ballistic missile programs, assistance that, for a while, Moscow did provide. In offering his guidance for the Chinese government's review of Soviet proposals for nuclear cooperation in early 1957, Chinese Premier Zhou Enlai established the principle that China's nuclear program would be "a complete set and form an independent nuclear force; but mainly we should solve the problem of 'having or not.' [T]herefore an excessive force would be unsuitable."[5]

China and the Soviet Union signed six cooperative agreements regarding defense technology, culminating in the October 1957 *Agreement on Producing New Weapons and Military Technical Equipment and Building a Comprehensive Nuclear Industry in China* (the New Defense Technical Accord), which among other things reportedly committed the Soviet Union to provide China with a prototype nuclear device.[6] Marshal Nie Rongzhen, writing in his memoirs, noted that "Although the agreement worked out quite well in the first two years, the assistance was short-lived."[7] For a variety of reasons, Sino–Soviet relations had begun to sour by early 1958, when the Soviet Union decided against shipping a prototype nuclear device, along with blueprints and technical data, to China. According to one account, the Soviets had prepared sealed railroad cars containing a prototype atomic bomb, documentation, and equipment. Upon learning of the preparations, however, the Soviet Communist Party Central Committee ordered the bomb removed and the documentation burned.[8]

Soviet assistance to China's nuclear program was terminated with a June 1959 letter from the Soviet Central Committee to its Chinese coun-

---

[4] Accounts of the meeting are provided in Lewis and Xue, *China Builds the Bomb*, pp. 35–39 and *China Today: Defense Science and Technology*, Xie Guang, ed. (Beijing, China: National Defense Industry Press, 1993) pp. 28–29.

[5] *China Today: Defense Science and Technology*, p. 181.

[6] This section is largely drawn from Nie Rongzhen, *Inside the Red Star: The Memoirs of Marshal Nie Rongzhen*, Zhong Rongyi, trans. (Beijing: New World Press, 1988), pp. 693–701; Lewis and Xue, *China Builds the Bomb*, pp. 39–72; and *China Today: Defense Science and Technology*, pp. 28–29.

[7] Nie, *Inside the Red Star*, p. 696.

[8] See Evgeny A. Negin and Yuri N. Smirnov, *Did the USSR Share Atomic Secrets with China?* (N.p.: Parallel History Project on NATO and the Warsaw Pact, October 2002) pp. 11–12.

terpart stating that due to test ban negotiations in Geneva, the Soviet Union would not provide China with a prototype nuclear device, blueprints, or technical data.

Amidst deteriorating Sino–Soviet relations, China's Central Military Commission issued one of the few published documents offering insight into early Chinese nuclear strategy. *The Guidelines for Developing Nuclear Weapons,* probably issued in 1959, established the basic parameters for the indigenous development of Chinese nuclear weapons.[9] The *Guidelines* endorsed a retaliatory operational doctrine based on an arsenal of "nuclear and thermonuclear warheads with high yields and long-range delivery vehicles," explicitly excluding the development of tactical nuclear weapons.

The general ideas about nuclear weapons expressed in the *Guidelines* have been noted by other scholars studying the Chinese leadership of the 1950s. In a study of Korean-War era Chinese-language materials—including articles in the Chinese mass media, civil defense and cadre manuals, and specialized journals—Mark Ryan concludes that the first generation of Chinese Communist leaders "early on developed a marked attitude of realism in their treatment of … not only the physical effects of nuclear weapons and how they might affect warfare, but also to the sphere of political assessment—how likely the enemy was to use nuclear weapons, what the political preconditions were for such use, and what the political repercussions might be stemming from such use."[10] Ryan argues that these attitudes "depended in part upon a measure of psychological realism, an ability to look clearly at both the enemy's and one's own advantages, disadvantages, hopes, fears, and general psychological deportment."[11] These attitudes continued to shape the Chinese leadership's decisions about the role for their own nuclear weapons, leading to the adoption of a minimum deterrent posture that remains dominant in Chinese strategic planning.

---

[9] The source of the guidelines, as Lewis and Xue note, does not provide a date for when they were issued. Lewis and Xue argue that the guidelines were issued in July 1958, but *China Today: Defense Science and Technology* suggests the decision to pursue nuclear weapons indigenously was not until 1959. Lewis and Xue, *China Builds the Bomb,* p. 71 and *China Today: Defense Science and Technology,* pp. 41–42.

[10] Mark A. Ryan, *Chinese Attitudes toward Nuclear Weapons,* p. 195.

[11] Ibid., p. 195.

The complete withdrawal of Soviet advisors from China in July 1960 and the turmoil of the Great Leap Forward (1958–1960) campaign complicated Chinese efforts to develop a nuclear weapon and ballistic missiles. In particular, China faced great difficulty in producing adequate amounts of fissile materials, particularly plutonium.[12] As a result of the Soviet withdrawal, the Chinese leadership halted construction on China's first plutonium production reactor between 1960 and 1962.[13] China's first nuclear weapon would, instead, use highly enriched uranium.

The budgetary and technical constraints imposed by the aftermath of the Great Leap Forward and of the Soviet withdrawal created divisions within the Chinese leadership about the wisdom of pursuing strategic programs; some senior officials argued that the expense of strategic programs had begun to "impede the development of other sectors of the national economy."[14]

In the summer of 1961, the Central Committee resolved the controversy during a meeting at Beidaihe, selecting strategic programs for modernization at the expense of conventional forces.[15] Advocates for slowing or suspending the strategic programs argued that large expenditures for strategic programs would jeopardize their other programs and priorities, including the modernization of conventional forces.[16] Nie Rongzhen carried the day, arguing that strategic programs would serve as a focal point for national science and technology, a rationale that linked the development of "sophisticated weapons" to the broader theme of China's national economic development.

Although bureaucratic wrangling over resources and control of the nuclear program would continue, the Central Committee had accepted

---

[12] On the difficulties created by the withdrawal of Soviet technical advisors, particularly in the production of fissile material, see Lewis and Xue, *China Builds the Bomb*, pp. 104–136 and [Author redacted], *China's Plutonium Production Reactor Problems: A Research Paper* (Central Intelligence Agency, January 1988), p. 1.

[13] *China Today: Defense Science and Technology*, p. 201.

[14] Nie, *Inside the Red Star*, p. 702.

[15] This meeting is summarized in Nie, *Inside the Red Star*, pp. 702–703; *China Today: Defense Science and Technology*, pp. 43–44; and Feigenbaum, *China's Techno-Warriors*, pp. 29–31.

[16] In the end, the Chinese nuclear program would cost 10.7 billion Yuan in 1957 prices over the period from 1955 to 1964—roughly equivalent to the entire defense budget for 1957 and 1958. Lewis and Xue, *China Builds the Bomb*, pp. 107–108.

Nie's national development rationale for strategic programs and would over the next few years create senior-level bureaucratic structures, including a fifteen-member Special Commission of the CCCPC (CSC), headed by Zhou Enlai in November 1962, to centralize control over the military science and technology industry.[17] This centralization resulted in the decision to prioritize ballistic missiles over aircraft, whose advocates had aligned themselves with opponents of the strategic weapons programs, as the delivery system for nuclear weapons.[18] Consequently, the CSC directed that "the research orientation of nuclear weapons should take mainly the missile-carried atomic warhead [as its first priority] while making [the development of the] aerial bomb subsidiary."[19]

This preference for missile-delivered warheads was presumably evident to China's nuclear weapons designers. In 1961, they settled on pursuing a relatively more sophisticated implosion device (A-1) instead of a simpler gun-type device because the former conformed better to the requirements of missile delivery and made more efficient use of China's fissile material stockpile.[20]

As China neared completion of a nuclear device that could be tested, Chinese officials became concerned that the United States might attempt to destroy their nuclear facilities—to "strangle the baby in the cradle" in Robert Komer's colorful phrase.[21] The CSC presented the Central Committee with two options in September 1964: test the device as soon as possible, or delay a test while making defensive preparations. The Central Committee, led by Mao Zedong and Liu Shaoqi, again made a decision that suggested that even a small nuclear capability would provide a significant deterrent: "Mao Zedong and others, looking at the issue from an

---

[17] *China Today: Defense Science and Technology*, pp. 43–44.

[18] On the competition for resources between ballistic missiles and aircraft, see Evan A. Feigenbaum, *China's Techno-Warriors: National Security and Strategic Competition from the Nuclear to the Information Age* (Stanford, CA: Stanford University Press, 2003), pp. 25–37.

[19] *China Today: Defense Science and Technology*, p. 200.

[20] Lewis and Xue, *China Builds the Bomb*, pp. 137–160.

[21] On China's planning for U.S. preemption, see Gordon H. Chang, "JFK, China, and the Bomb," *Journal of American History*, vol. 74, no. 4 (March 1988), pp. 1289–1310, and William Burr and Jeffrey T. Richelson, "Whether to 'Strangle the Baby in the Cradle': The United States and the Chinese Nuclear Program, 1960–1964" *International Security*, vol. 25, no. 3 (Winter 2001), pp. 54–99.

even wider strategic point of view, thought that the atomic bomb served as a deterrent force, it was therefore better to test early."[22]

China successfully tested a 15 kiloton (KT) implosion device utilizing uranium 235 (U-235) in October 1964. The Chinese government promptly issued a statement that outlined the major features of China's nuclear declaratory policy:

> China exploded an atomic bomb at 15:00 hours on October 16, 1964, thereby successfully carrying out its first nuclear test. This is a major achievement of the Chinese people in their struggle to strengthen their national defense and oppose the U.S. imperialist policy of nuclear blackmail and nuclear threats. ...
>
> China is developing nuclear weapons not because it believes in their omnipotence nor because it plans to use them. On the contrary, in developing nuclear weapons, China's aim is to break the nuclear monopoly of the nuclear powers and to eliminate nuclear weapons. ...
>
> China is developing nuclear weapons for defense and for protecting the Chinese people from U.S. threats to launch a nuclear war.
>
> The Chinese government hereby solemnly declares that China will never at any time or under any circumstances be the first to use nuclear weapons.[23]

This statement, received in the West largely as propaganda, accurately reflects the contents of the nominally secret 1959 *Guidelines for Developing Nuclear Weapons.* Both statements described the purpose of China's nuclear weapons as defensive and referenced broader goals such as safeguarding world peace and promoting disarmament. Perhaps most important, the 1964 statement, issued after China's first test, articulated the no-first-use pledge that remains the major doctrinal statement describing the structure of Chinese nuclear forces. This consistency between internal formulation and external formulation of nuclear strategy is not surprising, given China's interest in discouraging Soviet or U.S. preemption.

The 1964 statement contains a number of other elements that are interesting from a historical point of view. The statement describes the Limited Test Ban Treaty, an agreement among the Soviet Union, United States, and United Kingdom to refrain from testing nuclear weapons in

---

[22] *China Today: Defense Science and Technology,* p. 63.

[23] Statement of the Government of the People's Republic of China (October 26, 1964). An edited version of this statement is available as an appendix to Lewis and Xue, *China Builds the Bomb,* pp. 241–243.

the atmosphere, outer space, and under water, as "a big fraud" and "an attempt to consolidate the nuclear monopoly of the three nuclear powers." This is almost certainly a veiled reference to the June 1959 Soviet letter suspending assistance to the Chinese nuclear program in deference to test ban negotiations in Geneva. (In fact, China's first nuclear device had been code-named "596," for "June 1959," the date of the letter.) The statement also refers to Mao's aphorism that the "atom bomb is a paper tiger"—a comment that Ryan suggests symbolized the limited military utility and high political costs associated with the use of nuclear weapons.

The U.S. intelligence community had expected China to test a device using plutonium, rather than uranium-235.[24] Glenn Seaborg, chairman of the Atomic Energy Commission at the time, recalled that "to our surprise, the Chinese had detonated a device employing U-235. Further, we were persuaded that the Chinese bomb had been more sophisticated in design than our own Hiroshima U-235 weapon, employing an advanced form of implosion trigger to detonate fission materials."[25]

With its first nuclear test completed, China shifted resources into two parallel tracks, with one track dedicated to developing a thermonuclear warhead and another to "weaponize" nuclear devices for use with aircraft and ballistic missiles. Zhou Enlai established a three-step procedure by which China's nuclear weapon designs would be certified for serial production: a verification test, trial production based on revised design drawings and technical documents, and the submission of a summary report and technical documentation to the relevant state commission for review and approval.[26]

---

[24] The U.S. intelligence community was unaware that the gaseous diffusion plant at Lanzhou had begun enriching uranium in 1963. For an intelligence assessment from that period, see *The Chances of an Imminent Communist Chinese Nuclear Explosion*, Special National Intelligence Estimate 13-4-64 (Director of Central Intelligence, August 26, 1964). For a historical account of the Lanzhou facility, see Lewis and Xue, *China Builds the Bomb*, pp. 113–125.

[25] Glenn T. Seaborg with Benjamin S. Loeb, *Stemming the Tide: Arms Control in the Johnson Years* (Lexington, MA: Lexington Books, 1987), pp. 116–117. I have omitted a parenthetical note in the text reading "(The other four nuclear weapon powers had used plutonium devices for their first tests.)" Seaborg's passage is based on his diary entries for October 20 and 21, 1964, republished in *Journals of Glenn Seaborg*, Volume 9 (Berkeley, CA: Lawrence Berkeley Laboratory, University of California, 1979), p. 261.

[26] *China Today: Defense Science and Technology*, p. 203. The relevant state commission is described as the State Commission of Certification.

Just as Chinese designers had faced a choice between the relatively simple gun-type device and the more sophisticated implosion device, the weaponeers now chose between a simple "boosted" device, which would have had a yield on the order of hundreds of kilotons, and a multistage thermonuclear weapon with a yield of one megaton or more. Again, the Chinese designers chose the more technically complicated route, though this time the decision was inferred from broad guidance provided by Zhou Enlai in July 1964. That guidance reportedly reiterated the 1958 *Guidelines for Developing Nuclear Weapons* focus on developing "nuclear and thermonuclear warheads with high yields and long-range delivery vehicles," making clear the "high-level goal" of producing "thermonuclear warheads that would be fixed to our intermediate and long-range missiles." As one senior Chinese official recalled, "We thought we had to develop hydrogen bombs with deterrent force."[27]

Just as the chaos of the Cultural Revolution was beginning to overtake the country, China successfully tested a two-stage thermonuclear device in June 1967, dropping it from a bomber. The design contained an all oralloy (enriched uranium) primary stage and tuballoy (natural uranium) secondary stage.[28] *China Today: Defense Science and Technology* described the design, which was quite heavy, as "a step [toward] solving the problem" of mating a thermonuclear device to a ballistic missile.[29]

While Chinese designers were completing work on thermonuclear warheads, a second track was underway to develop operational air- and missile-delivered nuclear warheads. Over the 1965–1966 period, China reorganized ballistic missile programs into an eight-year program, established the Second Artillery Corps to operate China's nascent ballistic missile force, and tested deliverable nuclear fission devices, including a gravity bomb dropped from an H-6 aircraft in May 1965 and another fission weapon launched from a ballistic missile in October 1966.[30]

---

[27] This paragraph is drawn from Lewis and Xue, *China Builds the Bomb*, pp. 196–202.

[28] *Soviet and People's Republic of China Nuclear Weapons Employment Strategy*, (Washington, DC: Defense Intelligence Agency, March 1972). p. II-D-1.

[29] *China Today: Defense Science and Technology*, p. 236.

[30] The May 1965 and October 1966 tests are detailed in Lewis and Xue, *China Builds the Bomb*, pp. 207–210; Nie, *Inside the Red Star*, pp. 711–712; and *China Today: Nuclear Industry* JPRS-CST-88-002 (Foreign Broadcast Information Service, U.S. Department of Commerce Joint Publications Research Service, January 15, 1988), pp. 43–44.

The May 1965 aircraft-deliverable fission bomb was tested just once–following the verification test, the CSC canceled trial production of the design and focused on developing a device that could be mated to a ballistic missile.[31] Although Second Artillery units received the CSS-1 (DF-2) missile in September 1966, Chinese nuclear warheads were reportedly still too heavy for the CSS-1 until some time after the October 1966 test, when a CSS-1 delivered a 500-kilogram device with a 12 KT yield.[32] The October 1966 device was also tested only once, although *China Today* indicates this design seems to have been certified for "batch" production.[33]

The U.S. intelligence community did not detect CSS-1 deployments and troop training for several more years, not until *after* China had tested a three-megaton (MT) thermonuclear warhead. It is possible that Chinese leaders, as typified by Zhou Enlai's 1964 guidance to develop "nuclear and thermonuclear warheads with high yields and long-range delivery vehicles," intended to deploy an arsenal that exclusively comprised large-yield nuclear warheads delivered by ballistic missiles—essentially the same force that China has today.

China's unusual decision to test a missile armed with a live nuclear warhead deserves some consideration.[34] China's weaponeers initially intended to examine the effects of warhead reentry on China's ballistic missiles with an underground test. Owing in part to limited nuclear testing experience, however, they concluded that a live test of a nuclear weapon launched on a ballistic missile would be necessary, and in November 1965, the CSC approved such a test. The Chinese leadership claims to

---

[31] *China Today: Defense Science and Technology*, p. 68.

[32] Lewis and Hua estimate the mass of the device at 1,290 kilograms. This device, however, is widely believed to be the same design that China transferred to Pakistan in the early 1980s and that Pakistan transferred to Libya in the 1990s. That design is reported to weigh 500 kilograms, which is consistent with my estimates of mass from publicly available photographs of the Chinese device before launch in 1966. See Lewis and Hua, "China's Ballistic Missile Programs," p. 15; David Albright and Corey Hinderstein, "Unraveling the A. Q. Khan and Future Proliferation Networks," *The Washington Quarterly*, vol. 28, no. 2 (Spring 2005), pp. 111–128; and Jeffrey Lewis, "More on Libya's Bomb Design ..." *Arms Control Wonk.com*, October 8, 2005, Available at: http://www.armscontrolwonk.com/816/more-on-that-chinese-design-that-ended-up-in-libya.

[33] *China Today: Defense Science and Technology*, p. 69.

[34] This paragraph is drawn from *China Today: Defense Science and Technology*, pp. 226–232.

have undertaken extensive safety precautions for this test, including the evacuation of residents in areas under the missile's flight path and the installation of a self-destruct mechanism on the missile. Much as the Chinese leaders concluded that testing a nuclear device would provide a measure of deterrence, they also saw value in demonstrating the capability to build fission weapons deliverable by ballistic missiles.

China's First Generation of Strategic Systems, 1967–1981

Following the successful demonstration of the operational fission and thermonuclear devices, the Chinese nuclear program began, over the course of the 1970s and early 1980s, to certify thermonuclear designs for use with ballistic missiles.

According to *China Today: Defense Science and Technology*, China did not certify its first thermonuclear weapon for production until the early 1970s. This publication devotes substantial attention to the detrimental impact of the Cultural Revolution, particularly efforts by Lin Biao in the late 1960s and by the Gang of Four in the mid-1970s to exert control over China's strategic weapons programs. Judging by atmospheric tests, China appears to have conducted five full-yield tests of three-megaton thermonuclear devices between December 1968 and June 1974. These designs probably made extensive use of uranium.[35]

Beginning in 1971, China entered a new phase in its testing program, focusing on the development of warheads incorporating plutonium.[36] China tested a four-megaton device in September 1976 (most likely for use with the CSS-4, which would be deployed in 1980). According to one spectrographic analysis by the Swedish Defense Research Establishment, the device contained 7.7 kilograms (+/- 2.6 kilograms) of plutonium.[37] This number is quite high; if it is not an error, the design choice is interesting. Unlike their counterparts in the United States, Chinese designers might have chosen less efficient designs to enhance reliability.

---

[35] Data on Chinese nuclear testing in this period is derived from *Soviet and People's Republic of China Nuclear Weapons Employment Strategy*, pp. II-D-1-3.

[36] Basic information about the composition of China's nuclear devices tested in atmospheric tests during the 1970s is available from Lars-Erik De Geer, "Chinese Atmospheric Nuclear Explosions from a Swedish Horizon: A Summary of Swedish Observations of Chinese Nuclear Test Explosions in the Atmosphere, 1964–1980," paper prepared for the Scope-Radtest Workshop, Beijing, October 19–21, 1996.

[37] Lars-Erik De Geer, "The Radioactive Signature of the Hydrogen Bomb," *Science and Global Security*, vol. 2. no. 4 (1991), pp. 351–363.

The U.S. Defense Intelligence Agency (DIA) estimated that China had deployed three basic types of warheads by 1984: a fifteen-kiloton fission device, a three-megaton thermonuclear device, and a four- to five-megaton thermonuclear device.[38]

These warhead designs were largely intended for China's ballistic missiles. The privileged status of ballistic missiles, relative to aircraft, as a delivery vehicle for Chinese nuclear warheads appears to have been rooted in the notion that the development of nuclear weapons was linked to China's economic development. Indeed, the Chinese term for the program, *liang dan* or "two weapons," is often translated as "sophisticated weapons."[39]

Although work on ballistic missiles had begun with the onset of Soviet technical assistance in the 1950s, the modern outlines of China's ballistic missile program were set forth in the 1965 *Eight Year Plan for the Development of Rocket Technology*.[40] The *Eight Year Plan* specified a series of four *Dongfeng* (DF) missiles to be developed from 1965 to 1972: the DF-2 (CSS-1), DF-3 (CSS-2), DF-4 (CSS-3), and DF-5 (CSS-4). During the 1970s, Chinese leaders would focus on deploying its first generation medium-range ballistic missiles (DF-2/CSS-1 and DF-3/CSS-2), completing development of long-range ballistic missiles (DF-4/CSS-3 and DF-5/CSS-4), and developing solid-fueled ballistic missiles.[41] The missiles outlined in this plan, with some modification, continue to form the backbone of China's strategic forces today.

Although China tested the DF-2 (CSS-1) and DF-3 (CSS-2) on schedule and deployed these missiles at the beginning of the 1970s, the longer-range DF-4 (CSS-3) and DF-5 (CSS-4) would not enter China's arsenal until the 1980s. These delays largely reflect the turmoil of the Cultural Revolution. During the long development timelines of the CSS-3 and CSS-4, the changing strategic outlook of China's leaders, including a new

---

[38] Defense Intelligence Agency, *Defense Estimative Brief: Nuclear Weapons Systems in China*, DEB-49-84 (April 24, 1984) p. 1.

[39] The Chinese term *liang dan* in Marshal Nie's memoir, which roughly translates as "two weapons" and appears in modern descriptions of the Chinese program, is translated as "sophisticated weapons" in the New World Press translation, as well as in "How China Develops Its Nuclear Weapons," *Beijing Review*, no. 17 (April 29, 1985), pp. 15–18.

[40] *China Today: Defense Science and Technology*, p. 76.

[41] Unless otherwise noted, this section is drawn from Lewis and Hua, "China's Ballistic Missile Programs," pp. 5–40.

emphasis on the threat from the Soviet Union, was reflected in the changing technical requirements for these missiles.

China's nuclear posture in the 1970s reflected the aftermath of the 1969 border crisis between China and the Soviet Union, during which the Soviet leadership reportedly ordered extensive preparations for a disarming first strike against China.[42] These preparations may have reflected a serious consideration of a preventive strike, an effort to coerce Chinese leaders, or both. The aftermath of this crisis appears to have shaped Chinese decisions about force deployments in a number of ways.

In 1972, DIA concluded that China may have deployed the DF-2 (CSS-1) and DF-3 (CSS-2) in the aftermath of the 1969 Sino–Soviet crisis, although Lewis and Hua report that both missiles had entered the Second Artillery prior to 1972.[43] The deployment of the DF-2 may have been an emergency measure, since deployments were stopped after 1972 at around thirty missiles.[44] Rather than prompting early deployment of the DF-3, deteriorating relations with the Soviet Union may have accelerated easily detected activities, such as troop training or defensive measures at missile bases, that revealed existing deployments.

The 1969 crisis also affected the development of the DF-4 (CSS-3) and DF-5 (CSS-4) during the 1970s. Both missiles were modified to optimize their ability to target Moscow: the Chinese extended the range of the DF-4 (CSS-3) to 4,500 kilometers to bring Moscow within range of bases located in Qinghai province and designed a flight-testing program for the DF-5 (CSS-4) that improved the ability of the missile to penetrate the Moscow missile defense system.[45]

---

[42] Descriptions of Soviet preparations are available in Bruce Blair, *The Logic of Accidental Nuclear War* (Washington, DC: Brookings Institution, 1993) p. 25; Raymond Garthoff, *Détente and Confrontation* (Washington, DC: Brookings Institution, 1985), p. 209; and Arkady Shevchenko, *Breaking With Moscow* (New York: Knopf, 1985), p. 165.

[43] *Soviet and People's Republic of China Nuclear Weapons Employment Strategy*, table 5 (page number redacted). See also Lewis and Hua, "China's Ballistic Missile Programs," p. 15.

[44] *United States Military Posture for FY 1978* (Joint Chiefs of Staff, 1977), p. 31. The number estimate is derived from *Soviet and People's Republic of China Nuclear Weapons Employment Strategy*, table 5, and *Defense Estimative Brief: Nuclear Weapons Systems in China*, p. 5.

[45] Lewis and Hua suggest that China's decision to improve penetrability was a response to the declaration that the U.S. antiballistic missile (ABM) system was deployed against the Chinese arsenal, while the DIA concluded it was designed

During the 1970s, many of the decisions about modernizing China's nuclear forces focused on improving the survivability of the missiles using passive measures including hardening and dispersal. The United States intelligence community detected a "war preparations" campaign undertaken in China in 1969 as Beijing's relations with the Soviet Union deteriorated.[46] Passive civil defense measures to protect China's military and industrial facilities were already underway on a massive scale. The 1965–1971 "third front" program to build redundant industrial capacity in the country's remote interior consumed, at its peak, more than two-thirds of national budgetary industrial investment.[47]

Throughout the 1970s, China extensively pursued enhancements to reduce its nuclear arsenal's vulnerability. Improvements in U.S. and Soviet missile accuracy reportedly led the Chinese military to consider more survivable basing modes for its new generation of silo-based ballistic missiles (DF-4/CSS-3 and DF-5/CSS-4) and to accelerate development of the mobile, solid-fueled CSS-5/CSS-NX-3 (DF-21/JL-1) program. In 1975, China's senior civilian and military leadership approved a pair of reports that changed the DF-4 (CSS-3) basing mode to mountain caves and authorized studies on ship-mobile, rail-mobile, and various camouflaged fixed-based modes for both missiles. The Central Military Commission also approved a 1975 report entitled *Report on Arrangements for Research and Development on Nuclear-Armed Missiles* that called for the accelerated deployment of the CSS-3 (DF-4) and CSS-4 (DF-5) by 1977 and the JL-1 by 1980.[48]

Research on a solid-fueled ballistic missile to be launched from a submarine (the JL-1/CSS-NX-3) had been ongoing since the late 1960s, although the work "progressed somewhat haphazardly" through the years of the Cultural Revolution due to political upheaval and technological challenges associated with solid fuels, miniaturized warheads, and nuclear-powered submarines. The Central Military Commission reiter-

---

to penetrate Moscow's ABM system. Compare Lewis and Hua, "China's Ballistic Missile Programs," p. 21 with *Special Defense Intelligence Estimate: China's Evolving Nuclear Strategies*, DDE-2200-321-85 (Washington, DC: Defense Intelligence Agency, May 1985), p. 8.

[46] See *Soviet and People's Republic of China Nuclear Weapons Employment Strategy*, pp. II-15.

[47] Barry Naughton, "The Third Front: Defence Industrialization in the Chinese Interior," *The China Quarterly* no. 115 (September 1988), pp. 351–386.

[48] Described in Lewis and Xue, *China's Strategic Seapower*, p. 308 n. 19.

ated its concern about the arsenal's survivability in 1977, approving a *Report on the Arrangement of the Research and Development on Strategic Nuclear Missiles and Man-Made Satellites and Their Delivery Systems before 1980* that focused on deploying a limited number of CSS-3 (DF-4) and CSS-4 (DF-5) ICBMs, as well as attempting to complete the CSS-NX-3 (JL-1) SLBM program by "the first half of the 1980s."[49] The Central Military Commission settled on cave basing for the DF-4 (CSS-3) in 1977 and had probably settled on camouflaged silo basing for the DF-5 (CSS-4) by the time the Defense Science and Technology Commission ended rail-mobile trials in November 1978.[50] The Chinese leadership reportedly ordered the "emergency deployment" of the CSS-3 (DF-4) and CSS-4 (DF-5) near the end of 1979, although the CSS-4 silos would not be ready until August 1981. The basing modes gave Chinese officials sufficient confidence in the survivability of China's arsenal. Chinese officials would later reportedly express confidence to U.S. officials that this force would deter the Soviet Union "because the Chinese arsenal is so well-hidden that it ensures sufficient retaliatory capability to inflict intolerable damage to the USSR."[51]

That left the question of China's "mobile MRBM and IRBM (CSS-1/CSS-2)" force then "estimated at over 100 launchers, all of which possess a refire capability."[52] China accelerated work on a solid-fueled ballistic missile to replace the relatively vulnerable DF-3 (CSS-2). Although the DF-3 (CSS-2) was mobile, the missile required several hours of prelaunch exposure to load propellants and prepare the guidance systems. During the mid-1970s, the Second Artillery organized China's first "massive long-range firing practice with live warheads, involving moving operations, camouflaging, and launching."[53] By the late 1970s, Chinese units were reportedly able to reduce prelaunch exposure in exercises to two to three hours.

----

[49] Ibid., p. 308 n. 25.

[50] From 1978 to 1984, China also pursued a mobile, liquid fueled 8,000-kilometer IRBM called the DF-22.

[51] Jack Anderson, "China Shows Confidence in Its Missiles," *Washington Post*, December 19, 1984, p. F11.

[52] Lewis and Hua state that the CSS-1 was completely retired by 1979, although U.S. intelligence continued to credit the PRC with twenty-five CSS-1 ballistic missiles through 1984.

[53] Zhang Jiajun and Zao Zhi, "The Strong Contingent of Secret Rockets—The Historical Course of Development of China's Strategic Guided Missile Units," *Xinhua Hong Kong Service* (July 7, 1996), FBIS-FTS-1996-0707-000027.

After 1981: China's Second Generation of Strategic Systems

After 1981, the Chinese leadership turned its attention to deploying China's new ICBMs, the CSS-3 and CSS-4, and developing a second generation of ballistic missiles that used solid-propellant fuel to replace China's first generation of liquid-fueled ballistic missiles. In addition to developing solid-fueled ballistic missiles, China developed an SSBN and miniaturized nuclear warheads. Although we know little about actual Chinese expenditures during this period, DIA reported that China's 6th *Five Year Economic Plan* (1981–1985) devoted an "increasing share of [procurement] funds for ICBM deployment and SSBN/SLBM force development."[54] DIA predicted large deployments of both of China's longer-range ballistic missiles (CSS-3 and CSS-4), as well as its SLBM (CSS-NX-3), through the mid-1990s—at which point China was expected to deploy mobile ICBMs and a CSS-NX-3 follow-on SLBM (see Table 3-1).

Table 3-1: DIA Projection of Selected Chinese Strategic Forces, 1984–1994

	Actual & Projected in *Nuclear Weapons Systems in China* (1984)			Actual
	1984	*1989*	*1994*	*1994*
CSS-4 (DF-5)	2	*9*	*16*	7
CSS-3 (DF-4)	8	*31*	*32*	10
CSS-NX-3 (JL-1)	0	*24*	*48*	0

Projections are *italicized*.

Actual is from National Security Council, *Report to Congress on Status of China, India, and Pakistan Nuclear and Ballistic Missile Programs*, July 28, 1993.

In 1984, China maintained 110 CSS-2 MRBMs, which accounted for more than three-quarters of the country's total number of operationally deployed warheads. As a modified CSS-2 entered the inventory in 1986, the total number of CSS-2 missiles was allowed to decline to fewer than fifty launchers by 1993. ICBM deployments were halted after construction of a pair of CSS-4 silos in 1981. Following a modification program carried out from 1983 to 1986 to improve the range, operability, and reliability of the CSS-4, China reportedly deployed just four of the DF-5

---

[54] *Defense Intelligence Memorandum: Military Implications of China's Economic Plans*, DDE-1900-80-84 (September 1984), pp. 8–9.

modified ICBMs. By 1994, China had deployed just seven total CSS-4 (DF-5) and ten CSS-3 (DF-4) ballistic missiles.[55] China built just one SSBN, which never became operational. Total force levels declined from nearly 150 missiles in 1984 to less than seventy a decade later.

One factor may have been the increasing confidence among Chinese leaders that war, including nuclear war, was unlikely.[56] Threat perceptions clearly began to ease in the early 1980s. The defining symbol of Beijing's recognition of the relaxation of international tension was a 1984 statement, issued after the annual summer leadership conference at Beidaihe, stating that no world war would occur for at least ten to fifteen years. Over the course of the 1980s, the Chinese leadership would substantially reduce the size of the PLA and allow defense spending to atrophy.

China would have a decade or more to improve its first generation of ballistic missiles and develop its second. China's solid-propellant missile programs would progress slowly. Work had been underway in earnest since August 1978, when Deng Xiaoping expressed "the greatest interest in mobility on land; that is, in the use of modern weapons for fighting guerilla war."[57] The relative priorities given to the JL-1 (CSS-NX-3) and its land-based variant, the DF-21 (CSS-5), during this period remain unclear. During the mid-1980s, however, the Chinese leadership slowed investment in the SLBM/SSBN program as both the missile and the submarine programs experienced technical setbacks. The JL-1 testing program experienced three consecutive failures during a 1985 test series to demonstrate the missile's ability to ignite underwater, and, following a pair of successful tests in 1988, work appears to have stopped on this program.[58] The 092 *Xia* SSBN, which was to carry the missile, was reportedly so noisy during its initial sea trials that its crew was unable to sleep.[59] Although DIA speculated that the Chinese might deploy as many as four *Xia* submarines by 1994, the Chinese leadership delayed and then canceled construction of a follow-on ballistic missile submarine in 1985, shifting resources to long-term design efforts for a more advanced sub-

---

[55] National Security Council, *Report to Congress on Status of China, India and Pakistan Nuclear and Ballistic Missile Programs*, np.

[56] This paragraph is based on Lewis and Xue, *China's Strategic Seapower*, pp. 211–214.

[57] Lewis and Hua, "China's Ballistic Missile Programs," p. 26.

[58] Lewis and Xue, *China's Strategic Seapower*, pp. 200–202.

[59] Ibid., p. 120.

marine, still under development, that would carry the naval variant of the CSS-X-10 (JL-2).[60]

Even the CSS-5 (DF-21), which had a comparatively smooth testing program compared with the CSS-NX-3, was not deployed for many years following a series of successful tests in 1985. The Second Artillery created an operational CSS-5 unit in 1986, but unclassified U.S. intelligence estimates note that "deployment of this missile seems to have begun in the early 1990s."[61] In 1996, the U.S. intelligence community observed that China had deployed only a handful of the DF-21 missiles while R&D flight tests continued and that China planned to keep the CSS-2 (DF-3) in service until CSS-5 (DF-21) deployments were "adequately underway, ... perhaps by 2002."[62] As in the cases of China's ICBM and SLBM programs, the token deployments of the DF-21 in 1994 were substantially below DIA projections from the mid-1980s.[63]

The delay in CSS-NX-3/CSS-5 deployments may have been related to difficulty in developing a miniaturized warhead for the two missiles. Original design plans reportedly called for the CSS-5/CSS-NX-3 to carry a 600-kilogram warhead with a yield of more than 400 KT.[64] Although *China Today: Nuclear Industry* describes a testing program in the early 1980s to validate "new design principles for development of nuclear

---

[60] Projections of SSBN deployments are available in *Defense Estimative Brief: Nuclear Weapons Systems in China*, p. 4. The cancellation is noted in Lewis and Xue, *China's Strategic Seapower*, p. 121.

[61] National Security Council, *Report to Congress on Status of China, India and Pakistan Nuclear and Ballistic Missile Programs* (National Security Council, np). A later edition of *Chinese Military Power* expresses more confidence, noting the CSS-5 (DF-21) has been "operationally deployed since about 1991." See Department of Defense, *Future Military Capabilities and Strategy of the People's Republic of China, Report to Congress Pursuant to Section 1226 of the FY98 National Defense Authorization Act* (Washington, DC: Government Printing Office, 1998), p. 9.

[62] National Air Intelligence Center, *China Incrementally Downsizing CSS-2 IRBM Force*, NAIC-1030-098B-96 (November 1996) in Gertz, *The China Threat*, pp. 233–234.

[63] DIA anticipated twenty-eight MR/IRBM follow-on missiles by 1994. *Defense Estimative Brief: Nuclear Weapons Systems in China*, p. 4.

[64] Lewis and Xue, *China's Strategic Seapower*, p. 177. In "China's Ballistic Missile Programs," Lewis and Hua report that the warhead was to be 500 kilograms with a yield of 200-300 kilotons. See Lewis and Hua, "China's Ballistic Missile Programs," p. 30.

weapons," *Biographies of the Founders of the Nuclear, Missile and Satellite Program* suggests China had refrained from weaponizing the device given the expense involved.[65] *Biographies* also suggests that work on the warhead accelerated as the Chinese expected a test ban agreement among the superpowers.

The yield data from Chinese nuclear tests suggests a series of tests from 1987 to 1991 that appear to be high-yield warheads (200 KT to 1 MT). This warhead may have been superseded by an even smaller warhead for the CSS-X-10 that was completed during the test series from 1992 to 1996.[66] China also experimented with enhanced-radiation warheads (neutron bombs) during this period, although—as with China's low-yield tests in the 1970s—there is no evidence that China built or deployed the devices.

While China spent comparatively little on deployments of ICBMs and early solid-propellant ballistic missiles during the 1980s, the Chinese leadership set in place plans that govern China's current modernization, which relies on the CSS-X-10 family of solid-propellant ballistic missiles.[67] The Chinese leadership reportedly became concerned about the survivability of silo-based missiles following the U.S. deployment of the Trident II–D5, which the U.S. intelligence community assessed to be accurate enough to threaten Chinese silos.[68] Ballistic missiles with solid-propellant fuel remain fueled at all times, reducing prelaunch exposure and permitting mobile transporter-erector-launcher operations. With no nuclear war expected in the near future, the State Council and Central Military Commission in 1985 reorganized ongoing research into solid-propellant ballistic missiles. The broad features of that plan, like the 1965 *banian sidan* plan, continued to guide the development of China's missile program for more than a decade: The Central Military Commission settled on a pair of "second generation" solid-fueled ballistic missiles: the DF-31 and JL-2, with the land-based DF-31 receiving priority over the submarine-based

---

[65] This section is drawn from *Biographies of the Founders of the Nuclear, Missile and Satellite Program (Liangdan Yixing Yuanxunzhuan)*, (Tsinghua University Press, 2001), pp. 56–63.

[66] Dan Hoffman and Ian Stober, *A Convenient Spy: Wen Ho Lee and the Politics of Nuclear Espionage* (New York: Simon & Schuster, 2002), p. 226.

[67] Lewis and Hua, "China's Ballistic Missile Programs," pp. 28–30.

[68] Robert Walpole in *CIA National Intelligence Estimate of Foreign Missile Development ...*, S. Hrg. 107–467, p. 26.

JL-2. In 1986, the Chinese also began work on a mobile 12,000-kilometer range ICBM to follow the DF-31, which has variously been described as the DF-41 or merely as an extended-range DF-31.

The deployment of solid-fueled ballistic missiles would reduce Beijing's reliance on maintaining ambiguity about the number and location of its fixed deployment sites. During this period, China shifted resources from more near-term programs, such as the follow-on Xia-class submarine and a mobile, liquid-fueled ICBM (DF-22).

The Chinese leadership reportedly expected the CSS-X-10 (DF-31) and JL-2 systems to enter the Chinese arsenal in the late 1990s. Despite flight testing of the CSS-X-10 (DF-31) in 1999 and 2000, recent National Intelligence Council (NIC) estimates predict Chinese deployments of the DF-31, an extended-range DF-31, and the JL-2 in the last half of the decade—more than twenty years after the programs were inaugurated and almost a decade after initial flight testing.[69]

Delays experienced by the CSS-X-10 program may reflect the technical complexity of the endeavor or a lack of state support. Unfortunately, little public information is available about the DF-31 flight testing program or about Chinese budgetary allocations. Whatever the reason, China appears to have reassessed its ballistic missile deployments during the 1990s. Between 1994 and 1998, U.S. intelligence estimates of the number of China's CSS-4 (DF-5) ballistic missiles increased from "seven to ten" to "about twenty."[70] China may have increased the number of its ICBMs during that period, perhaps in response to delays in the CSS-X-10 program (either due to technical challenges or a decision to reduce investment).[71] China has also continued periodic upgrades on the CSS-4, per-

---

[69] The few official statements about the DF-31 flight testing program are provided in: Kenneth H. Bacon, Department of Defense News Briefings, August 3, 1999 and December 12, 2000. Available at: http://www.defenselink.mil/news/Aug1999/t08031999_t0803asd.html and http://www.defenselink.mil/news/Dec2000/t12122000_t1212asd.html. See also *Current and Projected National Security Threats to The United States*, S. Hrg. 107–597, p. 78.

[70] Compare *Report to Congress on Status of China, India and Pakistan Nuclear and Ballistic Missile Programs* and National Air Intelligence Center, *Ballistic Missile Programs* with *Ballistic and Cruise Missile Threat*, NAIC-1031-0985-00 (Washington: National Air Intelligence Center, 1998), http://www.fas.org/irp/threat/missile/naic/.

[71] Conversely, U.S. intelligence capabilities may simply have begun providing more detailed information about China's ballistic missile capabilities. In 1992, the United States launched the first of three advanced Keyhole (KH-11)

haps to extend the missile's service life beyond its reported 2010 with-drawal.[72]

Other manifestations of the Chinese leadership's interest in more sur-vivable forces during the 1980s included an effort to improve the coun-try's command-and-control system and the beginning of a "certain major defense project" to construct "a number of strategic missile positions that hold different types of missiles."[73] This project was completed in 1995.

The reduction in defense spending and personnel that the Chinese government undertook in the mid-1980s was part of a much larger pro-gram of professionalization that continues to shape the modern People's Liberation Army, including the Second Artillery. Lewis and Hua write that, "Until the early 1980s, there were no scenarios, no detailed linkage of the weapons to foreign policy objectives, and no serious strategic research." In the mid-1980s, the Second Artillery became vastly more professional, conducting its first "large-scale combined battle exercise" to assess the overall capability of the strategic missile units.[74] In 1984, the Central Military Commission ordered the Second Artillery to develop a system of what Lewis and Xue call "round-the-clock alerts." Such alerts are probably an effort designed to raise professionalism rather than readi-ness given the Chinese leadership's increasingly sanguine view of the international system. Indeed, the Second Artillery has made many efforts to increase professionalism within its ranks. By the mid-1990s, more than 70 percent of Second Artillery officers were college graduates.[75] The Second Artillery reportedly offers officer recruits with doctorates or doc-toral-level education salaries of 50,000 Renminbi and 30,000 Renminbi, as well as better living and working conditions.[76] Such salaries are rather

---

imaging satellites, which reportedly included a thermal infrared imagery system that offered improved ability to detect buried structures, such as missile silos.

[72] Continuing CSS-4 upgrades are noted in "Chinese Military Power," (July 2003), p. 31.

[73] "RMRB Summarizes Report on Jiang Praise for Second Artillery Corps," *Renmin Ribao* (March 21, 2002) FBIS-CPP-2002-0321-000103.

[74] Zhang and Zao, "The Strong Contingent of Secret Rockets."

[75] "Chinese Progress in Missile Research," *Xinhua News Agency* (July 21, 1997) FBIS-CHI-97-202.

[76] "160 People with Doctorates in Service for China's Strategic Missile Troops," *Xinhua News Service* (April 21, 2004), FBIS-CPP-2004-0420-000028. Avail-able at: http://fpeng.peopledaily.com.cn/200404/20/eng20040420_140929.shtml.

large in a country where a division commander in Beijing makes 36,000 Renminbi per year.[77]

A final, important change in the posture of the Second Artillery began with the development of tactical ballistic missiles in the 1980s.[78] *Operational Studies* reports that the PLA created the first conventional missile units within the Second Artillery during the early 1990s. This time period corresponds to the first deployments of the CSS-5 MRBMs (some of which were armed with conventional warheads) and CSS-6 SRBMs. The number of CSS-6 and CSS-7 SRBMs has grown dramatically from fewer than 200 in 1998 to more than 450 in 2003.[79]

PRINCIPLES OF DESIGN

The passage that begins this chapter asserts that China's nuclear deployments continue to reflect a set of principles. *Strategic Studies* suggests four principles have guided the development of China's nuclear forces:

> The nuclear strategy of our country has the following basic characteristics:
>
> Number one, it is defensive. From the first day of possessing nuclear weapons, our government solemnly stated that in any time, under any circumstance, we would not use nuclear weapons first. Our country has nuclear weaponry purely for the purpose of self-defense and breaking the nuclear monopoly and nuclear blackmail of hegomonism [sic].
>
> Number two, it is limited. The size of our nuclear force is limited. We do not involve ourselves in the nuclear arms race of other nations. The development of our nuclear force is completely in accordance with the active defensive military strategic guidance.
>
> Number three, it is effective. The fundamental purpose of developing nuclear weapons by our country is to stop a nuclear attack against our country. Once being attacked of this kind, we will firmly and effectively conduct destructive nuclear retaliation.

---

[77] "A Better Life for Common Soldiers," *People's Daily* (July 23, 2002). Available at: http://www.china.org.cn/english/FR/37476.htm.

[78] Lewis and Hua, "China's Ballistic Missiles," pp. 31–39.

[79] The 1998 estimate is from the Defense Intelligence Agency, *Chinese CSS-6 and CSS-X-7 Launchsite Coverage of Taiwan, October 1998* (1998), cited in Gertz, *The China Threat*, p. 232.

Number four, it is safe. Our nuclear force is under the direct command of the Central Military Committee. And we have taken strict management measures, so nuclear security has reliable safeguarding. All the strategic regions of our country are the strategic operational units under the centralized and unified leadership of the Central Military Committee. The main tasks of all the strategic regions in their strategic operational directions are to consider the reality of all the strategic directions according to the unified arrangement of the Central Military Committee to carry out the strategic intention of the Central Military Committee creatively and implement all the requirements of the military strategy.[80]

These four principles—that China's nuclear forces are defensive in their purpose, limited in size, effective, and safe—may appear somewhat anodyne, but their application in practice has produced an arsenal strikingly different from that of other nuclear states. Although many observers have anticipated imminent change in China's doctrine and force structure, Chinese nuclear forces continue to be structured around principles very much like the ones suggested in *Strategic Studies*, which themselves reflect the core notion that the deterrent effect of nuclear weapons is largely insensitive to changes in the size, configuration, and readiness of nuclear forces.

Chinese Nuclear Forces are 'Defensive'

Chinese leaders deliberately chose to maintain a defensive operational doctrine, marked by a no-first-use pledge, and declined to deploy battlefield or tactical nuclear weapons. The defensive orientation of China's nuclear forces was expressed within the no-first-use commitment in 1964, among the earliest doctrinal pronouncements to shape Chinese nuclear force decisions. Major General Pan Zhenqiang, (PLA-Ret) has argued that "The no-first-use doctrine provided a conceptual guideline for the development of China's nuclear force."[81] The commitment to a defensive arsenal comprising "nuclear and thermonuclear warheads with high yields and long-range delivery vehicles" in the 1958 *Guidelines for Developing Nuclear Weapons*, reiterated by Zhou Enlai in July 1964,

---

[80] *Strategic Studies* (*Zhanlue xue*) (Beijing, Academy of Military Sciences, 2000), chapter 19, p. 1.

[81] Pan Zhenqiang, "On China's No First Use of Nuclear Weapons," Pugwash Online, November 26, 2002, http://www.pugwash.org/reports/nw/zhenqiang.htm.

reportedly determined the decision to proceed with a multistage thermonuclear device and eschew deployments of relatively small fission
weapons for use by the People's Liberation Army Air Force.

China did not deploy warheads with yields of less than one megaton
until the 1990s. Work on these weapons began in the 1980s, when Chinese leaders outlined plans for a miniaturized warhead, with a 200- to
300-kiloton yield, for use with solid-fueled ballistic missiles, such as the
CSS-5 (DF-21) and CSS-NX-3 (JL-1), that had reduced throw-weight.
Research efforts in the 1970s and 1980s on nuclear weapons with yields
of a few tens of kilotons do not appear to have led to the deployment of
tactical nuclear weapons.

This trend continues to be evident in the design of China's nuclear
arsenal. Doctrinal documents and Second Artillery exercises continue to
emphasize defensive operations associated with a no-first-use commitment. The decision to outfit China's newest missiles—the CSS-5 (DF-21)
IRBM and M-9 and M-11 short range ballistic missiles—with conventional
payloads is particularly telling. Were Chinese planners considering tactical
use of nuclear weapons in a future crisis, one would expect China's newest
tactical missiles to be armed with nuclear weapons. Yet, Chinese planners
appear to have chosen conventional payloads, perhaps to free the Second
Artillery from constraints imposed by China's no-first-use pledge.

The retaliatory nature of China's deterrent does not preclude either the
targeting of military targets, such as U.S. bases in the Asia-Pacific region, or
limited retaliatory strikes. *Operational Studies* includes "enemy strategic
targets, political centers, and military installations" as potential targets to
"send the enemy a tremendous mental shock."[82] *Operational Studies* also
suggests that commanders prepare to retain a reserve force to continue to
provide a measure of intrawar deterrence.[83] Nevertheless, these elements of
China's operational strategy do not appear tied to purposes such as the
control of escalation or the creation of favorable exchange ratios.

Chinese Nuclear Forces are 'Limited'

China's leaders chose to deploy a small nuclear force. They were clearly
concerned about the survivability of their deterrent, making extensive
investments in passive defensive measures to camouflage, harden, and dis-

---

[82] *Operational Studies* (*Zhanyi xue*), chapter 14, p. 9.
[83] Ibid., chapter 14, p. 7.

perse industrial and military assets, including ballistic missile forces. The limited nature of China's deterrent has two elements: First, the number of nuclear warheads and delivery vehicles is small, even when compared to British and French nuclear forces that numbered in the 200 to 500 range. Second, the Chinese rely on a single basing mode for the country's nuclear deterrent, while both Britain and France maintained multiple modes of delivery for most of the Cold War.

China's ballistic missile production has consistently been below the country's industrial capacity, based on floor space estimates. Following large expenditures to develop nuclear weapons, China spent comparatively little on the deployment of ballistic missiles—perhaps as little as 5 percent of its total defense spending from 1965 to 1979.[84] Chinese leaders reportedly spent a greater percentage during the 1980s, although deployments of the CSS-3 (DF-4) and CSS-4 (DF-5) remained very limited, and investment in the SLBM/SSBN program probably remained below the DIA estimates based on China's Five Year Economic Plan for 1981 to 1985. China reportedly deployed fewer than ten ICBMs through the mid-1990s, although China produced ten ICBMs and space launch vehicles each year from 1978 to 1982.[85] Futron Corporation estimates the commercial price of a CZ-2 launch vehicle, the space launch variant of the CSS-4, at $25 million (in 2000 dollars). At this price, the cost of adding ten CSS-4 ballistic missiles per year would be modest—less than 5 percent of total equipment expenses in 2000.[86]

Chinese Nuclear Forces are 'Effective'

The Chinese leadership defined an "effective" nuclear force as one capable of delivering a limited retaliatory strike. Throughout the 1970s, Chinese leaders clearly expressed concern about the survivability of their strategic forces, undertaking campaigns to harden facilities and reduce

---

[84] Chinese spending estimates are from Ronald G. Mitchell and Edward P. Parris, "Chinese Defense Spending, 1965–1978," Joint Economic Committee, *Allocation of Resources in the Soviet Union and China—1979* (Washington: Government Printing Office, 1979), pp. 66–72.

[85] Schuyler Bissel, "Economic Assessment of the Soviet Union and China," in Joint Economic Committee, *Allocation of Resources in the Soviet Union and China—1983* (Washington: Government Printing Office, 1984), p. 104.

[86] *Space Transportation Costs: Trends in Price Per Pound to Orbit 1990–2000* (Bethesda, MD: Futron, September 6, 2002), Available at: http://www.futron.com/pdf/FutronLaunchCostWP.pdf.

prelaunch exposure. However, they did not increase the scope of deployments or the readiness of their strategic forces.

The sentiment expressed by six of President John F. Kennedy's advisors—that "American nuclear superiority was not in our view a critical factor, for the fundamental and controlling reason that nuclear war, already in 1962, would have been an unexampled catastrophe for both sides"—is also found in *Operational Studies,* which notes, "Though the United States was superior to the Soviet Union in nuclear weapons at that time, if a nuclear war broke out, no country could avoid the destiny of destruction. There is sharp conflict between the super destructive power of the means of war and the thinking of the war launcher who wants to get his interest on one hand, but fears destruction on the other."[87]

Mark Ryan, noting that Chinese leaders developed an accurate assessment of U.S. psychological attitudes during the Korean War, speculates that Chinese leaders continued to draw confidence from their assessment of Washington's likely fears about possible retaliation. Chinese confidence was evident in assessments by senior Chinese military officials, including Marshal Nie Rongzhen, during the 1969 border clashes with the Soviet Union. Although the Soviet Union was actively preparing for a disarming first strike against China and making public statements to pressure the Chinese leadership, Nie and his colleagues, in a report to the Central Committee, concluded that a Soviet preventive attack was unlikely because "It is not an easy matter to use a nuclear weapon. When a country uses nuclear weapons to threaten another country, it places itself under the threat of [the] other country's nuclear weapons...."[88]

Major General Pan suggested that such an attitude underpinned China's support for no-first use, explaining that "The idea was as long as you are able to give a devastating counter-attack against one or two U.S. big cities, the scenario was enough to make the attacker who had the intention of preemptive nuclear strike pause, and hopefully drop the plan."[89] China's decision to measure its arsenal's effectiveness as a func-

---

[87] *Strategic Studies (Zhanlue xue)*, chapter 20, p. 7.
[88] Nie et al., *Report to the Central Committee: A Preliminary Evaluation of the War Situation,* translated in Chen Jian and David L. Wilson, "All Under The Heaven Is Great Chaos: Beijing, The Sino-Soviet Border Clashes, And The Turn Toward Sino-American Rapprochement, 1968–69," *Cold War International History Project Bulletin no. 11* (1996) p. 167.
[89] Pan, "On China's No First Use of Nuclear Weapons," np.

tion of another country's psychological fear of retaliation, rather than a calculation based on the force balance, explains why it undertook extensive defensive measures to conceal, harden, and disperse military and industrial assets without also undertaking large deployments of land-based ballistic missiles and nuclear-capable aircraft.

John Lewis contends that Chinese nuclear strategy appears to have been driven more by technology than by the leadership's beliefs about deterrence.[90] Writing with Xue Litai, Lewis suggested the Chinese leadership "decisively endorsed the military-technical side of doctrine and a posture to deter nuclear attack."[91]

This is an important insight, but it perhaps understates the role that Chinese attitudes toward deterrence played in permitting military-technical considerations to dominate decisions about nuclear deployments. Moreover, the "military-technical side of posture" would not explain China's choices about alert postures, operational training, or targeting doctrines, all of which vary greatly from those in the other NPT nuclear weapons states.

Technological requirements were also altered to reflect changing political conditions. Following the 1969 border clashes with the Soviet Union, the Chinese government ordered the Second Artillery to accelerate troop training exercises and modified some programs to reflect a new focus on the Soviet Union. The CMC shifted emphasis from the JL-1 to the DF-21 and ordered the China's missile designers to extend the range of the DF-4 and test the DF-5 against simple missile defense systems. In these instances, leadership beliefs were clearly instrumental in altering technical requirements.

Finally, the Chinese leadership clearly favored some technologies over others. Chinese leaders focused their resources on developing land-based strategic ballistic missiles over aircraft and the development of tactical ballistic missiles (at least until the 1980s). In the mid-1980s, Chinese leaders shifted resources away from a sea-based deterrent. China has not deployed multiple reentry vehicle (MRV) or multiple independently targetable reentry vehicle (MIRV) ballistic missiles, possibly due to technological constraints on the size of warheads that existed into the 1980s. The U.S. intelligence community is currently divided over the question

---

[90] Lewis and Hua, "China's Ballistic Missile Programs," p. 20.
[91] John Lewis and Xue Litai, "Strategic Weapons and Chinese Power: The Formative Years," *China Quarterly,* vol. 112 (December 1987), p. 547.

of whether China will deploy multiple reentry vehicles on its CSS-4 ballistic missiles; the conclusion of this chapter is that such a deployment would be unlikely.

Chinese Nuclear Forces are 'Safe'

"Safe" refers to the degree of control that the Chinese leadership maintains over China's nuclear forces. The Chinese term for "safety" of nuclear weapons, *anquan*, is the same term used to describe the "security" of those weapons. Whether the term's dual meaning reflects a conceptual approach is a difficult question to answer.

The Chinese leadership has implemented operational practices that sacrifice readiness to preserve central control. China has never deployed nuclear-armed gravity bombs to airbases—despite the Chinese leadership's decision to rush the DF-5 into deployment in 1980. China continued to maintain separate storage for ballistic missiles and nuclear warheads, even after the decision to professionalize the Second Artillery in the 1980s and to institute "round-the-clock" alerts in 1984. There is substantial evidence that the Chinese leadership was acutely concerned about the vulnerability of the country's ballistic missiles, including its selection of storable fuels for the DF-2 based on analyses of the Cuban missile crisis, troop training exercises to reduce prelaunch vulnerability of the DF-3, and the investigation of multiple basing modes for the DF-4 and DF-5. Many of these concerns about the nuclear arsenal's survivability might have been met with the deployment of rudimentary missile warning radars and by operating Chinese nuclear forces on alert. Yet China did not take these courses of action, suggesting that the deterrent benefit from deploying more alert forces was overwhelmed by the inherent risk of the loss of control. Chinese leaders may not have made a conscious calculation, but one can easily imagine how senior leaders—in the aftermath of the leadership disputes of the Cultural Revolution, Lin Biao's death, and the arrest of the Gang of Four—may have reacted to suggestions that central control over nuclear weapons be loosened to enhance the deterrent effect.

Continuity over Time

These four principles of design appear consistent across changing threat perceptions and programmatic developments. They can be traced from the 1958 *Guidelines* to recent cadre training manuals like *Strategic Studies* (2000) and *Operational Studies* (2000).

This continuity can, in part, be traced to the slow generational turnover in China's leadership. For example, the current set of modernization programs was established in the mid-1980s under Deng Xiaoping, who, as party general secretary in 1956, would likely have been involved in the adoption of the 1958 *Guidelines*. Deng also selected Jiang Zemin and, reportedly, Hu Jintao to succeed him as China's paramount leader.

The longevity of senior Chinese leaders does not entirely explain this consistency in China's nuclear doctrine. Competing factions, particularly during the Cultural Revolution, continued to vie for control over the strategic programs, and disputes existed about the relative priority of conventional and strategic modernization. Strangely, though, little evidence suggests that any faction has proposed dramatic changes in the overall character of China's nuclear posture.

A Note on Organizational Bias

One alternative explanation for the unique nature of China's nuclear weapons deployment relies on the anticipated organizational bias of professional militaries. Some observers have suggested that professional militaries may "not develop invulnerable nuclear forces if left to their own devices" because programs to make arsenals less vulnerable to attack may

- Take resources away from more valued programs, such as bombers and missiles;
- Require new missions, systems, or even organizational units;
- Conflict with organizational preferences for preventive war; or
- Succumb to organizational routines and standard operating practices.[92]

Scott Sagan writes, "The influence of organizational biases on strategic weapons deployments can perhaps best be seen in the People's Republic of China," which, Sagan argues, "did not develop a confident and secure second-strike capability until the early 1980s."[93]

Sagan identifies two decisions to demonstrate this point. First, he suggests the Second Artillery "did not independently pursue the survivability

---

[92] Scott D. Sagan, "The Perils of Proliferation: Organization Theory, Deterrence Theory, and the Spread of Nuclear Weapons," *International Security* vol. 18, no. 4 (Spring 1994), pp. 66–107, especially pp. 90–91.

[93] Ibid., p. 90.

measures needed" for the CSS-3 (DF-4) and CSS-4 (DF-5) until Mao approved a report recommending cave- and silo-basing modes for the missiles.[94] Second, Sagan suggests that "the strong bureaucratic power of traditional People's Liberation Army interests in the party and the weapons institutes appears to have slowed the development of the Chinese navy's SLBM force."[95]

Although organizational and bureaucratic imperatives are undoubtedly an important part of the story, the two cases that Sagan cites are inadequate to explain the unique character of China's arsenal.

For example, Sagan describes Mao's approval of a recommendation by the Defense Science and Technology Commission (DSTC) to change the CSS-3 basing mode as "high level intervention by civilian authorities."[96] Sagan's source material, however, suggests the impetus for improving survivability came from *within* the defense community; the 1975 *Report on Arrangements for Research and Development on Nuclear-Armed Missiles*, prepared by the First Academy, contained several recommendations to accelerate work on more survivable basing modes. These recommendations were later approved by Mao.

China's broad interest in its nuclear arsenal's survivability is consistent with U.S. intelligence reports from the same period identifying an extensive campaign of dispersal and hardening across the Chinese military and industrial sectors, including the "third front campaign."[97] In the late 1980s, the Second Artillery completed another major engineering project to improve the survivability of ballistic missiles based in caves and silos.

Second, the Chinese decision to emphasize the land-based CSS-5 (DF-21) over the naval variant, the CSS-NX-3 (JL-1), did not, as Sagan suggests, prolong China's vulnerability "for a longer period of time than can be explained by the rationalist assumptions of proliferation optimists." First, Sagan implies that China eventually deployed the CSS-NX-3, but it actually did not do so for a variety of economic, political, and technical reasons outlined in the preceding section. The lack of urgency surrounding the JL-1 program that Sagan cites was not organizational, but technical. The slow progress made by other elements of the program, including

---

[94] Ibid., p. 91. Citing Lewis and Hua, "China's Ballistic Missile Programs," p. 24.
[95] Ibid., p. 90.
[96] Ibid., p. 90.
[97] See *Soviet and People's Republic of China Nuclear Weapons Employment Strategy*, pp. II-15.

miniaturizing a nuclear warhead for the JL-1 (which was not tested until the late 1980s) and developing an SSBN, obviated a crash program for this missile. As in the case of the basing mode for the CSS-5 (DF-21), the People's Liberation Army was concerned about this weapon's vulnerability—a concern piqued, no doubt, by the poor technical performance of the submarine and the limited range of the CSS-NX-3 (JL-1).[98]

A careful reading of these two cases suggests the Chinese military was, in fact, concerned with reducing the vulnerability of its forces. Yet that concern, which led to substantial investments in hardening, dispersal, and redundancy of national industrial capabilities, as well as the pursuit of survivable basing modes for land-based ballistic missiles, did not result in a more orthodox deployment pattern. In fact, the biases of professional military organizations identified by Sagan—particularly the value placed on hardware such as missiles and bombers and the preference for preventive war doctrines—should have created pressure for a larger and more diverse inventory of delivery vehicles, decentralized command and control, and a more flexible operational doctrine. Yet, the Chinese deterrent in 1994 that Sagan declared capable of surviving an attack was not materially different from the force of the 1970s that Sagan criticized as vulnerable. In 1994, the CIA estimates that China maintained only seven relatively inaccurate single-warhead ICBMs, some fifty medium- and intermediate-range missiles, and no submarine-launched ballistic missiles.[99]

CONCLUSION

The persistence of China's unorthodox nuclear deployment patterns—set against both the anecdotal evidence of the regime's concern with the survivability of its nuclear arsenal and the macroeconomic data suggesting substantial investments in defensive measures to protect national military forces, industrial capacity, and population against nuclear attack—appear to reflect a deliberate decision. Why did China undertake some measures, such as hardening and dispersal, but not others, such as building more delivery vehicles, placing forces on higher alert status, and adopting a more flexible operational doctrine?

---

[98] Lewis and Hua, "China's Ballistic Missile Program," p. 27.

[99] *U.S. Policy on Ballistic Missile Defenses and the Future of the ABM Treaty, Presidential Review 31* (1994) in Gertz, Betrayal, p. 233–236.

The quote by Sun Xiangli at the outset of this chapter suggests the simple answer: "a consistent framework of nuclear policy that is based on a clear understanding of the nature of nuclear weapons." The consistent framework, in this case, is a concern about accidental, unauthorized, or inadvertent launch or detonation of nuclear weapons rather than deliberate attack, and it is reflected in choices to invest in survivability measures that did not compromise party control of nuclear weapons. Even China's mobile ballistic missiles, which are dispersed around the country, do not appear to conduct regular patrols. Instead, nuclear warheads are stored separately from the ballistic missiles—a measure that seriously compromises the survivability of such deployments.[100] That compromise is fundamentally in the interest of the United States, even if that fact is not widely appreciated in the U.S. political system.

---

[100] China's lone SSBN does not patrol and is not believed to be operational.

CHAPTER 4

China's Participation in the Conference on Disarmament

The Conference on Disarmament, located along the Lac Leman in Geneva, is the single multilateral disarmament negotiating body in the world today, and as such, it plays an indispensable role in safeguarding world peace and security. What you are doing is an arduous but lofty work.

—Jiang Zemin, Address at the Conference on Disarmament, March 1999[1]

This chapter considers recent Chinese participation (from 1993 to 2003) in the United Nations Conference on Disarmament in Geneva, focusing on China's approaches toward two treaties designed to "freeze" global nuclear stockpiles in terms of sophistication and scope: the 1996 Comprehensive Test Ban Treaty and the proposed Fissile Material Cut-off Treaty (FMCT). The CTBT was negotiated at the CD from 1994 to 1996, and the FMCT has been under consideration by the CD since the conclusion of CTBT negotiations.

This period marked a shift in Chinese attitudes toward arms control and disarmament. Although official Chinese statements always paid homage to the goal of the "thorough" destruction of nuclear weapons, China shunned formal arms control negotiations until joining the Conference on Disarmament in 1980. The decision to negotiate and sign the CTBT was a particularly significant departure for China, which had denounced the 1963 Limited Test Ban Treaty as "a big fraud to fool the people of

---

[1] Jiang Zemin, "Promote Disarmament Process and Safeguard World Security, Address at the Conference on Disarmament," in *Final Record of the 822ⁿᵈ Plenary Meeting of the Conference on Disarmament*, CD/PV.822 (Geneva: March 26, 1999), p. 2.

the world."[2] China's leadership had viewed negotiations on the limited test ban as an excuse for the Soviet Union to deny technical assistance to the Chinese nuclear program. The CTBT represented the first time that China accepted an international constraint on its national military capabilities.[3] Any explanation of Chinese security policy must provide a coherent account of this decision as well as subsequent Chinese behavior toward the FMCT.

The Comprehensive Test Ban Treaty obligates signatories "not to carry out any nuclear weapon test explosion or any other nuclear explosion." Advocates of the CTBT believe that the test ban will prevent the development of increasingly sophisticated nuclear weapons. In this light, the CTBT has become a test of the nuclear weapons states' commitment under Article VI of the NPT to "pursue negotiations in good faith on effective measures relating to cessation of the nuclear arms race at an early date and to nuclear disarmament...."[4]

Where the CTBT places a qualitative constraint on nuclear arsenals through a ban on testing, the FMCT would impose a quantitative limit by prohibiting the production of additional fissile material for nuclear weapons. The 1995 NPT Review Conference identified the "immediate commencement and early conclusion of negotiations on a nondiscriminatory and universally applicable convention banning the production of fissile material for nuclear weapons or other nuclear explosive devices" as "important in the full realization and effective implementation of article VI" commitments to nuclear disarmament.[5]

---

[2] *Statement of the Government of the People's Republic of China* (October 16, 1964) in John Lewis and Xue Litai, *China Builds the Bomb* (Stanford, CA: Stanford University Press, 1988) pp. 241–243.

[3] Chinese participation in Chemical Weapons Convention (CWC) negotiations marked the first full participation of the Chinese delegation in an arms control negotiation. The institutional capacity developed during the CWC negotiations paid dividends during CTBT negotiations and Chinese positions on the CWC negotiations also foreshadowed some of the substantive positions that China would take on the CTBT, including proposals to limit the intrusiveness of on-site inspections.

[4] The connection between the CTBT and Article VI of the NPT was established in the *Final Document of the 1995 NPT Review Conference* (NPT/CONF.1995/32) making the treaty an important element of the nonproliferation regime that helps curb the spread of nuclear weapons. Available at: http://www.un.org/Depts/ddar/nptconf/162.htm.

[5] *Final Document of the 1995 NPT Review Conference* (NPT/CONF.1995/32/

Despite the similarity of the CTBT and the FMCT, China's behavior toward the two treaties has been radically different. China was an active participant in CTBT negotiations held at the CD. Although the Chinese delegation bargained hard, negotiations were completed on schedule with China among the first countries to sign the treaty. By contrast, China—in a dispute with the United States—blocked the adoption of a work program in the Conference on Disarmament for five years, foreclosing the possibility of negotiations on the FMCT.

A review of Chinese behavior in the CD from 1993 to the present is overdue; scholarly consideration of Chinese participation in the CD has been limited to a handful of small sections in journal articles.[6] Chapter five explores competing explanations of Chinese behavior at the CD, and this chapter offers a detailed history of the negotiations. Other accounts contain potentially significant factual errors regarding the sequence of events and the positions of the participants. I have conducted a limited number of interviews with U.S. and Chinese participants in the CD negotiations and made use of recently declassified U.S. documents regarding negotiating positions and unclassified assessments of China's testing program that emerged during the CTBT ratification debate and the allegations of Chinese nuclear weapons espionage. The Chinese delegation was prepared for a CTBT relatively early in the process: A 1986 report by two former directors of China's Institute of Applied Physics and Computational Mathematics (IAPCM) reportedly called for accelerating Chinese nuclear testing in anticipation of new U.S.-Soviet test-ban negotiations.

DEC.2). This statement was reaffirmed in the *Final Document of the 2000 NPT Review Conference* (NPT/CONF.2000/28).

6 Iain Johnston and Bates Gill, with various coauthors, are the only scholars who have dedicated any sustained attention to the question of why China signed the CTBT. Although each has published a number of articles and book chapters that include some discussion of the Chinese decision, the principle sources are Michel D. Swaine and Alastair Iain Johnston, "China and Arms Control Institutions," in Elizabeth Economy and Michael Oksenberg, ed., *China Joins the World* (New York: Council on Foreign Relations Press, 1999), pp. 90–135; Alastair Iain Johnston, "The Social Effects of International Institutions," in Daniel W. Drezner, ed., *Locating the Proper Authorities* (Ann Arbor: University of Michigan Press, 2003), pp. 145–196; Bates Gill, "Two Steps Forward, One Step Back: The Dynamics of Chinese Nonproliferation and Arms Control Policy-Making in an Era of Reform," in David Lampton, ed., *Making of Chinese Foreign and Security Policy in the Era of Reform, 1978–2000* (Stanford, CA: Stanford University Press, 2001), pp. 257–288.

As early as 1994, U.S. officials were briefed on Chinese plans to suspend testing by 1996.

Even less scholarly attention has been paid to the complete stoppage of work in the CD after the signature of the CTBT. The reasons for the deadlock appear to have been poorly understood at the onset, even by the participants. Some retrospective consideration is helpful to understanding the evolution of Chinese and U.S. policy in this regard. The section of this chapter concerning the FMCT is necessarily more speculative because the treaty is the subject of ongoing discussions about a potential work plan.

THE COMPREHENSIVE NUCLEAR TEST BAN TREATY

China's decision to negotiate and sign the CTBT was an important turning point for Chinese participation in international arms control regimes. On October 5, 1993, China committed to the completion of the CTBT "no later than 1996."[7] The October 1993 commitment to a test ban was rooted in decisions made during a major revision of Chinese security policy in the mid-1980s, decisions that are worth a short digression.

During the mid-1980s, China's security policy began to reflect the country's rapid economic development and China's growing confidence. Mikhail Gorbachev's ascension to power in the Soviet Union also affected China's security calculations. For example, in 1985, paramount leader Deng Xiaoping ordered a reduction in the size of the PLA by one million troops.[8] Deng allowed defense spending to decline as a percentage of GDP—a trend that would continue through the 1980s.[9] The number of operationally deployed nuclear forces declined as China reduced the number of CSS-2 MRBMs.

---

[7] Statement of the Government of the People's Republic of China on the Question of Nuclear Testing (October 5, 1993).

[8] Deng Xiaoping, *Speech at an Enlarged Meeting of the Military Commission of the Central Committee of the Communist Party of China* (June 4, 1985). Available at: http://english.peopledaily.com.cn/dengxp/vol3/text/c1410.html.

[9] For a review of military reforms instituted under Deng, see Dennis J. Blasko, "PLA Force Structure: A 20 Year Retrospective," in James C. Mulvenon and Andrew N.D. Yang, eds., *Seeking Truth from Facts: A Retrospective on Chinese Military Studies in the Post-Mao Era*, CF-160-CAPP (Santa Monica, CA: RAND, 2001), pp. 51–86.

Figure 4-1: Chinese Nuclear Tests, 1982–1996

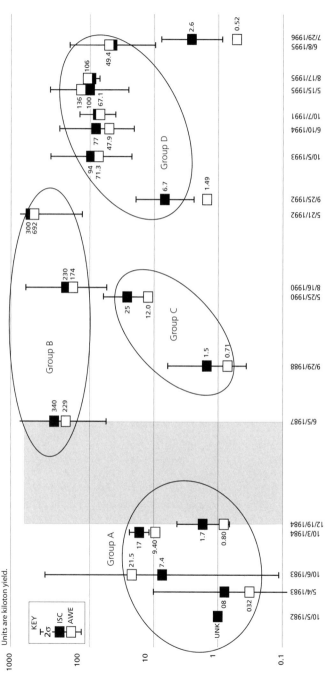

Notes: Yield estimates in black boxes and standard error are derived from data provided by the International Seismological Centre (ISC) Bulletin, available at: http://www.isc.ac.uk. Error bars represent one standard error. On the difficulty of using least squares method, see Ray Buland, "Uniform reduction error analysis," Bulletin of the Seismological Society of America, vol. 76, no. 1 (February 1986) pp. 217-230. White boxes are derived from data provided by the UK Atomic Weapons Establishment (AWE). See Aoife O'Mongain, Alan Douglas, John B. Young, "Body-wave Magnitudes and Locations of Presumed Explosions at the Chinese Test Site, 1967-1996," 22nd Annual DoD/DoE Seismic Research Symposium: Planning for Verification of and Compliance with the Comprehensive Nuclear-Test-Ban Treaty (Department of Defense/Department of Energy, 2000). Available at: http://www.ldeo.columbia.edu/res/pi/Monitoring/Doc/Srr_2000/.

Following a December 1984 nuclear test, China did not conduct another nuclear test for thirty months, until June 1987 (See Figure 4-1). This testing pause appears to have coincided with the completion of deployment goals for China's first generation of nuclear-capable ballistic missiles and the Soviet test moratorium that Gorbachev declared on July 1985 (and which lasted until February 1987).

During this period, two former directors of IAPCM, Yu Min and Deng Jiaxian, became concerned that the United States would accept calls for a Comprehensive Nuclear Test Ban Treaty.[10] Chinese designers had been pursuing miniaturization technologies slowly, in part because of the expenses involved. Although China had validated miniaturization principles in a series of tests during the early 1980s, the design had not been weaponized (See Figure 4-1, Group A). Deng Jiaxian had also been hospitalized repeatedly during the 1985–1986 testing pause. Just before his death in late 1986, he called Hu Side—later the head of China's nuclear weapons program—to the hospital and, after conferring with Yu Min and the other senior weapons designers, asked Hu to compose a report to the Central Committee of the Chinese Communist Party asking for support of an accelerated testing program that would complete a miniaturized warhead design in advance of a test ban.[11] The Central Committee approved the report, dated April 2, 1986, and placed Hu Renyu and Hu Side in charge of the overall planning for the test series.

Chinese leaders apparently believed additional U.S. nuclear weapons testing would not enhance U.S. deterrence. Deng and Yu argued that the United States was experiencing declining returns from testing and could, when politics required, agree to a test ban.[12]

----

[10] This section is drawn from *Biographies of the Founders of the Nuclear, Missile, and Satellite Program* (*Liangdan Yixing Yuanxunzhuan*), (Tsinghua University Press, 2001) pp. 56–63.

[11] In the 1990s, France would also accelerate its nuclear testing program in anticipation of the CTBT. China's decision is notable largely for its foresight—which seems to reflect the relative priority placed at the time on economic development and the central planning apparatus.

[12] An interesting analogue to this reasoning appears in a contemporary DIA analysis of Chinese attitudes about nuclear weapons: The DIA reported that Chinese leaders viewed U.S. Pershing II missile deployments in Europe as a purely political exercise and expected the United States—having defeated Moscow's efforts to undermine alliance cohesion with Soviet SS-20 missile deployments—to refrain from additional deployments for "political and psychological gains." In both cases, China anticipated that the United States

China's anticipation of test ban negotiations was evident in Chinese behavior in the CD. In 1985, China had expressed its willingness to "reconsider" its position on the CTBT if an *ad hoc* committee were convened. In March 1986, China announced that it would no longer conduct atmospheric nuclear testing and that it would participate in an *ad hoc* group on the CTBT if one were convened.[13]

The 1986 Deng-Yu report established a testing plan designed to lead China into a test ban. In 1984, the DIA assessed that the Chinese nuclear stockpile was based on a relatively small number of warhead designs (15 KT, 3 MT, and 4 to 5 MT warheads) that had been demonstrated in atmospheric nuclear tests.[14] The DIA speculated that further Chinese nuclear testing would be intended to

1. Increase reliability and warhead confidence;
2. Develop more compact warheads;
3. Increase hardening of warheads in a nuclear missile defense environment;
4. Develop tailored output devices, including enhanced radiation warheads; and
5. Improve safety, storage, and logistics procedures.[15]

China Today: Defense Science and Technology notes that China's nuclear tests between 1982 and 1988 were a single series of tests

---

would exercise restraint for the political gains it would bring, reasoning that the deterrent balance of strategic nuclear forces was insensitive to factors such as nuclear weapons testing and missile deployments. See *Special Defense Intelligence Estimate: China's Evolving Nuclear Strategies* DDE-2200-321-85 (Washington, DC: Defense Intelligence Agency, May 1985), pp. 9–10.

[13] On the commitment to cease atmospheric nuclear testing, see Zhao Ziyang's speech at the Chinese People's Rally for World Peace, quoted in "China Urges Superpowers to End Nuclear Testing," *United Press International* (March 21, 1986). On the commitment to participate in an *ad hoc* committee, see Qian Jiadong, "Statement at the Conference on Disarmament," in *Final Record of the 339th Plenary Meeting of Conference on Disarmament*, CD/PV.339 (Geneva: February 13, 1986), p. 32. China had, in 1985, expressed its willingness to "reconsider" its position on the CTBT if an *ad hoc* committee were convened. Qian Jiadong, "Statement at the Conference on Disarmament," in *Final Record of the 292nd Plenary Meeting of Conference on Disarmament*, CD/PV.292 (Geneva: February 19, 1985), pp. 32–33.

[14] *Defense Estimative Brief: Nuclear Weapons Systems in China*, DEB-49-84 (Defense Intelligence Agency, April 24, 1984), p. 2.

[15] *Defense Estimative Brief: Nuclear Weapons Systems in China*, pp. 2–3.

designed to help miniaturize China's nuclear weapons. The Chinese miniaturization effort seems to have employed similar approaches to those found in the U.S. W-70 warhead, including one modification which is referred to as an "enhanced radiation" warhead.[16] Some of these tests may also have been carried out to enhance the performance of the CSS-4 warhead for a nuclear anti-ballistic missile environment, improve reliability and confidence, and integrate safety features.

An analysis of Chinese test yields following the resumption of testing in 1987 suggests that Beijing implemented the recommendations from the 1986 Deng-Yu report and that China conducted three high-yield and two low-yield tests (See Figure 4-1, Groups B and C). The three high-yield tests were probably scaled tests of the warhead for the DF-21/JL-1 that was proposed in 1986 by Deng Jiaxian and Yu Min. One of the low-yield tests was reported to be an enhanced radiation device or "neutron bomb."[17]

In September 1992, China conducted a low-yield test that was reported to validate an aspherical primary—an innovation that allows construction of nuclear warheads with relatively small diameters like the U.S. W-88 warhead—for a miniaturized nuclear warhead that could arm the DF-31/JL-2.[18] China announced its intention to complete negotiations

---

[16] U.S. officials told the Associated Press that the classified version of the Cox Report "also discloses that U.S. intelligence detected that China tested 'a series' of neutron bombs in the 1980s with the last detonation occurring in 1988. One official put the number at about six." The reference to "neutron bombs" is probably a careless reference to the W-70. The unclassified version of the Cox Report notes that the W-70 design "contains elements that may be used either as a strategic thermonuclear weapon, or as an enhanced radiation weapon ('neutron bomb')." *Final Report of The United States House of Representatives Select Committee on U.S. National Security and Military/Commercial Concerns with the People's Republic of China*, House Report 105-851 (Washington, DC: Government Printing Office, 1999), p. 61. See also Dan Stober, "Chinese Neutron Bomb May Have Local Origin, FBI Suspects Theft of Livermore Lab Secrets," *San Jose Mercury News* (November 21, 1990), p. 1A.

[17] A small explosion of uncertain yield (10–30 KT) in May 1990 may have been a primary for the 200–300 KT warhead tested in June 1987 and August 1990, or a tactical warhead.

[18] For example, Sun Cheng Wei, a Chinese weapons scientist, gave a talk at Los Alamos in summer 1994 where he discussed China's work on spherical primaries, before noting "But these last few years, we've just been working at these watermelons." Ian Hoffman and Dan Stober, *A Convenient Spy: Wen Ho Lee and the Politics of Nuclear Espionage* (New York: Simon & Schuster, 2002), p. 109. See also *Statement of U.S. Representative Norm Dicks, Report of the Select*

on a CTBT "no later than 1996" following the first test of the complete design for a DF-31 warhead in October 1993.[19] Six tests in the 50 to 150 KT range probably completed validation for the design (See Figure 4-1, Group D). These tests were probably conducted with reduced-yield secondaries. The full yield of the DF-31 RV may be around 500 kilotons.[20]

The penultimate Chinese nuclear explosion may have been two tests, suggesting a lower yield consistent with tests for weapons effects and stockpile stewardship on the DF-31 RV.[21] China's final test, in July 1996, may have been a primary for an even smaller warhead.[22]

China's decision to conclude a CTBT "no later than 1996" appears to have been linked to the anticipated completion of the Chinese testing program, following the first successful test of the DF-31 RV. Based on the subsequent sequence of tests (six tests in the 50 to 150 KT range), the Chinese leadership appears to have approved a limited test schedule, probably in April 1991, that would permit the certification of a new warhead design by 1996.[23]

Committee on Technology Transfer to the People's Republic of China, (May 25, 1999).

[19] Chinese Foreign Minister Qian Qichen had told U.S. Secretary of State Warren Christopher in July 1993 that China would give "positive consideration" to a CTBT by 1996. "China, U.S. Hold Security Talks," *Agence France Presse* (July 27, 1993).

[20] China appears to have observed the 150-kiloton limit of the Threshold Test Ban Treaty, although it was not a signatory. One reason may have to do with the selection of the 150-kiloton threshold by the United States and the Soviet Union—a 150-kiloton threshold permits the development of new nuclear weapons with yields of 500 kilotons. See Harold Feiveson, Christopher Paine, and Frank Von Hippel, "A Low Threshold Test Ban is Feasible," *Science*, vol. 238, no. 4826 (October 23, 1987), p. 458.

[21] The June 1996 seismic event was reportedly two nuclear tests, which would reduce the yield to levels more compatible with effects and stockpile stewardship tests. In April 1995, *Jane's Defence Weekly*—citing unspecified but previously reliable sources—reported that China intended to conduct three nuclear tests in 1996. See "China Increases Test Total before Treaty," *Jane's Defence Weekly* (April 8, 1995), p. 3. The decision to conduct simultaneous nuclear explosions may have reflected international pressure to cease testing and agree to the CTBT. See "Latest Chinese Nuclear Test Involved Two Bombs," *Armed Forces Newswire Service* (June 12, 1996).

[22] "PRC Chief Engineer of Neutron Bomb Interviewed on Nuclear Weapons Development," *Chengdu Sichuan Ribao* (June 11, 2001), FBIS-CHI-2001-0613.

[23] The Xinhua news agency reported that "In the 1990s, Jiang Zemin personally inspected a nuclear weapons research and development base where he issued an

The U.S. intelligence community apparently believed that China was planning to suspend nuclear testing after 1996. A February 1994 U.S. State Department memorandum (now declassified), intended to prepare Undersecretary of State Lynne Davis for a meeting with her Chinese counterpart, cited "evidence that China plans to suspend testing in 1996."[24] Press reports indicated that Chinese officials privately confirmed to Undersecretary Davis that they would be ready to sign a CTBT by 1996.[25]

Chinese officials were also publicly stressing that their country's nuclear program was not open-ended. In early 1994, Chinese officials indicated that "five or six" tests remained in the ongoing testing sequence (in fact, six tests remained). In October 1994, a Chinese arms control official told reporters that China needed "a few more" nuclear tests.[26] After China's June 1996 test, Beijing officially announced that it would conduct one additional test.[27]

---

extremely important instruction on the nuclear weapons cause. Jiang also invited Zhu Guangya, Yu Min, Hu Renyu, Qian Shaojun, Hu Side, and some other scientists to Zhongnanhai where he held heart-to-heart talks and discussed with them the country's nuclear weapons development plan." Jiang Zemin made three visits to Sichuan province during the 1990s, including one in April 1991 that resulted in some consideration of the relationship between technology, modern weaponry, and national power. See "China's Nuclear Weapons History Viewed," *Beijing Xinhua Hong Kong Service* (September 19, 1999), FBIS-CHI-1999-0922 and "Text of 'Special Dispatch', 'Science, Technology Fever Triggered by the Central Authorities'," *Wen Wei Po* (May 21, 1991) in "CCP Leadership Encourages Technological Development," *BBC Summary of World Broadcasts* (May 22, 1991).

[24] This information appears in a declassified, but heavily redacted document with an incomplete citation, *China: CTBT/Nuclear Testing* (Department of State 1994), p. 2. Interestingly, this information does not appear to have been shared with the U.S. delegation in Geneva. Personal communication with Ambassador Stephen Ledogar, 2002.

[25] Vipin Gupta, "The Status of Chinese Nuclear Weapons Testing," *Jane's Intelligence Review* (January 1994), p. 34. One of the members of the Chinese delegation to Geneva, Zou Yunhua, authored an article in 1994 entitled "Comprehensive Nuclear Test Ban Treaty Inevitable in the Developing Circumstances ..." See Zou Yunhua, "Comprehensive Nuclear Test Ban Treaty Inevitable in the Developing Circumstances ..." *Guoji Wenti Yanjiu* [*International Studies*] (January 13, 1994), JPRS-CAR-94-030 (May 12, 1994), p. 1–4.

[26] "China to Conduct Just 'A Few More' Nuclear Tests," *Los Angeles Times* (October 21, 1994).

[27] See Gupta, p. 34; "China Increases Test Total before Treaty," p. 3; and "China

Negotiations on the CTBT commenced when the CD convened in January 1994. Although the negotiations were conducted under the auspices of the CD, the five nuclear weapons states (or P5 reflecting their status as the five permanent members of the UN Security Council) conducted regular talks as a group, and, in some instances, countries conducted bilateral negotiations.

China maintained three "treaty-killing proposals" that were designed to forestall an early CTBT. First, China insisted that any treaty permit "peaceful nuclear explosions [PNEs]."[28] The Chinese delegation must have been well aware that its position on PNEs would find little support among other states—permitting such nuclear explosions would make a treaty non-verifiable, and there was little international interest in PNEs.[29] Second, China argued that the treaty should contain negative security assurances, including a no-first-use pledge from the United States. The United States had long refused to adopt a no-first-use policy and made its position clear that the test ban treaty was an unacceptable forum to discuss these pledges. Third, China proposed an international satellite monitoring system that was widely considered unnecessary and cost-prohibitive. In subsequent interviews, Chinese participants in these negotiations confirmed that they were under instruction not to agree to a test ban before 1996.[30]

At the beginning of negotiations, the United States supported permitting nuclear tests with yields below four pounds (so-called hydronuclear tests), but this was unacceptable to the other nuclear states, which all lacked the test data and expertise to conduct useful tests at such low yields. The negotiations on the threshold for the test ban occurred principally among the P5 and lasted through August 1995, when the United States dropped its insistence on a four-pound threshold and committed

---

Stages Nuclear Test and Vows to Join Ban After One More," *The New York Times* (June 9, 1996), p. 14.

[28] For a review of various Chinese proposals for PNEs, see John Horgan, "'Peaceful' Nuclear Explosions: China's Interest in This Technology May Scuttle a Test-ban Treaty," *Scientific American*, vol. 274, no. 6 (June 1996), pp. 14–15.

[29] The *Final Document of the 1995 NPT Review Conference* (NPT/CONF.1995/ 32) recommended that the Conference on Disarmament "take … into account when negotiating a comprehensive nuclear test-ban treaty" that "peaceful applications of nuclear explosions envisaged in article V of the Treaty have not materialized."

[30] Personal communications, 2002.

to a "zero-yield" test ban. This essentially ended the negotiations over the threshold question, with the other members of the P5 agreeing to the U.S. proposal. The U.S. concession came amid mounting evidence that the test ban negotiations were entering their final phase.

In July 1995, France announced a final series of eight tests in advance of the test ban, beginning in September of that year.[31] Several states pushed a resolution through the UN General Assembly on December 12, 1995, stating that the General Assembly "strongly deplores" nuclear testing and calling for the immediate cessation of nuclear weapons tests. The proposal had lukewarm support—a majority of states abstained, asked to be counted as "not present," or voted against the resolution (including all of the P5). The French Ambassador to the UN called the resolution "unfounded, unfair, pernicious and useless."[32] China came under rather less pressure than France on the testing issue, perhaps because Chinese tests in Xinjiang lacked the obvious colonial overtones of French testing in the South Pacific. The Japanese Diet, however, suspended the grant portion of its overseas development assistance (ODA) to China in 1995 in response to China's continued nuclear testing. This was largely symbolic; the grants represented a small fraction of Japan's ODA contribution to China.

China announced in March 1996 that a "common understanding" had been reached among the P5 on including the phrase "any nuclear weapon test explosion" in the treaty—essentially signaling Chinese support for a zero-yield test ban and moving the negotiations into the so-called endgame phase during 1996.

In short order, the Chinese delegation began to drop the "treaty-killing" provisions that it had previously supported. At the beginning of the session, the rolling text of the treaty ran ninety-seven pages with 1,200 instances of bracketed passages signifying disputed language, and many of these bracketed passages were from proposals advanced by China. On May 28, 1996, Dutch Ambassador Jaap Ramaker tabled a

---

[31] On June 13, 1995, French President Jacques Chirac announced a series of eight nuclear tests in the South Pacific to run from September 1995 to May 1996. Two months later, in the face of negative international and domestic reaction, France announced that the tests would end more quickly.

[32] Eighteen states voted against the resolution with another forty-three states abstaining, and all the other nuclear weapons states either voted against the resolution or abstained. Another thirty or so states either failed to cast votes or asked for their votes to be recorded as absent.

clean draft text that proposed compromises on all the disputed language. China largely accepted this draft, which did not contain a provision for a satellite verification system, as the basis for future negotiations. In June, China indicated that it would agree to a "temporary" ban on PNEs and dropped its demand for negative security assurances to be included in the treaty.

The CD Chair's text proposed compromises on two issues—the treaty's entry-into-force provisions and on-site inspections—that were the subject of negotiations during the second session of the CD. These issues remained unresolved when negotiations were closed with the June 28 CTBT text.

The difficulty over the entry-into-force issue reflected competing interests between early entry-into-force on the one hand and universal application on the other. All parties agreed that the P5 would need to ratify the agreement for it to enter into force, but there were disagreements about whether the treaty's entry-into-force should depend on ratification by the three "threshold" states—India, Pakistan, and Israel. Various formulas were floated to require ratification by the three threshold states without naming them, including requiring ratification by all members of the CD. China initially insisted on ratification by all members of the CD as a condition for entry-into-force. After September 1995, China supported a Russian proposal that would require ratification by sixty-eight states listed by the International Atomic Energy Agency (IAEA) as having nuclear reactors or nuclear research programs. In the end, China accepted the Chair's compromise that the treaty would need to be ratified by the forty-four states that were members of the CD and had IAEA nuclear reactors and research programs, most likely because this formula ensured that India would be required to sign the treaty. New Delhi, however, objected to Indian ratification as a condition for entry-into-force and, after the Chair indicated that negotiations were closed with the June 28 text, withheld its consent to forwarding the treaty to the United Nations. In the end, Australia, rather than the CD, forwarded the treaty to the UN for signature.

China had better luck reopening the June 28 text on the issue of on-site inspections. The Chair's draft of June 28 accepted much of the Chinese position on inspections. The Chinese delegation had objected to initial U.S. proposals to use information collected by national technical means as a justification for an inspection and to automatically approve inspections unless opposed by a majority of the CTBT Executive Council (the so-called red-light procedure whereby a certain number of votes would be required to stop or "red light" an inspection). The Chinese delegation wanted national technical means limited to a "supplementary" role in triggering an inspection, and for each inspection to be approved—or "green lighted"—by an affirmative two-thirds of the treaty's proposed Executive Council. The June 28 Chair's text (the official working draft) permitted national technical means to be used as a justification for inspections as the U.S. delegation wished, but it adopted the green-light procedure preferred by the Chinese, requiring only a simple majority of votes in the Executive Council. The United States indicated at that point that it would accept the compromise proposal in the Chair's text.

The Chinese delegation indicated that the June 28 draft still did "not reflect China's positions on some important issues," such as the basis for on-site inspections and the decision-making procedure of the Executive Council. The Chinese delegation put forward their own amendments to the Chair's text and expressed concern about the possible abuse of inspections. Interview data suggests that the members of the Chinese delegation had different emphases among themselves on how to revise the text of the treaty. Concern about the abuse of inspections was shared by "many" states that were "adamantly opposed to giving the U.S. what they considered was . . . a license to spy."[33] Inspections might reveal sensitive technical data about a country's testing program as well as provide cover for espionage efforts directed at nearby facilities. Moreover, inspections were hypothetical at the time of negotiation. No delegation or observer could be certain how common or intrusive inspections would actually be. The United States was itself concerned about such espionage and, in its own interagency process, favored restricting access to U.S. facilities during inspections.[34]

In response to the standoff over procedures for on-site inspections, Chinese President Jiang Zemin reportedly sent a letter dated July 12, 1996 to U.S. President Bill Clinton expressing his "hope that the two sides can reach agreement on this matter prior to the resumption of the Conference on Disarmament on 29 July with a view to avoiding the

---

[33] *Final Review of the Comprehensive Nuclear Test Ban Treaty (Treaty Doc. 105–28)*, Hearing before the Committee On Foreign Relations, S. Hrg. 106-262 (October 7, 1999), p. 18.

[34] Ibid., p. 18.

reopening of talks on the chairman's text during the resumed meeting and to facilitating the signing of a CTBT within this year."[35]

In August 1996, the United States opened intensive bilateral negotiations with China over the treaty's provision for on-site inspections. This decision by Washington was based on a belief that China would not sign the treaty without further compromise on the issue of inspections. Whether or not the Chinese delegation would have signed the agreement without this compromise is difficult to say. Interview data suggest the delegation was divided over the issue of on-site inspections, and Chinese participants provide different answers to a counterfactual question regarding whether China would have signed without the compromise. But the U.S. belief that China would insist on a compromise with regard to on-site inspections seems to have been based on some evidence. Chinese representative Sha Zukang had publicly told the Conference on Disarmament that the "success or failure" of the negotiations would hinge on the issue of on-site inspections. One member of the Chinese delegation recalled that "Chinese ambassador Sha Zukang made it clear in the discussions that China would be unable to sign the treaty without this concession."[36] In all likelihood, the decision would have been made at the most senior levels of the Chinese government. On August 6, the United States and China indicated that China accepted the use of information from national technical means as a basis for inspections, but that inspections would require a supermajority of the treaty's Executive Council (thirty of fifty-one members).[37] This compromise was submitted on August 14, 1996.

After signing the treaty in 1996, the Chinese government continued to express concerns about the possible abuses of the inspection regime. The official Chinese government statement that accompanied the Chinese signature reaffirmed Beijing's opposition to "the abuse of verification rights by any country, including the use of espionage or human

---

[35] This apparently responded to Clinton letters dated June 26 and July 8, 1996. See Zou Yunhua, *China and the CTBT Negotiations* (Stanford, CA: Stanford University Center for International Security and Cooperation, 1998), p. 24.

[36] Zou, *China and the CTBT Negotiations*, p. 24.

[37] "US, China Say They Have Made Progress on CTBT," *Agence France Presse* (August 6, 1996). AFP later reports that, in exchange for setting the trigger at thirty votes, China committed to secure Pakistani support and push the CTBT through to the UN General Assembly. "US, China Agree to Get around Indian Opposition to CTBT," *Agence France Presse* (August 9, 1996).

intelligence, to infringe upon the sovereignty of China and impair its legitimate security interests in violation of universally recognized principles of international law." U.S. Secretary of State Warren Christopher appears to have sent a letter to Chinese Vice Foreign Minister Qian Qichen expressing that "the United States understood China's concern on NTM [national technical means] and was committed to compliance by all parties to the CTBT with these CTBT provisions against possible abuse."[38] China appears to have been serious in its concern about abuse and proposed drafting a "permitted activities" list that would reduce suspicion and the risk of mutual recrimination.[39]

In September 1996, the CTBT was opened for signature. After signing the CTBT, President Clinton told the United Nations General Assembly that the United States was ready to begin "negotiating a treaty to freeze the production of fissile materials for use in nuclear weapons" and suggested that the "Conference on Disarmament should take up this challenge immediately."[40]

FISSILE MATERIAL CUT-OFF TREATY

In contrast to the period from 1993 to 1996 when the CD energetically worked toward a CTBT, the CD has not adopted a program of work to negotiate a FMCT—in fact, the CD has been deadlocked since the end of 1996 (with a three-week exception in 1998). Disputes in the first two years following the conclusion of the CTBT (1997–1998) focused on the scope of the proposed treaty on fissile materials. Many developing nations wanted to link FMCT negotiations with broader negotiations toward nuclear disarmament; this linkage was in large measure a proxy for the more contentious issue of whether the treaty ought to be a nonproliferation measure that banned future production, or whether it would be a more general disarmament measure subjecting existing fissile material stockpiles of the nuclear weapons states to regulation.

The nuclear weapons states all strongly oppose the inclusion of existing stockpiles in the treaty. China is especially sensitive about subjecting its stockpile to international regulation. Beijing ceased production of plu-

---

[38] Zou, *China and the CTBT Negotiations*, p. 24.

[39] The document is said to be classified because it might have complicated negotiations with non-nuclear states. Citation available from author.

[40] William Jefferson Clinton, "Address to the United Nations," *Public Papers of the Presidents* (1996), vol. 2, p. 1648.

tonium for military uses around 1990, apparently as part of a larger effort to convert defense industries to civilian production.[41]Most estimates of Chinese fissile material production credit China with one to four tons of plutonium and twenty tons of highly enriched uranium (HEU).[42] Most of China's currently deployed nuclear weapons rely heavily on plutonium. Though the size of China's plutonium stockpile cannot be estimated with precision, it may constrain the size of the Chinese nuclear arsenal.

China has never disclosed the amount of plutonium it has produced. Western estimates are largely derived from the capacity of China's two plutonium production facilities. Classified estimates by the U.S. Department of Energy (DoE), leaked to the press, approximate the Chinese plutonium stockpile (including weapons) to be 1.7 to 2.8 tons.[43] Assuming 3 to 5 kilograms of plutonium per warhead, 1.7 to 2.8 tons of plutonium could support a force of 340 to 930 weapons. If China uses substantially more than 5 kilograms per warhead, its stockpile might only support a few hundred weapons. These estimates probably form the basis of the assessment from *Proliferation: Threat and Response* that China "has a stockpile of fissile material sufficient to improve or increase its weapons inventory."[44] The DoE estimate is consistent with a detailed, unclassified estimate of Chinese plutonium production that has placed the Chinese plutonium stockpile at two to five tons.[45]

Limited information about the production facilities themselves, as well as the power and operating histories of the reactors, can significantly change the estimates of the total size of the stockpile. U.S. intelligence estimates of South African HEU production in the 1980s, for example, were significantly higher than actual production, in part because South Africa's facilities encountered substantial difficulties.[46]

---

[41] David Wright and Lisbeth Gronlund, "A History of China's Plutonium Production," *Science and Global Security,* vol. 11, no. 1 (2003), pp. 61–80. See also *Proliferation: Threat and Response,* (Washington, DC: Department of Defense, 2001), p. 14.

[42] David Albright, Frans Berkhout, and William Walker, *Plutonium and Highly Enriched Uranium 1996: World Inventories, Capabilities, and Policies* (New York: Oxford University Press, 1997), pp. 126–130.

[43] Robert S. Norris and William M. Arkin, "World Plutonium Inventories," Bulletin of the Atomic Scientists vol. 55, no. 5 (September/October 1999) p. 71.

[44] *Proliferation: Threat and Response,* p. 14.

[45] Wright and Gronlund, p. 74.

[46] Robert E. Kelley, "The Iraqi and South African Nuclear Weapon Programs: The Importance of Management," *Security Dialogue,* vol. 27, no. 1 (March 1996), p. 37.

Declassified U.S. intelligence documents suggest Chinese plutonium production facilities encountered significant technical problems, possibly resulting from the withdrawal of Soviet assistance in 1960.[47] If one of the plutonium production facilities suffered operating problems—such as a rumored fire during the 1970s—the total amount of plutonium in the Chinese stockpile could be significantly lower.[48] If the Chinese plutonium stockpile is closer to one ton, China may face a serious constraint on its ability to expand its arsenal beyond the projected modernization plans.[49]

Non–nuclear weapon states have supported the much broader concept of a "Fissile Material Treaty" that would cover both existing stockpiles and future production. Algeria, Egypt, Iran, and Pakistan have been particularly keen to include existing stockpiles as a way to curb Israeli and Indian nuclear arsenals. There were (and are) also disagreements over other matters such as transparency, civil reprocessing of plutonium, and verification measures. The 1996–1998 period ended with an agreement on an agenda and program of work in late 1998. Although there was a general sense that the agreement on a program of work was largely symbolic (as the year was drawing to a close, there would be little time for negotiations before the year ended, and a new work plan would be necessary), a compromise on the scope of negotiations appeared feasible.

This modest progress was soon halted. In January 1999, U.S. Secretary of Defense William Cohen announced a major restructuring of the U.S. national and theater missile defense programs. Cohen announced, among other changes, that the Clinton administration would seek $6.6 billion over 2000–2005 for *deployment* of a national missile defense system (previous funding had been restricted to research and development) and would explore the "nature and scope" of modifications to the ABM Treaty.[50] In March 1999, the Chinese delegation began to link negotiations on a fissile material cut-off treaty with negotiations on "preventing an arms race in outer space" (PAROS) as part of a "balanced and comprehensive" plan of work. This procedural position reflected a substantive

---

[47] Central Intelligence Agency, *China: Plutonium Production Reactor Problems* (Washington, DC: January 1988).

[48] Wright and Gronlund, "A History of China's Plutonium Production," p. 74.

[49] Modern Chinese pits are made with plutonium. The use of Highly Enriched Uranium in pits would seem a very unlikely option for China.

[50] Craig Cerniello, "Cohen Announces NMD Restructuring, Funding Boost," *Arms Control Today* (January/February 1999), p. 20.

dispute between Beijing and Washington over China's objections to U.S. military activities in outer space, particularly to anticipated missile defense deployments.

The U.S. delegation did not expect this linkage when the CD convened in January 1999 (with the United States holding the presidency), and was slow to recognize its significance. The proposed program for this round of CD negotiations clearly did not anticipate Chinese demands for outer space negotiations. China's decision to link the FMCT and PAROS agendas occurred against the backdrop of a difficult period in Sino–American relations, marked by sharp disputes over NATO's intervention in Yugoslavia (Operation Allied Force). In March, the Rambouillet talks to determine the status of Kosovo collapsed. In the days between the collapse of the talks and the beginning of Operation Allied Force, Li Changhe, China's Ambassador for Disarmament Affairs, advanced a strong Chinese demand that any program of work include an *ad hoc* committee to "negotiate and conclude an international legal instrument banning the test[ing], deployment and use of any weapons, weapon systems and their components in outer space, with a view to preventing the weaponisation of outer space."[51] Two days after the United States began Operation Allied Force, Chinese Premier Jiang Zemin addressed the CD. His remarks focused on looming U.S. missile defense deployments and Operation Allied Force—but not the specific Chinese proposal to link the FMCT with PAROS.[52]

In retrospect, the tensions in the U.S.–China relationship may have obscured the degree to which the Chinese position reflected less ephemeral concerns. As the tension over Operation Allied Force began to ease after the cease-fire in June 1999, Ambassador Dembri of Algeria proposed a compromise formula: negotiations on a fissile materials convention and discussions on nuclear disarmament and PAROS. Accepting the Dembri formula for an *ad hoc* committee to discuss disarmament would have exceeded the negotiating instructions given to the U.S. representative; the authority to agree to an *ad hoc* committee appears to have been removed from his instructions the previous winter. Although he

---

[51] Li Changhe, "Statement at the Conference on Disarmament," in *Final Record of the 818th Plenary Meeting of Conference on Disarmament,* CD/PV.818 (Geneva: March 11, 1999), p. 15.

[52] Jiang Zemin, "Promote Disarmament Process and Safeguard World Security," pp. 2–5.

pledged to "work with [the delegations] to take advantage of any flexibility that may exist on the part of my government," that flexibility was constrained and did not encompass a subsequent June 2000 Chinese draft mandate for the *ad hoc* committee that called for negotiations. Although the United States might have agreed to a mandate that convened an *ad hoc* committee, Washington was unlikely to accept a mandate that created an obligation to negotiate a treaty.

By 2000, China insisted that the *ad hoc* committee to discuss outer space must have a mandate that included the word *negotiate*. The United States refused. As one U.S. participant explained, "It's just that one word—*negotiate*." In another effort at compromise, Ambassador Celso Amorim of Brazil suggested supplementing the Dembri formula with a declaration by the CD president stressing that the CD was a disarmament *negotiating* forum and that the mandates and work of the bodies should be "understood in that light."[53] Again, the Chinese rejected this proposal and insisted that the mandate itself include some form of the word *negotiate*.

After taking office in January 2001, the Bush administration maintained the Clinton Administration commitment to negotiating a fissile material cut-off treaty through November 2003.[54] Robert Grey, a Clinton appointee, remained as Ambassador to the CD through the end of 2001 and received approval to commit the United States to the Amorim formula. The Chinese delegation continued to insist on negotiations, proposing that the discussions take place "with a view to negotiating a relevant international legal instrument." The stalemate continued. As the new U.S. Ambassador to the CD, Eric Javits, took office, the Chinese delegation offered another formulation—this time modifying the mandate for an *ad hoc* committee to discuss a number of issues related to an arms race in outer space, "including the possibility of negotiations."

---

[53] The Amorim proposal was published as CD/1624 (August 24, 2000).

[54] See for example, Avis T. Bohlen, *Statement in the First Committee of the General Assembly United Nations, New York* (October 10, 2001). The Bush administration would later review and revise its support for the FMCT. See "U.S. Reviewing FMCT Policy," *Arms Control Today* (November 2003), and Jackie W. Sanders, Permanent Representative to the Conference on Disarmament and Special Representative of the President for the Nonproliferation of Nuclear Weapons, Remarks to Conference on Disarmament, Geneva, Switzerland (July 29, 2004).

This Chinese initiative appears to have been too late—it might have been enough to gain agreement from the Clinton administration, but the Bush administration did not accept it. The reasons are not clear, and judgments about the U.S. response are highly politicized. Some observers claim that Javits was removed by the Bush administration (he was transferred to the Organization for the Prohibition of Chemical Weapons) over a dispute with Undersecretary of State John Bolton, and that Javits had wanted more flexibility to negotiate with the Chinese. This judgment has gained the status of conventional wisdom, in part because Washington did not nominate a successor to Javits for more than a year.

Although some CD delegations are, no doubt, happy to have the excuse for inaction provided by the United States and China, the vast majority of states appear ready to begin FMCT negotiations. For example, the Italian Ambassador to the CD noted that:

> The deadlock we are experiencing for so long a time is not due to the inflexibility of the greatest majority of the States here represented.... Therefore, we expect that the major players will not let this last attempt [to reach consensus] down. In this context we applaud, as a first step, the political consultations on CD held recently in Beijing between the United States and China. We expect in fact that the major players honor their high responsibilities in front of international community and history....[55]

In 2003, the Chinese government moved again, this time significantly, accepting a "research mandate" where the CD would merely examine issues related to the prevention of an arms race in outer space. The Bush administration did not accept this compromise, but rather announced a "review" of the administration's commitment to achieving the FMCT. In August 2004, the Bush administration reiterated its support for the FMCT, but without provisions for verification and under a "clean" mandate that did not include the *ad hoc* committees in the previous initiatives. This marked a new phase in the CD, where principal responsibility for the deadlock fell solely on the United States. In accepting a "research mandate" Chinese leaders may be responding to international pressure or attempting to enmesh the United States in international negotiations once again.

---

[55] Angelo Persiani, "Statement at the Conference on Disarmament," in *Final Record of the 917th Plenary Meeting of Conference on Disarmament*, CD/PV.917 (Geneva: January 28, 2003), p. 15.

CONCLUSION

China began preparations for a CTBT in the mid-1980s, much earlier than most observers realize. Those preparations reflected a decline in Chinese threat perceptions. Mirroring the new emphasis on quality over quantity throughout the PLA, China reduced the size of its operationally deployed nuclear forces and shifted resources toward a much longer-range modernization that included a test ban.

China's participation in CTBT negotiations marked a dramatic change for the country that, in the statement accompanying its first nuclear test, called the 1963 Limited Test Ban Treaty "a big fraud to fool the people of the world." In the end, the state that warned the test ban would "tie the hands of all peace-loving countries" ended up drafting the list of permitted activities for the five nuclear powers. China's subsequent opposition to a program of work in the CD represented not so much a return to its original position, but a culmination of China's increasing confidence that it had a right to participate in setting the global arms control and disarmament agenda. This conclusion is at odds with much of the current scholarship emphasizing skepticism about China's motives; the next chapter attempts to compare these competing explanations.

CHAPTER 5

Competing Explanations for China's Arms Control Behavior

> *Signing the CTBT was in line with China's consistent stand in support of "the complete prohibition and thorough destruction of nuclear weapons." This was one of the major reasons China supported an early conclusion of the treaty.*
>
> *Of course, China's desire to meet the trend of the modern world also motivated it to sign. Because economic development had long been Beijing's top priority, China needed a peaceful security environment in order to devote itself completely to the modernization of the nation. To this end, its defense buildup had been steadily subordinated to national economic development.*
>
> *Beijing's decision on the CTBT negotiations stemmed also from its self-defense and no-first-use nuclear policies. China had established an effective nuclear force for self-defense.*
>
> —Zou Yunhua, *China and the CTBT Negotiations*, 1998[1]

Given China's current force configuration and its past participation in the Conference on Disarmament, one might expect China to be an active participant in arms control negotiations. Yet most U.S. analysts would agree with three authors of a recent study for the Council on Foreign Relations, who conclude: "In the current climate, however, we have a sense of pessimism about the prospects for

---

[1] Zou Yunhua, *China and the CTBT Negotiations* (Stanford, CA: Stanford University Center for International Security and Cooperation, 1998), pp. 6–7.

Chinese participation in nuclear arms control beyond the [Comprehensive Test Ban Treaty]."[2]

This pessimism is partly rooted in the conventional account of China's attitudes toward nuclear weapons. Chinese participation in international arms control negotiations and regimes since the late 1980s is typically explained as an adaptation to external changes in China's security environment that do not reflect a fundamental change in Chinese attitudes toward nuclear weapons—attitudes that reportedly emphasize the value of nuclear weapons and the sensitivity of deterrence to changes in the balance of capabilities.[3] China's accession to certain arms control regimes is frequently explained as a concession to international pressure in spite, rather than because, of China's attitudes about nuclear weapons and arms control.

Skeptics of Chinese participation in international arms control regimes generally believe that Chinese leaders highly value the military power of nuclear weapons—a materialist outlook that fits comfortably with academic conceptions of realism.[4] For policymakers—presumably interested in the interaction of U.S. and Chinese force deployments, as well as the prospect for arms control solutions—casting the debate as one between realism and its critics is not helpful: Realists hold a range of views regarding the sensitivity of deterrence to changes in the balance of forces and a range of views on the need and purpose for arms control arrangements.[5] The more crucial question is how the Chinese planning system treats choices about deterrence and arms control.

---

[2] Robert A. Manning, Ronald Montaperto, and Brad Roberts, *China, Nuclear Weapons, and Arms Control: A Preliminary Assessment* (New York: Council on Foreign Relations, 2000), p. 66.

[3] For example, see Alastair Iain Johnston, *Cultural Realism: Strategic Culture and Grand Strategy in Chinese History* (Princeton, NJ: Princeton University Press, 1988) and Thomas J. Christensen, "Chinese Realpolitik," *Foreign Affairs,* vol. 75, no. 5 (September/October 1996), pp. 37–52.

[4] Alastair Iain Johnston, "Learning versus Adaptation: Explaining Change in Chinese Arms Control Policy in the 1980s and 1990s," *The China Journal,* no. 35 (January 1996), pp. 29–30.

[5] For example, see Kenneth Waltz, "The Spread of Nuclear Weapons: More May Be Better," Adelphi Papers, no. 171 (London: International Institute for Strategic Studies, 1981); and Charles L. Glaser, "Realists as Optimists: Cooperation as Self-Help," *International Security,* vol. 19, no. 3 (Winter 1994/1995), pp. 50–90.

The first few chapters of this book suggest that China maintains smaller, less diverse, and less ready strategic forces because Chinese leaders believe the stability of deterrence is largely unaffected by such factors. China's almost existentialist approach is philosophically compatible with arms control agreements and other constraints on strategic forces. In fact, recent Chinese participation in the Conference on Disarmament (1993–2003) suggests that Chinese leaders are more interested in formal arms control than Americans generally believe. U.S. policymakers may have overestimated the impact of international pressure on the Chinese security agenda.

Inadequate appreciation of Beijing's readiness for arms control efforts may have been responsible for much of the recent deadlock at the CD in Geneva, as well as for the rather gloomy assessments of the prospects for future U.S.–China arms control negotiations. China's behavior toward the 1996 CTBT and the proposed Fissile Material Cut-off Treaty offers an interesting comparative test of this hypothesis. Both treaties ask Beijing to accept significant restrictions on Chinese nuclear force structure in exchange for more general improvements in the international security environment, yet Chinese behavior toward the two treaties has been radically different. On the CTBT, China was an active participant in the treaty negotiations held at the CD. Although the Chinese bargained hard, negotiations were completed on schedule, and China was among the first countries to sign the treaty. By contrast, China—in a dispute with the United States—blocked the adoption of a work program in the Conference on Disarmament for five years, foreclosing the possibility of negotiations on a FMCT during that period.

SKEPTICAL EXPLANATIONS FOR CHINA'S PARTICIPATION IN ARMS CONTROL

U.S. observers are generally skeptical about China's motives for participating in arms control regimes. This skepticism rests on the belief that China remains the "high church of realpolitik in the post–Cold War world," meaning that Chinese leaders are very concerned about the material aspects of power and the relative balance of military capabilities.[6] Skeptics of China's participation in arms control regimes assume that the realpolitik worldview ascribed to the Chinese leadership will necessarily

---

[6] Christensen, p. 37.

render Chinese leaders acutely sensitive to changes in the deterrent balance. "Realpolitik world views are associated with a keen sensitivity to relative power capabilities, since these are critical for preserving the territorial integrity of the state," Iain Johnston notes. "Given this world view, it is not surprising that China's decision-makers have generally accorded a great deal of status and military value to nuclear weapons."[7]

China, however, has expanded participation in international arms control and nonproliferation regimes despite its policymakers' reputed sensitivity to changes in relative capability. In the process, China has undertaken at least one significant obligation—the Comprehensive Nuclear Test Ban Treaty—that constrains its military forces.

To account for the decision to sign the CTBT, while preserving the assumption that Chinese leaders are acutely concerned with managing the deterrent balance, skeptics argue that the "changes are mostly tactical in nature, [and] reflect a recalculation of the most effective means to avoid placing China's capabilities on the arms control tables, and that they are designed to preserve and improve its relative capabilities."[8] This argument reproduces the debate that occurred in the late 1980s over the nature of the changes occurring in the Soviet Union, particularly the changes in foreign policy that Mikhail Gorbachev implemented starting with the redefinition of "peaceful coexistence" at the 27th Party Congress in February and March 1986. That debate broke into roughly two camps: One camp argued that Gorbachev was merely "adapting" to new situations without altering the fundamental character of Soviet policy, while a second camp suggested that the changes reflected "new thinking" about Soviet interests (academics called this "learning" to reflect the fundamental nature of the change).

There are limits to the value of the distinction between adaptation and learning. First, locating the changes in Soviet foreign policy implicitly accepted a crude (and probably incorrect) caricature of pre-Gorbachev Soviet foreign policy.[9] Second, the model also presents a suspiciously

---

[7]Alastair Iain Johnston, "Prospects for Chinese Limited Nuclear Force Modernization," *China Quarterly*, no. 146 (June 1996), p. 550.

[8] Johnston, "Learning versus Adaptation," p. 28.

[9] On the roots of "new thinking" in Soviet foreign policy, see Celeste Wallander, "Lost and Found: Gorbachev's 'New Thinking,'" *The Washington Quarterly*, vol. 25, no. 1 (Winter 2002), pp. 117–129.

clean distinction between motivations and actions that led one academic to declare the discipline a "conceptual minefield."[10] Whatever its merits, the entire debate about learning and adaptation has been transferred to the question of China's participation in international arms control regimes, with most U.S. academics adopting a variant of the "adaptation" view that China participates in international regimes solely for reputational or image reasons.[11]

The argument that Chinese leaders are very susceptible to international pressure takes two forms. The most straightforward account concerns China's reputation—Chinese leaders worry that an image as a non-cooperative state will leave it isolated amid a highly threatening international system. A second version of the argument suggests that the concern for image evinced by the Chinese leadership is not connected to material rewards, but rather reflects sensitivity to "back-patting and opprobrium."[12] This sensitivity is said to be accentuated by a tendency among Chinese elites to conflate their identities with that of the state. Academics call the process either anthropomorphism or isomorphism.

How well do skeptical theories that posit that China is attempting to optimize either reputation or "back-patting" explain Chinese behavior in international arms control regimes? Is the skeptical explanation more parsimonious than the explanation that Chinese leaders, having concluded that deterrence is robust, are pursuing their security interests cooperatively? The next section considers skeptical explanations for Chinese behavior in the CD during the CTBT negotiations, and then tests those explanations against subsequent Chinese behavior in that forum.

---

[10] Jack Levy, "Learning and Foreign Policy: Sweeping a Conceptual Minefield," *International Organization*, vol. 48, no. 2 (Spring 1994), pp. 279–312.

[11] Johnston warns that "While reputation and image are often used interchangeably in international relations theory literature, they are in fact different concepts." Unfortunately, he himself uses the concepts interchangeably, e.g. when he argues that the most important "variable appears to be international image. The costs to reputation from backing out of these kinds of processes are extremely high, while the benefits from remaining inside—reinforcing China's image as a responsible major power—are also high." Johnston, "Prospects for Chinese Limited Nuclear Force Modernization," *China Quarterly*, no. 146 (June 1996), p. 576.

[12] Johnston, "The Social Effects of International Institutions," p. 173.

The Comprehensive Nuclear Test Ban Treaty

The idea that China is acutely sensitive to social pressure is principally employed to explain Chinese participation in the CTBT negotiations. Signing the CTBT was the "first instance where [China] sacrificed potential military capabilities for the sake of formal multilateral arms control."[13] A Chinese leadership, keenly aware of the relative balance of technical capabilities, should be very reluctant to sign such an agreement. Therefore, it would seem that an additional variable is necessary to explain this supposedly anomalous behavior by Beijing: skeptics argue that China's reluctant participation in the CTBT was driven by the fear that outright obstruction would damage its reputation or image:

> Until late summer 1996, outside observers did not sense much strong support in China for the CTBT. Indeed, Beijing's position in the CTBT talks seemed to have been largely designed to slow down the process, in the view of many CD delegates and nongovernmental observers. Specifically, China had posed several preconditions for successful completion of the treaty that were generally unacceptable to other participants in the talks and that would seriously delay its signing and implementation.... China had little choice once it was clear that the CTBT was supported by an enormous majority of states who saw it as a pillar of the nuclear nonproliferation regime.... China's signature was consistent with its being a responsible major power, and joining the treaty was part of a "global atmosphere," such that China would have been isolated had it opposed or sabotaged the treaty.[14]

This account is straightforward, but stylized and inaccurate. Although "outside observers did not sense much strong support in China for the CTBT" before "late summer 1996," apparently long-running internal preparations for a test ban date to a report issued by Deng Jiaxian and Yu Min in 1986. This report concluded that the declining marginal utility of additional refinements to U.S. and Soviet nuclear weapons would render nuclear testing obsolete.[15] Contrary to the claim that "It was clear from the start that China's decision makers were not especially interested in a test ban treaty," the Chinese testing program anticipated an end to nuclear

---

[13] Johnston, "Learning versus Adaptation," p. 54.

[14] Ibid., p. 108.

[15] See chapter 4.

modernization in 1996—something that the U.S. State Department was reporting in early 1994 and that Chinese officials confirmed in private meetings reported in the press.[16] Moreover, the Chinese leadership geared its nuclear modernization to achieve a more survivable version of its current deterrent posture, most likely based on judgments that the United States and the Soviet Union (later Russia) would negotiate a test ban based on the declining utility of further strategic force modernization.

Some skeptics suggested that China completed its testing program by the end of 1996, perhaps with the assistance of espionage, which is consistent with the hypothesis that pressure played a crucial role in China's decision. To be clear, the CTBT imposes two constraints on the further modernization of the Chinese arsenal. Unclassified U.S. intelligence assessments conclude that China would require additional nuclear tests in "the yield range needed to develop a more nearly optimum (lighter weight and perhaps more efficient use of fissile material) warhead" similar to the W-88.[17] China might need to make more efficient use of its fissile material stockpile (for example, by using composite pits of both plutonium and highly enriched uranium) to expand the size of its nuclear arsenal without resuming production of fissile material. China might also want to further miniaturize its nuclear warheads to place multiple RVs on its new solid-fueled mobile missiles. Although China might achieve further miniaturization through engineering advances in the power supply, arming, fuzing, and firing systems, the U.S. intelligence community has assessed that China is unlikely to deploy such a warhead without additional testing.[18] If one assumes that China is keenly sensitive to the tech-

---

[16] Vipin Gupta, "The Status of Chinese Nuclear Weapons Testing," *Jane's Intelligence Review* (January 1994), p. 34.

[17] John Holdren et al., *Technical Issues Related to the Comprehensive Nuclear Test Ban Treaty* (Washington, DC: Committee on Technical Issues Related to Ratification of the Comprehensive Nuclear Test Ban Treaty, Committee on International Security and Arms Control, National Academies of Sciences, 2002), p. 72.

[18] The National Intelligence Estimate concludes that developing such a warhead without testing would "encounter significant technical hurdles and would be costly." *Foreign Missile Developments and the Ballistic Missile Threat Through 2015* (Washington, DC: National Intelligence Council, December 2001), p. 8. In his capacity as special advisor to the president and secretary of state for the Comprehensive Test Ban, former Chairman of the Joint Chiefs of Staff General John Shalikashvili concluded that the test ban would "impede China from

nical details of the deterrent balance, the CTBT would require Beijing to make substantial sacrifices.

The claim that "China had posed several preconditions…that would seriously delay [the CTBT's] signing and implementation" is also misleading. This argument is employed to explain the "interesting decision" by China's leaders to enter negotiations in 1994. One author notes that "China could probably have blocked the treaty before its negotiations had started, linking with the other two medium-sized nuclear powers to prevent a P-5 agreement to negotiate a treaty in the CD." The same author speculated that "if costs to its image preclude" blocking a CTBT, "there are good reasons for China to…at least slow down the process."[19]

There is no evidence, however, that China slowed negotiations. In 1994, China committed to a CTBT "no later than 1996" and, in fact, the treaty was completed when the UN General Assembly convened in 1996. Interview data does suggest that the Chinese delegation at the CD in Geneva was not authorized to agree to a test ban before the completion of China's ongoing testing program in 1996.[20] Although the Chinese delegation adopted positions that would allow it to slow negotiations if necessary, in the end China did not need to obstruct negotiations. The United States agreed to a zero-yield test ban in August 1995, meaning that the treaty could not have been completed and forwarded to the General Assembly any earlier than it was—when the General Assembly convened again in September 1996. Rather than slowing negotiations, China dropped its obstructionist positions and focused on core concerns about the procedures for on-site inspections as negotiations entered the endgame.

---

placing multiple warheads on a mobile missile." See John M. Shalikashvili, *Findings and Recommendations Concerning the Comprehensive Nuclear Test Ban Treaty* (Department of State, January 2001), p. 7. These assessments were echoed by former Los Alamos Director Harold Agnew, who concluded, in reference to allegations of Chinese nuclear espionage, that "No nation would ever stockpile any device based on another nation's computer codes…. If China doesn't resume testing, no harm will possibly have been done other than to our egos." See Harold M. Agnew, "Looking for Spies in Nuclear Kitchen," *Wall Street Journal* (May 17, 1999), p. A27.

[19] Johnston, "Learning versus Adaptation," p. 55. Johnston defines an "early" test ban as 1996, noting "suspicions in the Conference on Disarmament that at a minimum China hopes the negotiations are delayed past 1996…."

[20] Personal communication. Citation available upon request.

There are three problems with the claim that "China had little choice once it was clear that the CTBT was supported by an enormous majority of states who saw it as a pillar of the nuclear nonproliferation regime." First, the claim is unnecessary; the arguments in the previous paragraphs suggest that China was ready to stop testing in 1996.

Second, there is no evidence that the Chinese leadership "felt" or was susceptible to pressure on the testing issue. A declassified 1994 U.S. State Department memorandum is revealing:

> In the meantime, China is pursuing an accelerated test series to sat-isfy the military's minimum requirements for strategic forces mod-ernization, and there is evidence that China plans to suspend test-ing in 1996. We are unlikely to persuade China not to conduct its next test (probably in the spring). Our past protests have met with a stock reply. Nonetheless, to maintain consistency in our position and to place the onus on China, we should continue to press China to halt its tests.[21]

This resigned attitude was certainly noticed by foreign diplomats—the lack of conviction in U.S. protests over China's nuclear testing was recorded in a report commissioned by the French government. The report relayed French diplomats' suspicion that the United States and China had reached a private understanding in advance of negotiations.[22] If Chinese diplomats were operating to minimize image costs, they might have agreed to a moratorium in lieu of the treaty. Such an approach would have defused an overwhelming amount of international pressure, without requiring China to accept the possibility of on-site inspections that were apparently a major concern for the Chinese leadership.

Third, China's behavior in negotiations over the verification regime suggests that China would not have signed the treaty if it did not meet certain minimal conditions. Skeptics argue that the endgame negotiations were political theater:

> That the Chinese bargained hard over verification issues—in partic-ular on-site inspection—even in the face of considerable dismay among delegations, does not undermine the argument about social

---

[21] Department of State, *China: CTBT/Nuclear Testing* (1994), p. 2.

[22] Rene Galy-Dejean et al., *La simulation des essays nucleaires*, Rapport d'infor-mation n. 847 (December 15, 1993), pp. 33–34.

influence. Bargaining to dilute the verification elements of the treaty in the last months of negotiations was premised on the existence of a basic acceptance of the core "distributional" features of the treaty.[23]

The claims that China was "bargaining to dilute the verification elements of the treaty" and accepted "the core 'distributional' features of the treaty," however, are both problematic.

The Chinese position would not "dilute the verification elements" of the CTBT because China would not have improved its ability to conduct militarily significant clandestine testing. The National Academy of Sciences' authoritative study on technical issues related to the verification of the CTBT (hereafter, Holdren et al.) concluded that the "very limited nuclear testing [China] could plausibly conceal [from the International Monitoring System] would not add significantly" to China's military capability (See Figure 5-1).[24]

Chinese proposals concerning on-site inspection focused on the number of states needed to approve an inspection. The impact of the Chinese proposal was to reduce the frequency of inspections so that they became a "rare" event. Yet, inspections in a test ban treaty need not be frequent to have the desired impact.[25]

Inspections would not contribute to the monitoring regime, except as a deterrent. Holdren et al. suggest that "it is impossible to quantify the likelihood that [inspections] would succeed" in demonstrating that a clandestine test had occurred, but "a violator would not be able to anticipate how to conceal all potential evidence."[26] As a result, a state that had violated the treaty would be unlikely to accept an inspection—which would itself be suspicious. Holdren et al. conclude "the right to on-site inspection provided by the CTBT constitutes a deterrent to treaty viola-

---

[23] Alastair Iain Johnston, "Explaining Chinese Cooperation in International Security Institutions," in Deepa M. Ollapally, ed., *Controlling Weapons of Mass Destruction: Findings from USIP-Sponsored Projects*, Peaceworks no. 41, (Washington, DC: United States Institute of Peace, September 2001), pp. 49–53.

[24] Holdren et al., p. 68.

[25] Some analysts argue that the political difficulties involved in proposing and conducting inspections generally outweigh their value. See Steve Fetter, *Toward a Comprehensive Test Ban* (Cambridge, MA: Ballinger, 1988), pp. 132–136.

[26] Holdren et al., p. 55.

Table 5-1: Purposes and Plausible Achievements for Chinese Nuclear Testing at Various Yields

Yield	Purpose
Subcritical testing only (permissible under a CTBT)	Equation-of-state studies
	High-explosive lens tests for implosion weapons
	Development and certification of simple, bulky, relatively inefficient unboosted fission weapons
	Limited insights relevant to designs for boosted fission weapons
Hydronuclear testing (yield < 0.1 ton TNT, likely to remain undetected under a CTBT)	One-point safety tests
	Validation of design for unboosted fission weapon with a yield in the ten-ton range
Extremely-low-yield testing (0.1 ton < yield <10 tons, likely to remain undetected under a CTBT)	Validation of design for unboosted fission weapon with a yield in the 100-ton range
	Possible overrun range for one-point safety tests
Very-low-yield testing (10 tons < yield < 1-2 kilotons, concealable in some circumstances under a CTBT)	Proof tests of compact weapons with a yield of up to one to two kilotons
	Partial development of primaries for thermonuclear weapons
Low-yield testing (1-2 kilotons < yield < 20 kilotons, unlikely to be concealable under a CTBT)	Development of low-yield boosted fission weapons
	Development and full testing of some primaries and low-yield thermonuclear weapons
	Proof tests of fission weapons with a yield of up to 20 kilotons

Adapted from Technical Issues Related to the Comprehensive Nuclear Test Ban Treaty (Washington, DC: Committee on Technical Issues Related to Ratification of the Comprehensive Nuclear Test Ban Treaty, Committee on International Security and Arms Control, National Academy of Sciences, 2002), p. 68.

tion whether or not the inspection actually takes place...."[27] Inspections, then, may occur infrequently and still have a deterrent value—some analysts have suggested that less than a single annual inspection of Russian test sites would resolve ambiguous seismic events.[28] In this regard, the Chinese proposals do not appear to have been a serious threat to the integrity of the inspection regime.

---

[27] Ibid., p. 56.
[28] Fetter, p. 136.

Yet, the Chinese delegation appears to have been ready to reject the CTBT unless the United States reopened negotiations on the July 28 Chair's text (the official working draft) and increased the number of states necessary to approve an inspection from twenty-six to thirty. Contrary to the claim that "prestige, image and relative...gains in security can prevail...over narrow technical and military considerations," narrow technical and military considerations were doing rather well. Yet the technical and military considerations at issue concerned the prevention of frivolous inspections, not the continued conduct of nuclear testing.

There is some evidence that China's decisions on the CTBT reflected international pressure. A Chinese participant, in a monograph, mentions "the necessity of maintaining [China's] international image" as "*a reason*" for China's decision to sign the CTBT.[29] However, China's image is one of six reasons the author cites. The list also includes equally plausible motivations such as the role of arms control negotiations in promoting peace and security, the subordination of military modernization to economic development, the limited testing requirements to maintain a minimum nuclear deterrent, and the value of the CTBT as a nonproliferation measure.

The second piece of evidence is what one observer described as the "consistent refrain in interviews...that China could not stay out of, or in the end sabotage, the CTBT because of the costs to China's international image."[30] I have also noticed this refrain in my own interviews. Although much of the language used is in fact status-oriented, Chinese interlocutors also cite a range of other reasons. When asked about the precise role of international pressure, these interlocutors deny that it was a significant factor in their decision. Others have noticed this phenomenon: "In some cases, when I followed up with questions specifically on the role of image concerns, my interlocutors would downplay what they had just said, since this implied that China was indeed susceptible to external pressure."[31] Instead of positing a psychological motive for the conflicting answers, a simpler explanation is that the subjects were being truthful that status was a significant but not determining factor. This conclusion is consistent

---

[29] Zou, *China and the CTBT Negotiations*, pp. 6–7. Emphasis added.

[30] Alastair Iain Johnston, "The Social Effects of International Institutions on Domestic (Foreign Policy) Actors" in Daniel Drezner, ed., *The Interaction of Domestic and International Institutions* (Ann Arbor: The University of Michigan Press, 2001), p. 183

[31] Ibid., p. 196 n. 66.

with the overall tone of the interviews, the assessments of U.S. negotia-
tors in the process, and actual Chinese behavior during negotiations. As
the next section indicates, it also explains Chinese behavior in the CD
since the conclusion of the CTBT negotiations.

The Fissile Material Cut-off Treaty

This section attempts to test the predictions of the social influence
hypothesis against subsequent Chinese behavior in the CD. Most of the
literature concerning China's decision to negotiate and sign the CTBT
was written in the early stages of FMCT negotiations, and some of these
articles offer tentative predictions about China's behavior.

If material and image costs determine China's strategies toward arms
control negotiations, Beijing should adopt similar strategies for treaties
that pose similar cost calculations. Cases (such as the CTBT and the
FMCT) where China has adopted very different approaches suggest either
dissimilar cost calculations or the irrelevance of material and image costs.

Although the CTBT and FMCT are typically associated with qualitative
and quantitative constraints, respectively, the two treaties pose the same
basic question for China's leaders: Should China sacrifice its flexibility to
reconfigure its nuclear arsenal to maintain its image as a cooperative and
responsible power? In fact, proponents of the social influence hypothesis
have suggested that China's behavior toward the two treaties should be
similar:

> It is fairly clear that China would prefer not to be in CTBT negotia-
> tions or the talks on a fissile material production ban.... Yet China
> is involved in these negotiations, even though there is no external
> material coercion compelling its participation.... So there must be
> some additional factor that is altering the cost-benefit analysis, a
> factor that compels China to participate in a process the end point
> of which it would prefer to avoid. This variable appears to be inter-
> national image. The costs to reputation from backing out of these
> kinds of processes are extremely high, while the benefits from
> remaining inside—reinforcing China's image as a responsible major
> power—are also high.[32]

---

[32] Alastair Iain Johnston, "Prospects for Chinese Nuclear Force Modernization:
Limited Deterrence Versus Multilateral Arms Control," in David Shambaugh
and Richard H. Yang, eds., *China's Military in Transition* (Oxford: Clarendon
Press, 1997), pp. 311–312.

This is a strong *prima facie* case for expecting similar behavior from China on the two treaties. The burden of proof ought to rest with those who suggest that the CTBT and FMCT pose dissimilar choices for Chinese leaders.

Although the FMCT and CTBT impose different technical constraints on the Chinese arsenal, both treaties limit China's ability to reconfigure its nuclear forces—whether China wants to optimize its deterrent to anticipate U.S. missile defense deployments or adopt an entirely new strategy of limited nuclear deterrence. Both treaties constrain on the size of China's arsenal—building more weapons would either require expanding the stock of fissile material through production or stretching a fixed stock through new designs (such as composite pits) that require testing. Presently, China has a sufficient stock of fissile material to complete the modernization anticipated in unclassified intelligence estimates and could restart production in advance of a ban to produce any additional fissile material.[33] As a result, a ban on the production of fissile material that does not deal with past production would impose a relatively light burden on Chinese modernization plans.[34]

A fissile material cut-off treaty with provisions for past production would require a fairly intrusive verification regime that might reveal sensitive information about the Chinese nuclear program. Nevertheless, some Chinese academics have argued that in the event of such an agreement, Beijing would accept the verification procedures likely to attend an FMCT based on the location and type of facilities. Although this is a matter of conjecture, the technical assessments that support this hypothesis are confirmed by Western analysts.[35]

---

[33] Yitzhak Shichor, *Peaceful Fallout: The Conversion of China's Military-Nuclear Complex to Civilian Use*, Bonn International Center for Conversion Brief no. 10 (November 1997), pp. 30–39.

[34] This would not be the case if China were pursuing a move toward a "limited" deterrent, as argued by Alastair Iain Johnston, that would require tripling the size of the China's nuclear forces to, perhaps, rough parity with U.S. and Russian forces. See Johnston, "Prospects for Chinese Nuclear Force Modernization," in Shambaugh and Yang, eds., p. 299, and Alastair Iain Johnston, "China's New 'Old Thinking': The Concept of Limited Deterrence," *International Security*, vol. 20, no. 3 (Winter 1995/96), p. 39.

[35] See Hui Zhang, "Uses of Commercial Satellite Imagery in FMCT Verification," *The Nonproliferation Review*, vol. 7, no. 2 (Summer 2000), pp. 120–135; Hui

In addition to imposing similar material constraints, the treaties should pose similar image considerations for the Chinese leadership. The conditions for these costs are well defined in the adaptation literature: "Beijing wishes to avoid appearing as an outlier or violator of arms control norms when these are supported by a large group of politically significant nations."[36] Moreover, this sensitivity is greatest in the CD:

> Sensitivity to these image costs and benefits would not be as great if the 'audience' were smaller or less important. But the CD is the only UN-related multilateral arms control negotiating body. All the major powers, and a critical mass of developed and developing states[,] are members. In front of this particular audience China's identity is not unequivocally that of an underdog or a have-not, so it has to be more careful about not appearing as a self-interested major power like all the others.[37]

Although we do not know the lower bound of China's susceptibility to pressure, if image matters at all, the consensus in the CD for a program of work centered on a fissile materials production ban clearly should have forced Chinese participation well before it did. Only the United States and China have rejected programs of work for the CD over the five-year period from 1998 to 2003.

The reason for normative pressure is not entirely related to affinity for the FMCT. The CD has been essentially inactive since the end of 1996; some states are considering options for negotiating outside the CD. Anecdotal evidence suggests that countries are beginning to reduce their staffs in Geneva, while others have stopped sending representatives entirely. Washington, in particular, left the post of ambassador vacant for a year, choosing instead to send a parade of officials through to berate the CD

Zhang, "Civil Remote-sensing Satellites and a Fissile Material Cutoff Treaty: Some Case Studies on Verifying Nonproduction," *Journal of Nuclear Materials Management*, vol. 30, no. 1 (Fall 2001), pp. 20–28; and Lisbeth Gronlund, Yong Liu, and David Wright, "The China Card: Will China Agree to Cut off Fissile Material Production?" *Nucleus: The Magazine of the Union of Concerned Scientists*, vol. 17, no.2 (Summer 1995), Available at: http://www.ucsusa.org/Nucleus/95sum.chinacard.html.

[36] Swaine and Johnston, p. 119.

[37] Johnston, "Prospects for Chinese Nuclear Force Modernization," *China Quarterly*, no. 146 (June 1996), p. 576.

for inaction. Presumably, China would not want to be seen as sharing the blame, even in equal measure with the United States, for the slow, agonizing death of a forum that many developing nations view as an important guarantee of their representation in international security discussions. This forms an important "second front" of pressure on Beijing, which should be especially sensitive to charges that it was helping to collapse the CD as a negotiating forum.

Skeptics also predicted that China, once having failed to keep the FMCT off the agenda, would work with the other nuclear powers to keep past production out of the talks. If this strategy were unsuccessful, China would have been expected to shift toward limiting the intrusiveness of the treaty's verification regime. Skeptics did not anticipate China's decision to link work on an FMCT to outer space negotiations. They focused "on whether and when" China might sign a fissile materials convention.[38] Obstruction by China was not considered a likely outcome because "once these issues are on the international agenda, China is loathe to back out even when the process is not necessarily in its military interests."[39]

China's decision to back out of negotiations and then to block work in the CD for several years undermines the hypothesis that China is largely motivated by concerns about its reputation or image. At most, China attempted to shield itself from criticism by offering amendments to various proposals, issuing working papers of its own, and issuing a 2002 joint working paper with six other countries including the Russian Federation. Chinese leaders, however, would seek to minimize the diplomatic costs of any strategy. Yet China was not "entrapped" as skeptics predicted.[40]

The Chinese decision to obstruct the FMCT negotiations is not damning to skeptical argument. Given China's focus on external factors, the adaptation hypothesis suggests that the United States will be a critical actor in defining the international arms control agenda.[41] A dramatic change in U.S. policy might reasonably explain the change in Chinese

---

[38] Swaine and Johnston, p. 110.

[39] Ibid., p. 124.

[40] "so sensitive": Johnston, "Prospects for Chinese Nuclear Force Modernization," in Shambaugh and Yang, eds., p. 312 n. 93; "has become trapped ..." Johnston, "China's New 'Old Thinking,'" pp. 38–39.

[41] Swaine and Johnston, p. 125.

policy.[42] In particular, U.S. decisions to test and deploy missile defense and withdraw from the ABM treaty were possible candidates to ensure that the international arms control agenda "gets nowhere."[43]

The role of the United States as an agenda setter on arms control with the power to determine the reputational and image costs facing China opens two possible explanations consistent with the adaptation hypothesis. If the changes in U.S. policy have been substantial, China may be responding to a more threatening environment by implementing a less cooperative, more obstructionist strategy; if U.S. policy has changed only slightly, perhaps China used outer space issues to obstruct the FMCT and deflect international criticism. Either modification protects the view that the "standoff on the FMCT reflects the Chinese desire to keep as many options open as possible for the modernization of its nuclear weapons program."[44]

U.S. failures to address China's security concerns could, at some point, undermine Chinese support for an arms control agenda set in Washington. If Chinese leaders viewed deterrence as sensitive to changes in capability and were also motivated by image costs, China's obstruction of the FMCT should have been one aspect of a general subordination of image benefits in favor of greater emphasis on managing the balance of forces. This overall change would manifest across Chinese security behavior, including a shift toward a more flexible nuclear posture and a general decline in China's compliance with arms control agreements. The outlook for arms control, therefore, would be quite pessimistic—and Chinese obstruction of the FMCT would be explained. As three skeptics warned:

> China is unlikely to welcome any formal U.S. arms control initiative at this time. It probably perceives the drift toward TMD and NMD [national missile defense] as inevitable. Beijing recognizes that Washington's decisions on the status of its offensive forces will

---

[42] Ibid., pp. 125–126.

[43] Johnston, "Prospects for Chinese Nuclear Force Modernization," *China Quarterly*, no. 146 (June 1996), p. 575.

[44] Alastair Iain Johnston, *Sources of Conflict in the Sino-US Arms Control Relationship*, paper originally prepared for the Fairbank Center for East Asian Research-Chinese Academy of Social Sciences Institute of American Studies Project on Issues in Sino–U.S. Relations (Cambridge, MA: July 2002), p. 10.

be driven almost entirely by developments in the U.S.-Russian relationship. But it also sees START [the Strategic Arms Reduction Treaty] on prolonged hold. It is probably also thinking through the consequences of a possible collapse of the CTBT and NPT regimes.[45]

Is there evidence that Beijing has altered China's security policy to adapt to what it perceives as threatening changes in U.S. policy? Perhaps the most important evidence supporting the "major change" explanation would be a dramatic shift in China's nuclear posture. The changes in the international security environment that allowed China to begin undermining the FMCT should also have prompted China's Second Artillery to redress numerical, readiness, and operational imbalances, perhaps by abandoning its no-first-use pledge and developing plans to use nuclear weapons in a broader array of contingencies. Skeptics suggest "the primary constraint on China's nuclear modernization" will come from external factors such as "multilateral arms control processes and particularly American commitments to those processes," because China's own internal dynamics are pushing in the opposite direction.[46] If China's internal motivations are guided by a keen sensitivity to the deterrent balance, the Chinese state ought to seek *ceteris paribus* a limited nuclear deterrent. In that case, China might be expected to deploy:

> ...a greater number of smaller, more accurate, survivable missiles including ICBMs, SLBMs, cruise missiles, and tactical and theater

---

[45] Manning, Montaperto, and Roberts, p. 73. Johnston, too, argues, "The pessimistic prediction would be that an interactive downward spiral in Sino-US relations will eventually lead China to reconsider its support for various arms control regimes. Just as the US has abandoned the ABM, and there are arguments in Washington in favor of abandoning its nuclear testing moratorium (so as to develop third generation of warheads), so too it is easy to imagine that China could decide to resume nuclear testing (particular if the US abandoned the moratorium first) on the grounds that it needs to fully develop its second generation warheads, as well as electromagnetic pulse and enhanced-radiation capabilities to deal with different kinds of escalation scenarios in a Sino-US war over Taiwan." See Johnston, *Sources of Conflict in the Sino-US Arms Control Relationship*, p. 10.

[46] Johnston, "Prospects for Chinese Nuclear Force Modernization," in Shambaugh and Yang, eds., p. 311.

weapons; ballistic missile defence systems to improve survivability; space-based early warning and command and control systems; and [anti-satellites] to hit enemy satellites and a civil defense system that can reduce the number of urban and industrial centre casualties, thus enhancing the state's ability to recover from nuclear war.[47]

Without the external constraints imposed by arms control agreements, China's nuclear posture should move to reflect its own internal orientation—which the adaptation hypothesis predicts will be a limited nuclear deterrent. A decline in the U.S. commitment to arms control "may well also have the unintended consequence of dramatically reducing Chinese incentives to participate in the extant agenda in the CD. Certainly it will provide added incentives for China to speed up its nuclear modernization programme."[48]

Following China's active obstruction of the FMCT, however, there has been little evidence that China has simultaneously accelerated its adoption of limited nuclear deterrence. China has not begun "doubling, possibly tripling" the size of its nuclear forces.[49] At a time when China is expressing concerns that its future defense needs will be impinged upon by U.S. deployments, it has not taken even the rudimentary steps to give its leaders the option of expanding their arsenal beyond current modernization plans. China has not resumed production of fissile material (which would be expensive), suggesting that the Chinese leadership is not yet committed to a substantially larger arsenal. It is difficult to believe that China would obstruct the FMCT to "keep its options open" without simultaneously expanding its stockpile of fissile material. In the case of the CTBT, realists can claim that Chinese negotiating behavior was designed to buy time for an ongoing testing program. There is no comparable object or goal to explain China's delay in the case of the FMCT.

---

[47] The typesetter misprinted ICBM as ICMB; I have corrected it in the text. Johnston, "Prospects for Chinese Nuclear Force Modernization," in Shambaugh and Yang, eds., pp. 292–293.

[48] Johnston, "Prospects for Chinese Nuclear Force Modernization," *China Quarterly*, vol./no. 146 (June 1996), p. 575.

[49] Johnston, "Chinese Nuclear Force Modernization," p. 299. Johnston is also clear, however, that a shift toward a limited deterrent "may or may not entail a dramatic short-run increase in the absolute numbers of warheads and delivery systems: the pace will depend on whether the United States proceeds with TMD deployment." See Johnston, "China's New 'Old Thinking,'" p. 41.

Nor did China deploy "over the next decade or so" other elements of a limited nuclear deterrent: missile defense systems, space-based early warning systems, and upgraded command, control, and intelligence systems, or anti-satellite weapons—although research continues in these areas.[50]

Skeptics also predicted that in the absence of a strong U.S. commitment to the arms control process, China would turn against a number of other arms control arrangements that might inhibit the development of a limited nuclear deterrent. China's particular strategy for obstructing the FMCT, however, focuses on expanding, rather than shrinking, the overall arms control agenda to include an *ad hoc* committee to negotiate a legal instrument regarding the "prevention of an arms race in outer space." The next chapter directly addresses this proposal, but the essential features are noted here. First, China has incurred strong image costs by pursuing this strategy, sharing equal blame with the United States for undermining the viability of the CD year after year. Second, the decision to accept negotiations by the United States would impose a "dramatic constraint on China's limited deterrent" by restricting the development of China's ballistic missile defenses and anti-satellite weapons.[51] This is a significant constraint, particularly if China were to target U.S. command and control performance rather than theater forces. Third, a legal agreement to prohibit space weaponization might require transparency measures and relatively intrusive verification procedures that would reveal sensitive information about the state of China's ballistic missile and space-launch programs. Transparency, particularly for China's space and missile programs, is a high cost concession for Beijing.

Although China has neither rejected the CTBT nor resumed nuclear testing, it has yet to ratify the treaty formally. This is a major puzzle for the skeptics—if China were concerned about the size of its stockpile, one option would be to resume nuclear testing to improve the distribution of fissile material in its nuclear warheads. Manning et al. confess, "We were left wondering how deeply China remains committed to the CTBT....Beijing's perceptions of its nuclear future might have changed significantly since its signature of the CTBT in 1996."[52] Yet, China has not resumed testing. Instead, having "taken notice" of a Bush administration trial bal-

---

[50] "China's New 'Old Thinking,'" p. 41.
[51] Ibid., p. 39.
[52] Manning, Montaperto, and Roberts, pp. 66–67.

loon to resume nuclear testing, China expressed its continued support for the "early coming in force of the CTBT."[53]

If the Chinese leadership's threat perception has dramatically changed, these changes are not yet evident in policy. Consistency despite changes in the external environment runs contrary to the prediction of a China that supports arms control arrangements as "a short run policy of accommodation, to be reconsidered" when external factors change.

Skeptics might also argue that the changes in U.S. policy have been minor and that China has adopted a correspondingly minor revision of its own position: linking PAROS with the FMCT to pass some image costs from obstruction to the United States. Yet this would be a very high risk strategy for a China motivated by realpolitik—the United States might agree to the Chinese proposal on PAROS. This would leave China to face the worst of all possible worlds from a realpolitik perspective: a set of comprehensive restrictions on its stockpile of fissile material, as well as restrictions on ballistic-missile defense programs and anti-satellite weapons to complement the ban on nuclear testing. Successful conclusion of this agenda would preclude China from developing the limited deterrent necessary from a realpolitik point of view; blocking such an agreement would provide Chinese diplomats a much bigger hurdle than merely keeping the scope of the FMCT limited to future production.

In sum, China does not appear to have abandoned arms control for limited deterrence—even in the face of what could charitably be described as U.S. neglect of the international arms control agenda and Chinese interests. China's commitment to the process appears to be serious and its actions seem to be motivated by more than an effort to solicit "social back-patting" or to avoid opprobrium.

TOWARD AN ALTERNATIVE EXPLANATION

Skeptics have attempted to explain China's participation in arms control negotiations as the result of an extrinsic factor—in this case, China's acute concern about its external image. Their account, however, does not withstand scrutiny. This section explains China's participation in arms control regimes largely as a function of contemporary Chinese attitudes toward nuclear weapons, particularly the belief that the balance of deterrence is

---

[53] Zhu Bangzao, *Foreign Ministry Regular Press Conference* (September 4, 2001), Available at: http://www.chinaembassy.org.zw/eng/17580.html.

largely impervious to changes in the balance of capabilities. If Chinese leaders believe that deterrence does not depend on the fine details of the technical balance, they should view arms control as potentially beneficial.

The idea that deterrence is not sensitive to changes in the technical balance implicitly leads to support for arms control measures. If additional offensive capability (in the form of more weapons, more ready forces, etc.) does not significantly enhance the deterrent effect of a nuclear arsenal, such measures merely create inadvertent dangers. A policymaker who believes deterrence is easily achieved would see little reason to participate in arms races and would want to make sure that operational practices reinforce, rather than degrade, crisis stability. This policymaker would also be far more sensitive to the diplomatic and political implications of nuclear weapons deployments.

Many, although not all, of these efforts can be undertaken unilaterally. China certainly deployed an arsenal that reflected these priorities while simultaneously criticizing U.S–Soviet arms control efforts. Few states, however, are likely to count entirely on the stability of deterrence irrespective of the balance of capabilities, as even the modest Chinese nuclear force modernization suggests. As long as nuclear deployments interact, new deployments can lead to arms race effects and operational practices that undermine crisis stability. Arms control agreements may help constrain such conduct—a fact evident in Beijing's appreciation of the benefits that China received, as a third party, from the ABM Treaty (in spite of Chinese statements of hostility toward U.S.–Soviet arms control agreements at the time).

Arms control agreements may also reinforce deterrence by constraining weapons programs and operational practices that may "strengthen the illusion that a nuclear war could be fought and won, without altering the underlying reality that all would lose."[54] China's confidence that the United States would not use nuclear weapons in Korea was based, in part, on the political costs of using such weapons. Mark A. Ryan suggests that Chinese leaders saw disarmament campaigns (though not arms control campaigns) as a means to increase the political costs of nuclear weapons use, as well as a method to control their own fear of such weapons.[55] Opponents of arms control also sometimes note this effect,

---

[54] Fetter, p. 167.

[55] Mark A. Ryan, *Chinese Attitudes toward Nuclear Weapons: China and the United States during the Korean War* (New York: ME Sharpe, 1989), p. 180.

warning that arms control efforts undermine the (delicate) balance of terror by promoting the idea that nuclear weapons are not usable.

Advocates of the two treaties considered in this section—the Comprehensive Nuclear Test Ban and Fissile Material Cut-off treaties—often suggest that their support for the two treaties reflects the belief that deterrence is easy to maintain. As good-faith tests of the commitment of the nuclear weapons states to the "early cessation of the arms race," these measures are designed to impose some constraint on national nuclear arsenals as part of an effort to marginalize the role of nuclear weapons in providing international security. In technical terms, the CTBT complicates the development of new nuclear weapons, although much data could be obtained from computer simulations. A treaty to prohibit the production of fissile material would limit the size of nuclear arsenals, while a treaty that regulated existing stockpiles of fissile material would make nuclear reductions more permanent.

Interview data, as well as an assessment of China's security situation, suggests that the Chinese leadership viewed the CTBT and FMCT in much the same manner as advocates of both treaties within the Clinton administration. For Washington and Beijing, the further development of nuclear weapons was seen to contribute very little to either country's security, particularly compared to the benefits from enhancing the nonproliferation regime.

The Comprehensive Nuclear Test Ban Treaty

The fragmentary documentary record suggests that the Chinese leadership viewed nuclear testing as increasingly irrelevant. The 1986 report that Deng Jiaxian submitted to the Central Committee concluded that the "nuclear superpowers' technology level had approached the theoretical limits and needed no further development." The report's conclusion that the Soviet Union and the United States would support a test ban "out of political needs" suggests that Chinese leaders believed that Washington shared their basic judgment about the insensitivity of deterrence.[56] The report's recommendation for an accelerated test schedule to complete a warhead for the first generation of Chinese solid-fueled

---

[56] Hu Side et al., "Ten Years, We Cherish the Memory Every Moment: For the Tenth Anniversary of the passing away of Dr. Deng Jiaxian, 1924–1986" *Guangming Daily* (July 21, 1996), p. 1.

mobile ballistic missiles is evident in the subsequent test series with one change—the apparently successful development of an RV with an aspherical primary for the DF-31 eliminated the need for additional testing to develop new warhead designs. This testing program completed China's requirements for nuclear warheads, leading one Chinese participant in the CTBT process to conclude:

> China supported the CTBT negotiations in part because it had the capability to undertake the obligations of the treaty. China has long assumed a policy of building limited nuclear weapons for the purpose of self-defense only....Because of its stated no-first-use policy, China does not need to build a large number and variety of nuclear weapons and therefore does not necessarily need to conduct many nuclear tests.[57]

During the Cold War, advocates for a test ban argued that it would demonstrate that the United States and the Soviet Union were not arming to "fight and win" a nuclear war.[58] In the past, the Chinese government has been particularly interested in similar assurances. In 1994, China sought a bilateral no-first-use pledge from the United States (the two sides negotiated a non-targeting agreement), and several Chinese academics have written papers on other measures that the United States might take to reassure Beijing that it was not attempting to develop the capacity to undertake a disarming first strike.[59]

In interviews, Chinese participants in CD negotiations were clearly aware of the constraints that a CTBT would impose on the development of nuclear weapons. Chinese participants often remarked that "China signed the CTBT to promote disarmament." When asked precisely how the CTBT does this, Chinese participants offered sophisticated arms control explanations familiar to scholars such as the role that the CTBT could play in halting proliferation to new nuclear states and the impact this would have on the development of existing nuclear arsenals.

---

[57] Zou, *China and the CTBT Negotiations*, pp. 6–7.

[58] Fetter, p. 169.

[59] Li Bin, "Visible Evidences of No-First-Use Nuclear Strategies" *INESAP Information Bulletin*, no. 17 (August 1999), pp. 44–45; Wu Jun, "On No-First-Use Treaty" (Shanghai: The Sixth ISODARCO Beijing Seminar on Arms Control, October 1998); and Pan, "On China's No First Use of Nuclear Weapons," np.

Chinese observers were also aware of the limitations of the CTBT, particularly that the treaty's ability to constrain the United States is largely political in nature. One Chinese arms control expert noted that the treaty "would have more political than military significance."[60] Another Chinese academic echoed this reasoning:

> As a token, the CTB will bring nuclear testing to a halt, but one cannot take for granted that a CTB will automatically bring efforts to develop and modernize nuclear weapons to a stop. The CTB in itself does not address this issue. Halting development and modernization is a much different—and more difficult—matter… Within the context of a test ban, what is important is the political intention of complying with the treaty.[61]

Even China's then–Vice Foreign Minister, Wang Guangya, emphasized the normative impact of treaty: "The past four years have shown that though the Treaty has not come into force, it has already played an important regulatory role in the international community. Any breach of the Treaty would inevitably come under unanimous condemnation by the international community."[62]

The test ban is a necessary, but not sufficient, condition for the United States to demonstrate that it is not planning to "fight and win" a nuclear war. The relationship between testing and such preparations is an indirect one.[63] Chinese interlocutors usually emphasize the nonproliferation benefits of the treaty when discussing the Chinese decision to sign the CTBT. The symbolic connection between the test ban and what some Chinese observers have called "nuclear warfighting" is apparent, however, when Chinese interlocutors discuss the U.S. decision to reject the test ban.

China would gain a very substantial nonproliferation benefit from a test ban that entered into force. Although new nuclear states might

---

[60] Liu Huaqiu, "No-First Use and China's Security," *Henry L. Stimson Center Electronic Essay* (no date, c. 1998).

[61] Shen Dingli, "Toward a Nuclear-Weapon-Free World: A Chinese Perspective," *Bulletin of Atomic Scientists* (March/April 1994), pp. 52.

[62] Wang Guangya, *Remarks at the Opening Ceremony of the Regional Workshop for CTBTO International Cooperation and National Implementation/Ratification Procedures*, Beijing: June 6, 2000.

[63] Fetter, p. 169.

develop crude fission weapons without testing, more advanced designs—such as thermonuclear weapons—do require testing. The yield estimates associated with India's May 1998 nuclear test, for example, are difficult to reconcile with New Delhi's claims to have tested a "thermonuclear" device.[64] China would clearly have an interest in restraining India's development of thermonuclear weapons. A member of the Chinese CTBT delegation frankly noted the impact of China's conventional and nuclear capabilities on India's decisions to develop nuclear weapons and noted Beijing's interest in pressing "India and Pakistan to stop nuclear tests, observe the Comprehensive Nuclear Test Ban Treaty, and make a firm commitment not to deploy nuclear weapons or missiles capable of delivering nuclear warheads."[65]

The hypothesis that China viewed the CTBT as compatible with its national security interests helps explain the major puzzle that bedevils the international pressure hypothesis: why China accepted a treaty that entailed inspections (rather than a moratorium) and then almost scuttled negotiations over the *frequency* of those inspections. This puzzle has two parts:

• *Why did China sign the treaty, rather than agree to a moratorium?* In the previous section, I have argued that the pressure on China during CTBT negotiations largely resulted from continued testing of nuclear weapons; China might have defused that pressure by agreeing to a moratorium. Without signing the treaty, China would not have been obligated to accept on-site inspections, which were apparently a high-value concession for the Chinese.

• *Why did China almost walk out over on-site inspections?* Although we cannot know if China would have signed the CTBT without concessions from the United States regarding on-site inspections, the Chinese delegation clearly considered the matter to be of great importance. Chinese

---

[64] For yield estimations, see Brian Barker et al., "Monitoring Nuclear Tests," *Science* vol. 281, no. 5385 (September 25, 1998), pp.1967–68; Gregory van der Vink et al., "False Accusations, Undetected Tests, and Implications for the CTB Treaty," *Arms Control Today*, vol. 28, no. 4 (May 1998), pp. 7–13; and Terry C. Wallace, "The May 1998 India and Pakistan Nuclear Tests," *Seismological Research Letters*, no. 69 (September 1998), pp. 386–393.

[65] Zou Yunhua, *Chinese Perspectives on the South Asian Nuclear Tests* (Stanford, CA: Stanford University Center for International Security and Arms Control, January 1999), p. 17.

brinksmanship over a small issue such as the frequency of inspections is hard to fathom if the regime were under duress, particularly since the obvious motive would have been to scuttle the negotiations, using the prospect of inspections as a pretext.

China's decision to sign a treaty only makes sense if a formal agreement has intrinsic value beyond the avoidance of opprobrium—in this case, the treaty was a nonproliferation measure, as well as a form of reassurance that the United States was not contemplating the use of nuclear weapons for coercion. The nonproliferation rationale was probably very important, as the Chinese leaders could have anticipated that their signature would be a necessary condition for securing Indian compliance. Like their counterparts in the Clinton administration, Chinese leaders also viewed the CTBT as a necessary, but not a sufficient, step toward the larger, amorphous goal of reducing the role of nuclear weapons in international security. A third benefit from the treaty may have been prestige, but Chinese brinksmanship over on-site inspections suggests it was probably not the dominant factor.

The intrinsic, but limited, value of the CTBT explains China's almost obsessive focus on the frequency of inspections; to the extent that the test ban reflected a partial reassurance from the United States, there was considerable internal debate about what level of transparency was acceptable. Intrinsic value also explains China's efforts to gain additional assurances from the United States about the potential for abuse of inspections *after* the treaty was signed, as well as the subsequent decision to withhold International Monitoring Systems data in response to the U.S. Senate's rejection of the CTBT.

The Fissile Material Cut-Off Treaty

A fissile material cut-off would limit the size of potential nuclear arsenals by preventing the production of additional fissile material for the manufacture of nuclear weapons. Whereas the CTBT attempted to constrain the qualitative improvement of nuclear weapons by preventing testing, an FMCT would prevent quantitative enhancements by banning the production of plutonium and highly enriched uranium for weapons.

A cut-off treaty might also regulate the large stockpiles of fissile material currently held by the United States and the Russian Federation. International oversight of fissile material stockpiles would be useful in verifying warhead dismantlement and would render reductions irreversible if fissile material from dismantled weapons was placed under international safe-guards. Further efforts by nuclear weapons states to reduce the large disparities in fissile material stockpiles might be a precondition to the successful negotiation of the FMCT. The cut-off would provide a direct non-proliferation benefit by preventing the production of fissile material, as well as an indirect benefit from promoting deep reductions and subjecting nuclear facilities in all states to international inspection.

In contrast to China's behavior toward the CTBT, Beijing withheld its consent to a work program on the FMCT in the Conference on Disarmament from 1999 to 2003 because the United States refused to negotiate a treaty on "preventing an arms race in outer space" that would constrain U.S. missile defense and other military activities in outer space. This dispute has blocked the beginning of FMCT negotiations, although China has not indicated any opposition to such a treaty in principle. Revealing the calculus behind China's decision to obstruct negotiations is difficult for a number of reasons. First, participants are naturally more reluctant to provide information about an ongoing negotiation than a completed one such as the CTBT. Second, the size and composition of China's fissile material stockpile is a sensitive national security subject. Finally, Chinese academics have authored very few papers about the subject, in part because of the way that the Chinese nuclear weapons establishment is structured. The principle locus of arms control expertise is in China's weapons complex, which is a consumer of fissile material.

Interview data suggest that Chinese and U.S. leaders basically support a Fissile Material Cut-off Treaty for the same reason: Neither plans to expand the size of its arsenal beyond its current stock of fissile material. Despite the disparity between Chinese and U.S. stockpiles, China might benefit from U.S. reductions undertaken to build political support for the treaty. An FMCT would also constrain the size of India's nuclear arsenal, providing a straightforward nonproliferation benefit to China analogous to the CTBT. These benefits would accrue largely cost-free to China, which is no longer believed to be producing fissile material for military use. China would have to accept a verification regime, but most Chinese scholars appear to believe that this would not be an insurmountable hurdle. While Beijing might consider controls on future fissile material production, it shares the view of the other nuclear weapons states that national security considerations preclude a treaty that would regulate existing stockpiles. This would be particularly true if China's stockpile of fissile material may also be smaller than current estimates suggest. [66]

China's decision to obstruct CD negotiations on the FMCT is the principal puzzle. The image constraints that allegedly compelled Chinese participation in the CTBT should also have compelled Chinese participation in FMCT negotiations. If China viewed the balance of terror as delicate, it is unlikely that Chinese officials would choose to insist on more negotiations (in this case, an agreement concerning military activities in outer space) for missile defense deployments. Instead, China's obstruction in the CD ought to have been accompanied by more significant efforts to enhance its arsenal. Conversely, if Chinese leaders viewed the deterrent balance as relatively insensitive to changes in the balance of forces, they would focus on reaching additional agreements to address the broader security issues in question.

In this case, the security problem driving China's obstruction at the CD is Beijing's perception that U.S. strategic modernization efforts are intended to pose a threat to China's deterrent. It is in this context that the demand for a "balanced and comprehensive plan of work"— the linkage between PAROS and fissile material stockpiles—makes sense. If the strategic modernization envisioned by the United States involves significant space-based elements, then China's willingness to agree to a constraint on its fissile material stockpiles would require some assessment of the prospects for U.S. military activities in outer space. In the case of the CTBT, China's decision to suspend testing was premised on the judgment that U.S. leaders shared China's assessment that further nuclear testing would not alter the balance of deterrence. It would be surprising if the decision to cease fissile material production were not based on similar assessments about the impact that this decision would have on the strategic balance.

The nature of this linkage is largely symbolic and about conveying reassurance. Chapter 6 suggests that the current U.S. strategic modernization program, when matched to its Chinese counterpart, is unlikely to result in a substantial change in the strategic situation. The United States has not committed to a fixed architecture for missile defenses and other elements of its strategic modernization, permitting China to defer deci-

---

[66] Steve Fetter and Frank von Hippel, "A Step-by-step Approach to a Global Fissile Materials Cutoff," *Arms Control Today*, vol. 25, no. 8 (October 1995), pp. 3–8.

sions about specific countermeasures. Yet, the Chinese leadership must worry that U.S. policymakers may one day believe they could build strategic forces that are capable of disarming the Chinese arsenal in a crisis. China's refusal to enter FMCT negotiations underscores the point that the Chinese leadership believes that a much larger Chinese arsenal must remain an option under these circumstances.

The timing of China's decision to link its positions on outer space and fissile material is particularly telling. The decision was announced in early 1999—immediately following U.S. Secretary of Defense William Cohen's announcement that the United States would increase funding to develop a more capable national missile defense system that might require revision of the ABM Treaty. In March 1999, Chinese President Jiang Zemin strongly condemned U.S. missile defense plans in an address to the Conference on Disarmament. Jiang made a veiled reference to outer space, referring to the impact of missile defense systems on extending the arms race into "new areas."[67] Although this linkage might have appeared obvious to Chinese delegates at the time, interview data suggests that its significance was lost on the U.S. delegation against the backdrop of U.S.–Chinese disagreement regarding Operation Allied Force, the NATO deployment in Kosovo.

Similarly, China's announcement in June 2002 relaxing its demand for negotiations on outer space appears to have been formulated as a response to openings provided by the United States. This June 2002 announcement immediately followed the conclusion of the Moscow Treaty, a high profile arms control agreement between Washington and Moscow. Although Chinese observers were less than impressed with the terms of the treaty, the general consensus appears to have been that the decision to commit to an agreement was a substantial step for the Bush administration.

China's obstruction of negotiations in the CD poses a major challenge to the idea that Beijing participates in arms control agreements largely to avoid costs to its international image. Instead, China's behavior is best explained in terms of its national security interests. China's reluctance to

---

[67] Jiang Zemin, "Promote Disarmament Process and Safeguard World Security, Address at the Conference on Disarmament," in *Final Record of the 822nd Plenary Meeting of Conference on Disarmament*, CD/PV.822 (Geneva: March 26, 1999), pp. 2–5.

enter into fissile material cut-off negotiations appears to reflect a judgment about the need to balance constraints on the size of its nuclear arsenal with constraints on U.S. strategic capabilities. Chinese proposals for outer space negotiations—covered in more detail in a subsequent chapter—may therefore reflect a serious assessment of China's security situation rather than a stalling tactic.

CONCLUSION

The motivations behind China's participation in the CTBT and obstruction of the FMCT are important. They determine the broader prospects for arms control arrangements to manage the evolving deterrent relationship between the strategic offensive forces maintained by Washington and Beijing.

Skeptics suggest that China's support for arms control is ephemeral and a function of the Chinese leadership's acute sensitivity to international pressure. This explanation is offered to account for Chinese participation in CTBT negotiations despite the assumption that China's leaders are obsessed with the balance of forces. It fails to account for the fact that China began to prepare for a test ban as early as 1986, or for China's strong reluctance to agree to an inspections regime requiring a simple majority to approve an on-site inspection. Moreover, this explanation fails to predict China's behavior toward the FMCT.

A simpler explanation for China's support for arms control and the country's modest nuclear deterrent lies in China's relative confidence in the stability of deterrence. In other words, Chinese officials largely meant what they said about their motives for agreeing to the CTBT and for obstructing the FMCT. The Chinese leadership is motivated by the security benefits of arms control agreements rather than by international pressure. Beijing's decision to accept the constraints imposed by the CTBT on its strategic offensive force modernization, and the relative high priority assigned to preventing frivolous inspections, suggest that the Chinese leadership cautiously accepts the foundational principles of arms control. China's decision to obstruct negotiations on the FMCT appears to reflect concern that such an agreement, in the face of U.S. missile defense deployments, would seriously jeopardize China's national security. In the case of the FMCT, the timing of both China's decision to obstruct negotiations and to offer a key compromise suggests that Chinese decisions are, in large part, designed to entice the United States into serious discussions about the changing relationship between both arsenals.

The implications of this relationship are profound: At a time when China is modernizing, albeit modestly, its nuclear arsenal, the United States is essentially ignoring an opportunity to shape Chinese policies in ways that would be beneficial to the security of both countries. Subsequent chapters in this book consider Chinese perspectives on U.S. strategic forces modernization and arms control proposals.

CHAPTER 6

U.S. Nuclear Posture and the Logic of Restraint

I think [the United States has] not been very responsible at all. You know it's against their own principles which they are [acting in regard to missile defense]. They themselves … were propagating this idea to oppose missile defense [in the 1972 ABM Treaty]. Now all of sudden because of the collapse of the former Soviet Union, suddenly they change their mind and they want the world to listen to them. Of course, the US can be right and on many times or occasions they are right, but you cannot monopolize the truth. So we only want US to heed to the views of others and the views of themselves before.

—Sha Zukang, PRC Ambassador at Large for
   Disarmament Affairs, 2001[1]

The evolving capability and declaratory doctrine of U.S. strategic forces pose a challenge for China's nuclear posture. While Chinese planners view their limited nuclear arsenal as sufficient to maintain a mutual deterrent relationship with the United States, U.S. officials continue to reject mutual deterrence in the U.S.–China context. As articulated in the Pentagon's 2001 *Nuclear Posture Review*, the United States seeks strategic forces that would provide credible options for preventive and preemptive operations.[2] This modernization could

---

[1] This statement has been edited for spelling, punctuation, and clarity. Sha Zukang, interview with Chris Masters, Australian Broadcasting Company (August 6, 2001). Available at: http://abc.net.au/4corners/roguestate/interviews/kang.htm.

[2] The 2001 *Nuclear Posture Review* is officially classified. The Department of Defense provided an unclassified cover letter and briefing by Assistant Secretary of Defense for International Security Policy J.D. Crouch that are available at:

substantially increase the perceived willingness of the United States to subject China to coercion and, as a result, complicate China's efforts to maintain restraint under Beijing's apparent rationale that a small strategic force provides adequate deterrence.

China has not yet revised the deployment pattern of its strategic forces, nor does it need to. Despite U.S. investments in missile defense and non-nuclear strategic strike systems, China will continue to maintain a modest retaliatory capability. Overall, changes to China's nuclear posture are probably more likely to arise from internal domestic factors related to Chinese politics and bureaucratic interests rather than from changes in the objective balance of capabilities such as, to suggest one example, U.S. deployment of capable missile defenses.

The *Nuclear Posture Review* presents the United States with an opportunity cost. If Chinese leaders, for their own reasons, begin to lose confidence in their deterrent capability, Washington might attempt to reassure China's leadership that Beijing's nuclear forces are sufficient. The U.S. strategic forces outlined by the 2001 *Nuclear Posture Review*, however, appear designed to undermine, rather than enhance, China's confidence. As a result, the U.S. nuclear posture may unintentionally increase nuclear dangers to the United States. In particular, the logic of preemption inherent in the counterforce doctrine articulated by the 2001 *Nuclear Posture Review* may interact dangerously with more capable Chinese strategic forces, particularly if those forces are kept on higher rates of alert or if China fields systems to target U.S. command, control, and intelligence (C2I) assets.[3]

---

http://www.defenselink.mil/news/Jan2002/t01092002_t0109npr.html. Some sections of the 2001 *Nuclear Posture Review* were leaked to the press and are available at: http://www.globalsecurity.org/wmd/library/policy/dod/npr. htm.

[3] The 2001 *Nuclear Posture Review* uses the simpler "C2I" rather than other, more complex formulations like "C4ISR" (command, control, communications, computers, intelligence, surveillance, and reconnaissance) to describe systems designed to support a commander's exercise of command and control across the range of military operations. That practice is adopted here.

IMPLICATIONS OF CHANGES IN THE U.S. NUCLEAR
POSTURE FOR CHINA

The United States has embarked on a major transformation of its strategic forces, driven in part by concerns about the modernization of China's
strategic forces. China is prominently featured in the 2001 *Nuclear Posture Review*, having returned to U.S. nuclear planning in 1998 after a
long absence.[4] After unsuccessful efforts by U.S. Strategic Command to
include China in the 1994 *Nuclear Posture Review*, the 2001 *Nuclear
Posture Review* identifies China as one of seven countries "that could be
involved in an immediate or potential contingency" with nuclear
weapons.

China's strategic forces are increasingly supplanting Russia's arsenal as
the primary benchmark for determining the size and capabilities of U.S.
strategic forces, particularly as the Bush administration seeks to justify its
decisions to sign the Moscow Treaty and withdraw from the ABM Treaty
on the grounds that the United States no longer maintains an adversarial
relationship with Russia.[5] Secretary of Defense Donald Rumsfeld stated
that future reductions in the U.S. nuclear arsenal below the 1,700 to
2,200 range that is outlined in the Moscow Treaty, for example, are pre-
cluded by the size of Chinese nuclear forces:

---

[4] Presidential Decision Directive 60 (PDD-60) (1998) returned China to the
SIOP—the "Single Integrated Operational Plan" for a nuclear attack—after a
reported sixteen-year absence. Although PDD-60 was/is still classified, the
Washington Post reported that PDD-60 directed the "the military to plan attacks
against a wider spectrum of targets in China, including the country's growing
military-industrial complex and its improved conventional forces." See R. Jeffrey Smith, "Clinton Directive Changes Strategy on Nuclear Arms Centering
on Deterrence, Officials Drop Terms for Long Atomic War," *Washington Post*
(December 7, 1997), p. A1, and Hans M. Kristensen, *The Matrix of Deterrence:
U.S. Strategic Command Force Structure Studies* (Berkeley, CA: Nautilus Institute, May 2001), pp. 14–15. The revelation produced a confidential State
Department memorandum, now partially declassified, concerning targeting policy. See U.S. Department of State, *Targeting Policy* SEA-23820.9 (March 17,
1998).

[5] Bruce Blair, for example, estimated that the 2001 *Nuclear Posture Review*
would result in "a 50 percent reduction in Russian targets and a 100 percent
increase in China targets." See Walter Pincus, "U.S. Considers Shift in Nuclear
Targets: Defenses to Focus on China, Experts Say," *Washington Post* (April 29,
2001), p. A23.

I think it would be a mistake to leave the impression…that either the [Single Integrated Operational Plan] or the 1,700 to 2,200 is premised on Russia. The reality is we live in the world, there is a security environment. Russia exists and has capabilities to be sure, but so does the People's Republic of China, and they are increasing their defense budget and they are increasing their nuclear capabilities purposefully.[6]

In response to criticism that the proposed 1,700 to 2,200 nuclear warhead figure exceeds potential targeting requirements,[7] Secretary Rumsfeld warned that further reductions might encourage China to attempt what he termed a "sprint to parity"—a rapid increase in nuclear forces to reach numerical parity with the United States.[8] In an exchange with Senator Joseph Biden (D-Del.) concerning the disparity in size between the U.S. and Chinese nuclear forces, Rumsfeld explained the relationship between the Chinese strategic forces and their much larger U.S. equivalent:

BIDEN: [But Chinese strategic are forces are in the] multiples of
    10 right now, Mr. Secretary.
RUMSFELD: Very low, very low.
BIDEN: I mean, you know, 2,200…
RUMSFELD: I understand. We have—I'm coming to that.… To
    the extent you lower down so low that it looks like some coun-

---

[6] *Treaty on Strategic Offensive Reduction: The Moscow Treaty, Hearings before the Committee on Foreign Relations, United States Senate*, S. Hrg. 107–622 (July 9, 17, 23 and September 12, 2002), p. 111.

[7] For criticism of overkill in the *Nuclear Posture Review*, see John Steinbruner and Jeffrey Lewis, "The Unsettled Legacy of the Cold War," *Daedalus*, vol. 131, no. 4 (Fall 2002), pp. 5–10. See also David Mosher and Michael O'Hanlon, *The START Treaty and Beyond* (Washington, DC: Congressional Budget Office, October 1991), p. 21.

[8] In his prepared statement, Rumsfeld makes the "sprint to parity" argument explicit, though he does not specify China as the "would-be peer competitor" in question: Some have asked why, in the post-Cold War world, we need to maintain as many as 1,700–2,200 operationally-deployed warheads? The end of the Soviet threat does not mean we no longer need nuclear weapons. To the contrary, the U.S. nuclear arsenal remains an important part of our deterrence strategy, and helps to dissuade the emergence of potential or would-be peer competitors, by underscoring the futility of trying to sprint toward parity with us or superiority. See *Treaty on Strategic Offensive Reduction: The Moscow Treaty*, p. 81.

try can, in fact, sprint and get up to a level, then the deterrent effect of having your capability is probably less persuasive.[9]

Assumptions about the configuration and purpose of China's nuclear arsenal determine not just the overall U.S. force level, but also the mix of capabilities identified in the 2001 *Nuclear Posture Review*. The 2001 *Nuclear Posture Review* concludes that "a strategic posture that relies solely on offensive nuclear forces is inappropriate for deterring the potential adversaries we will face in the 21st century." Instead, the 2001 *Nuclear Posture Review* suggests a "New Triad," characterized by the addition of two capabilities.

- "The addition of defenses (along with the prospects for timely adjustments to force capabilities and enhanced C2 and intelligence systems) means that the U.S. will no longer be as heavily dependent on offensive strike forces to enforce deterrence as it was during the Cold War."

- "The addition of non-nuclear strike forces—including conventional strike and information operations—means that the U.S. will be less dependent than it has been in the past on nuclear forces to provide its offensive deterrent capability."

The capabilities in the New Triad, which include a revitalized defense infrastructure as the third aspect, are "bound together by enhanced command and control (C2) and intelligence systems."[10]

Missile Defense

Missile defenses are perhaps the most important element of the 2001 *Nuclear Posture Review* in the near term—as evidenced by Secretary Rumsfeld's claim that "our decision to undertake such deep reductions [as the ones outlined in the Moscow Treaty] was predicated, in part, on the assumption that we would deploy missile defenses."[11] The Bush administration has significantly increased the funding available for missile defense efforts (see Figure 6-1). The Bush administration has also made a

---

[9] *Treaty on Strategic Offensive Reduction: The Moscow Treaty*, p. 111.

[10] These quotations are drawn from the unclassified cover letter that accompanied the 2001 *Nuclear Posture Review*. See Donald H. Rumsfeld, "Foreword," *Nuclear Posture Review Report* (January 2002), http://www.defenselink.mil/news/Jan2002/d20020109npr.pdf.

[11] *Treaty on Strategic Offensive Reduction: The Moscow Treaty*, p. 120.

number of programmatic changes, including elevating the Ballistic Missile Defense Organization (BMDO) to the agency level, abolishing the distinction between theater and strategic defenses, and adopting an evolutionary approach that does "not envision a final or fixed missile defense architecture."[12]

Figure 6-1: U.S. Missile Defense Appropriations, 1985–2005

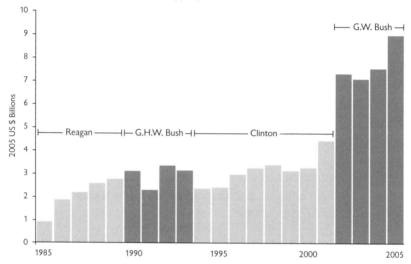

Missile Defense Agency, *Fiscal Year (FY) 2005 Budget Estimates*, Press Release (February 18, 2004), p. 7.

Despite enhanced levels of funding, the initial operational capability that the Missile Defense Agency intended to "stand up" on October 1, 2004 was not substantially different from the first level of capability or "C1" architecture proposed by the Clinton administration (See Figure 6-2).[13] The Bush administration significantly scaled back the Clinton

[12] Assistant Secretary Of Defense J.D. Crouch II, *United States Missile Defense Policy*, Statement Before The House Armed Service Committee United States House Of Representatives, (March 18, 2003). Available at: http://armed-services.senate.gov/statemnt/2003/March/Crouch.pdf.

[13] For a summary of the Clinton C1 architecture, see Walter B. Slocombe, "The Administration's Approach," *The Washington Quarterly*, vol. 23, no. 3 (Summer 2000), pp. 79–85. On the October 1, 2004 deployment date, see David Ruppe, "Rumsfeld Directs Missile Defense to Operate Oct. 1," *Global Security Newswire* (July 13, 2004), http://www.nti.org/d_newswire/issues/2004_7_13.html#90FC8434.

2005 C1 architecture in order to meet the 2005 deployment deadline. As the Department of Defense indicated in 2002:

- The Bush administration will place only twenty interceptors instead of 100, with sixteen in Alaska and four in California.

- Instead of building an X-band radar in Shemya, Alaska, the Bush administration will build a sea-based X-band radar and upgrade the early warning radar at Shemya.

- The Bush Administration restructured the Space-based Infra Red System (SBIRS) program, creating two satellite systems that will not be part of the Ballistic Missile Defense System's initial operational capability. The Missile Defense Agency plans to launch elements of the former "SBIRS-high" component, now simply called SBIRS, in 2007 and in 2010. The Air Force intends to launch a pair of "research and development" satellites, formerly known as "SBIRS-low" and now called the Space Tracking and Surveillance System (STSS), followed by the delivery of the first operational (non-R&D) satellite expected in 2012–2013.[14]

Non-nuclear Strike

The *Nuclear Posture Review* also contains recommendations for the development of non-nuclear strike capabilities, as well as new nuclear capabilities, to attack a variety of difficult targets—including "hard and deeply buried targets" (HDBTs) and mobile, relocatable targets. Conventional options offer practical advantages in certain scenarios and the political advantage of not requiring the initial use of nuclear weapons.

The Pentagon has repeatedly outlined requirements for a "prompt global strike" capability, which is the ability to hit a target anywhere in the world in a matter of hours.[15] These capabilities could be particularly threatening to the Chinese, who will continue to rely on hardening to protect command-and-control networks and who are investing in mobile ballistic missiles. The Pentagon is considering a range of programs to improve non-nuclear strike capabilities, including the Common Aero

---

[14] The major changes are derived from the Department of Defense, *Missile Defense Operations Announcement*, no. 642-02 (December 17, 2002).

[15] Matt Bille (ANSER) and Major Rusty Lorenz (AFSPC/DRM), *Requirements for a Conventional Prompt Global Strike Capability*, NDIA Missile and Rockets Symposium and Exhibition, Arlington, VA, May 2001.

Table 6-1: Notional U.S. Missile Defense Architectures

Architecture (Initial Operational Capability)	C1 (2005)	C2 (2007)	C3 (2010–2015)
Ground Based Interceptors (GBI)	100 Alaska	100 Alaska	125 Alaska 125 Grand Forks, ND
Upgraded Early Warning Radar (UEWR)	Beale, CA Clear, AK Cape Cod, MA Fylingdales, UK Thule, Greenland	Beale Clear Cape Cod Fylingdales Thule	Beale Clear Cape Cod Fylingdales Thule
X-Band Radars	Shemya, AK	Shemya Clear Fylingdales Thule	Shemya Clear Fylingdales Thule Beale Cape Cod Grand Forks Hawaii South Korea
Space Sensors	Defense Support Program (DSP) SBIRS-High	DSP SBIRS-High SBIRS-Low	SBIRS-High SBIRS-Low
In Flight Interceptor Communications System (IFICS)	Alaska Shemya Caribou, ME	Alaska Shemya Caribou Munising, MI	Alaska Shemya Caribou Munising Hawaii

Sources: C1-C3 architecture is derived from "C1/C2/C3 Architecture—Preliminary," briefing slide TRSR 99-082 25 (Ballistic Missile Defense Organization, March 3, 1999), in Andrew M. Sessler et al., *Countermeasures: A Technical Evaluation of the Operational Effectiveness of the Planned US National Missile Defense System* (Cambridge, MA: Union of Concerned Scientists, 2000), p. 21.

Vehicle (CAV), Space Radar (SR), and Transformational Communications Satellite (TSAT).

- *Common Aero Vehicle:* The CAV is a hypersonic glide vehicle designed to carry a payload 3,000 nautical miles (5,500 kilometers) downrange, with reentry speeds of approximately 4,000 feet per second (1,200 meters per second) and an accuracy (circular probable error) of three meters. The accuracy and cross-range would make the CAV particularly capable against mobile ballistic missiles. In the near term, the CAV will be delivered by a ballistic missile or by a space launch vehicle; it was expected to achieve initial operating capability from a ballistic missile in 2010. In December 2002, the deputy secretary of defense directed the Air Force and the Defense Advanced Research Projects Agency (DARPA) to establish a joint program office to accelerate the CAV effort in order to meet the DoD mission requirement for "conventional global, prompt response" with a total response time of "hours."[16]

Table 6-2: Selected Programs Supporting the Non-nuclear Strike (U.S. $ millions)

	2005	2006	2007	2008	2009	2010	2011	Total
PE 0604856F Common Aero Vehicle	16.1	27.0	33.4	32.4	40.8	44.0	82.4	276.1
PE 0603858F Space Radar	67.8	98.3	266.4	1565.4	1068.1	1316.4	1410.3	4227.3
PE 0603845F Transformational Communications Satellite	444.0	429.2	867.1	1536.0	2051.1	2308.3	2588.3	10224.0

FY 2007 President's Budget Request. Available at: http://www.defenselink.mil/comptroller/defbudget/fy2007.

- *Space Radar (SR):* The most promising program for space-based intelligence, surveillance and reconnaissance is the Space Radar program. SR is "designed to transform surveillance by providing persistent, all-weather detection, tracking, and imagery of time-critical targets."[17] SR has been designated by the Office of the Secretary of Defense as "as a key Transformational Space program inextricably linked" to its ISR requirement for transformational forces.[18] The U.S. Air Force estimates that annual funding for the SR could reach $1.4 billion by 2011, before the first satellite is ever launched. The Air Force is considering different radar constellations in low- and medium-earth orbits (MEO), including a mixed constellation with satellites in both.

---

[16] Defense Advanced Research Projects Agency, "FALCON: Force Application and Launch from CONUS Technology Demonstration PHASE I SOLICITATION 03-XX," (June 17, 2003), p. 7.

[17] John A. Tirpak, "The Space Based Radar Plan," *Air Force Magazine* (August 2002), p. 68.

[18] Northrop Grumman, *Program Description: Space-based Radar,* http://www.capitol.northgrum.com/programs/sbr.html.

- *Transformational Communications Satellite:* TSAT, formerly the Advanced Wideband System, will replace the Wideband Military Satellite Communications and supplement the Advanced EHF (extremely high frequency) system. The TSAT is expected to integrate a number of technologies, including laser communications, that would dramatically improve the rate of data transmission in much the same way that fiberoptic cables have improved ground-based data transmission.[19] The Air Force is still conducting an analysis of alternatives to determine the final architecture of the system. The first launch is targeted for 2014.[20]

Enhancing Deterrence

The mechanism by which new offensive and defensive capabilities would enhance deterrence is somewhat obscured by the language of the 2001 *Nuclear Posture Review.*[21] The document conceptualizes the problem of deterrence under conditions of asymmetry: The United States is presumed vulnerable to nuclear coercion because the risks inherent in regional conflicts often exceed the stakes. New offensive and defensive capabilities, as Keith Payne argued shortly before his nomination as deputy assistant secretary of defense for forces policy (with responsibility for overseeing the *Nuclear Posture Review*), would allow the United States to undertake offensive actions to "neutralize enemy military capa-

---

[19] Kerry Gildea, "Transformational Satellite Communications Architecture Almost in Place, Lord Says," *Defense Daily*, vol. 217, no. 11 (January 17, 2003).

[20] Peter B. Teets, *Testimony before the U.S. Senate Armed Services Committee*, Hearing on National Security Space Programs, S. Hrg. 108–18 (March 12, 2003).

[21] Clear statements about the logic implied by the addition of non-nuclear strike and defenses can be found in a series of articles and papers by Keith Payne, deputy assistant secretary of defense for forces and policy and principal author of the 2001 *Nuclear Posture Review*. On the general logic see "Victory is Possible," (written with Colin S. Gray) *Foreign Policy* (Summer 1980), pp. 14–27; *Deterrence in the Second Nuclear Age* (Lexington: University Press of Kentucky, 1996); Keith Payne et al., *Rationale and Requirements for U.S. Nuclear Forces, Vol. I, Executive Report* (Arlington, VA: National Institute of Public Policy, January 2001); and *Strategic Offensive Forces and the Nuclear Posture Review's "New Triad"* (Arlington, VA: National Institute of Public Policy, March 2003). On China's role in determining required capabilities, see *The Fallacies of Cold War Deterrence and a New Direction* (Lexington: University Press of Kentucky, 2001) and "Post-Cold War Deterrence and a Taiwan Crisis," np.

bilities, especially nuclear and other WMD forces" in order "to deter aggression, coerce compliance, and limit the damage that enemy forces can inflict."[22] This extends to the capability to target "Chinese nuclear forces, including intercontinental forces, [which] give 'teeth' to their diplomacy and vastly complicate U.S. planning to deter a conventional conflict in the Strait of Taiwan."[23]

Implicit in each of these missions—deterring aggression, coercing compliance, and limiting damage—is the ability to use offensive capabilities to neutralize an adversary's ballistic missiles prior to launch (either directly or by disrupting command-and-control networks), with missile defenses to "shoulder some of the burden of a counterforce strategy" by intercepting any ballistic missiles that survive a first strike.[24] For example, the Defense Science Board refers to "synergies between ballistic missile defense systems (BMDS) and offensive actions that offer the possibility for different consequences when considered together....BMDS could reduce the risk of some offensive options and thus permit a future strategic strike option with fewer detrimental consequences."[25] As Payne has argued:

> Depending on the circumstances, the U.S. might exploit non-nuclear and/or nuclear capabilities for attacking silo-based and mobile missiles. Unless the Chinese employed WMD against U.S. targets, however, *the U.S. National Command Authorities almost certainly would be highly reluctant to authorize preventive nuclear strikes against such targets....Consequently, offensive operations against ballistic missiles would need to be complemented by Ballistic Missile Defense (BMD)*, and other active and passive defenses for U.S. forward-deployed forces....[26]

This strategy is premised on preemption, as is evident by the fact that the effectiveness of a first strike declines substantially as an adversary's forces are raised to higher levels of readiness.

---

[22] Payne et al., *Rationale and Requirements for U.S. Nuclear Forces*, p. 5.

[23] Payne, *Strategic Offensive Forces and the Nuclear Posture Review's "New Triad,"* p. 4.

[24] Payne et al., *Rationale and Requirements for U.S. Nuclear Forces*, p. 8.

[25] *Report of the Defense Science Board Task Force on Future Strategic Strike Forces* (Washington, DC: Defense Science Board, February 2004), pp. 3–17.

[26] Payne, *The Fallacies of Cold War Deterrence and a New Direction*, p. 181. Emphasis Added.

The idea that a counterforce strategy emphasizing preventive or preemptive strikes is necessary to extend deterrence is hardly new. Writing with a colleague in 1981, Payne argued:

> However, American strategic forces do not exist solely for the purpose of deterring a Soviet nuclear threat or attack against the United States itself. Instead, they are intended to support U.S. foreign policy, as reflected, in the commitment to preserve Western Europe against aggression. Such a function requires American strategic forces that would enable a president to initiate strategic nuclear use for coercive, though politically defensive, purposes.[27]

POSSIBLE CHINESE RESPONSES

China, of course, has no guarantee that the United States will only use nuclear coercion for politically defensive purposes. Chinese leaders are likely to greet such assurances with skepticism, particularly given concerns about so-called nuclear blackmail during the 1950s. The Chinese government professed to be "deeply shocked" by the contents of the 2001 *Nuclear Posture Review*.[28] One Chinese analyst observed that the "New Triad would provide the United States with not only offensive strike capability but also missile defense capability against China. This would reduce China's nuclear retaliatory capability to impotence and thus neutralize China's limited nuclear deterrent forces. Thus the United States would be less cautious about drifting into a Taiwan Strait crisis."[29] Just as the *2001 Nuclear Posture Review* refers to "synergies" between offensive and defensive forces, Sha Zukang, China's then–ambassador-at-large for disarmament affairs, referred to efforts by some countries "to strengthen both their sword and shield in an attempt to gain their own absolute security in disregard of others' security."[30]

---

[27] Gray and Payne, "Victory is Possible," p. 20.

[28] Foreign Ministry spokesman Sun Yuxi told reporters in Beijing that the Chinese government says it is "deeply shocked" at reports China was one of seven countries mentioned by name in the 2001 *Nuclear Posture Review*. See "China 'Shocked' to be on U.S. Nuke Hit List," cnn.com (March 13, 2002): http://www.cnn.com/2002/WORLD/asiapcf/east/03/12/china.nuclear/.

[29] Tian Jingmei, *The Bush Administration's Nuclear Strategy and Its Implications for China's Security* (Stanford, CA: Center for International Security and Cooperation, March 2003), p. 3.

[30] Sha Zukang, *Statement at the Conference on Facilitating the Entry into Force of*

The possibility of preemptive strikes, implicit in the 2001 *Nuclear Posture Review*, demonstrate the risk inherent in China's nuclear strategy. Beijing's arsenal is limited because Chinese leaders appear to have confidence that the U.S. aspiration expressed in the 2001 *Nuclear Posture Review* remains infeasible. There is little sign—as yet—that Chinese choices about force modernization reflect the implicit threat posed by this aspiration.

The visible elements of China's current strategic forces modernization have been programmed since the mid-1980s and are not responses to recent changes in U.S. strategic policy. Although members of the U.S. intelligence community believe that this shift in China's strategic forces was driven in part by China's silo vulnerability, Beijing began design work on solid-fueled ballistic missiles in the late 1960s. China settled on the current modernization program, with its emphasis on solid-fueled ballistic missiles, in the mid-1980s.[31] Similarly, China has been developing countermeasures to U.S. and Russian missile defense systems for decades.[32] Although the technical parameters of China's nuclear arsenal may have been adjusted to account for the changing international geopolitical situation—for example, as the Soviet Union displaced the United States as the principle threat to Chinese security, Chinese designers extended the range of the CSS-3 to bring Moscow into range of bases in

---

the *Comprehensive Nuclear-Test-Ban Treaty* (October 7, 1999), http://www.nti.org/db/china/engdocs/sha1099.htm.

[31] John W. Lewis and Xue Litai, *China's Strategic Seapower: The Politics of Force Modernization in the Nuclear Age* (Stanford, CA: Stanford University Press, 1994), pp. 211–214, and Lewis and Hua, "China's Ballistic Missile Program," pp. 26–31. When asked "Is there any relationship or correlation between our withdrawal from the ABM Treaty on what [the Chinese] are doing?," Robert Walpole, national intelligence officer for strategic and nuclear programs, responded that "the modernization program to develop the two mobile ICBMs and the one SLBM that I talked about date clear back to the 1980's." *CIA National Intelligence Estimate of Foreign Missile Developments and The Ballistic Missile Threat through 2015*, Hearing before the International Security, Proliferation, and Federal Services Subcommittee of the Committee on Governmental Affairs, United States Senate, S. Hrg. 107–467 (March 11, 2002), p. 27.

[32] *Foreign Missile Developments and the Ballistic Missile Threat to the United States through 2015* (National Intelligence Council, September 1999), p. 8 in *National Intelligence Estimate on the Ballistic Missile Threat...*, S. Hrg. 106–671, p. 98. The Chinese countermeasures program, which dates to the beginning of work on ballistic missiles, is also mentioned in Lewis and Hua, pp. 21–22.

Qinghai province—the overall character of the modernization programs appears to be driven by a general determination to have technically competent forces in line with the "minimum means of reprisal."

The U.S. intelligence community projects that over the next decade China will increase the number of warheads targeted at the United States by adding new mobile ballistic missiles and, perhaps, by placing multiple warheads on existing silo-based ballistic missiles. This estimate is speculative; there is no evidence that China has either deployed solid-fueled ballistic missiles or placed multiple warheads on existing ballistic missiles. As U.S. intelligence officials have emphasized, the Chinese "do not have to commit themselves to specific countermeasures they will employ. Until they see what system the United States would deploy as a missile defense, they have the luxury at this point of pursuing multiple types of countermeasure options." Sha Zukang made the same point in a press briefing regarding missile defense issues:

> As I said earlier, even Americans need time to decide what kind of NMD they want. And Americans will need more time to design it and to resolve technical problems. So it's too early to say what kind of countermeasures China will take.[33]

One important factor in determining countermeasures will be the effectiveness of China's solid-fueled ballistic missiles and penetration aids in dealing with improvements in U.S. strategic strike and missile defenses.

China's existing modernization program should be sufficient to overcome threats posed by the most plausible deployments of new U.S. offensive and defensive strategic systems. Some combination of China's current and improved penetration packages, in particular, will be effective against near-term U.S. missile defense deployments. The U.S. Missile Defense Agency admits that its initial missile defense architecture "could not defend against a massive attack involving hundreds of warheads nor is it intended to defeat a more sophisticated set of countermeasures." The Defense Science Board, considering the range of possibilities for strategic strike and missile defense capabilities, has concluded that achieving "effective and comprehensive protection is likely to be a matter of decades."[34]

---

[33] Sha Zukang, *Transcript Briefing on Missile Defense Issue* (Beijing, China: March 23, 2001).

[34] *Report of the Defense Science Board Task Force on Future Strategic Strike Forces,* pp. 1–3.

China has advanced countermeasures programs comparable to those in Russia. A 1995 BMDO study suggested that China has developed several countermeasures, including electronic countermeasures, decoys, and radar cross-section reduction.[35] China presumably has the capacity to deploy all of the "readily available" technologies for simple countermeasures available to states like Iran and North Korea, including "separating reentry vehicles, spin stabilized RVs, RV reorientation, radar-absorbing material, booster fragmentation, low-powered jammers, chafe, simple or balloon decoys."[36]

Most Chinese ballistic missiles have either been deployed or tested with one or more penetration aids:

- The CSS-4 RV was reportedly designed with electronic countermeasures and light exoatmospheric decoys.[37] The U.S. intelligence community expects China to develop "improved penetration packages for its ICBMs."[38]

- CSS-5 RV flight tests in November 1995 and January 1996 each included "two probably endoatmospheric reentry decoys...designed to survive harsh atmospheric reentry conditions, and to simulate characteristics of the actual RV."[39]

- The CSS-X-10 RV apparently employs "similar decoys and other types of penetration aids."[40] An August 1999 CSS-X-10 flight test reportedly included an unknown number of decoys, although this is unconfirmed.[41]

The U.S. intelligence community seems to have little information about precise types of Chinese penetration aids, apart from decoys that are visi-

---

[35] Ballistic Missile Defense Organization Countermeasure Integration Program, *Country Profiles: China* (April 1995), pp. 12–18.

[36] Walpole in *National Intelligence Estimate on the Ballistic Missile Threat*, p. 10.

[37] Lewis and Hua, p. 21

[38] Defense Intelligence Agency in *Current and Projected National Security Threats to the United States...*, S. Hrg. 107–597, p. 321.

[39] National Air Intelligence Center, *Chinese ICBM Capability Steadily Increasing*, NAIC-1030-098B-96 (November 1996) in Bill Gertz, *Betrayal: How the Clinton Administration Undermined American Security*, (Washington, DC: Regency Publishing, 1999), p. 254.

[40] Ibid.

[41] Bill Gertz, "China Develops Warhead Decoys to Defeat U.S. Defenses," *Washington Times* (September 16, 1999), p. 1.

ble in ballistic missile flight tests. Penetration packages appear to vary by ballistic missile, depending on target and missile defense threats.[42]

Similarly, China's solid-fueled ballistic missiles are likely to be relatively secure from U.S. precision-strike capabilities, given the low requirement implicitly set by Beijing for the size of the retaliatory force that must survive a U.S. strike. In the estimate of the Defense Science Board (DSB), the United States will not achieve a decisive preemptive capability against Russian and Chinese HDBTs and mobile ballistic missiles. The DSB projected that the overall capability of U.S. forces against such targets would be only 54 percent of the "ideal" force—in other words, the U.S. capacity to conduct offensive operations against Russian and Chinese strategic forces will be little better than half the force that the DSB suggests is necessary. The DSB explained that most of the shortfall results from limitations in space-based C2I systems.[43] These limitations plague even the notional capabilities of future U.S. space assets—notional capabilities that are themselves probably optimistic given the technological and budgetary challenges facing so-called transformational systems such as Space Radar and TSAT.[44]

Nevertheless, the U.S. *aspiration* expressed by the 2001 *Nuclear Posture Review* is likely to seem threatening to Chinese leaders, even if the actual technologies described in the document remain some years away.

---

[42] Ballistic Missile Defense Organization Countermeasure Integration Program, *Country Profiles: China*, p. 18.

[43] How one ought to interpret the "ideal" capability is just one of many methodological issues that caution making extensive use of the study. Another is the decision to treat the capability of Russian and Chinese strategic forces as essentially equivalent, despite the evident difference in force size and sophistication. Although the DSB provides only a very rough measure, 54 percent leaves sufficient "room for improvement" beyond 2015 to suggest U.S. policymakers will, given the magnitude of retaliation, continue to be deterred by Russian and Chinese strategic forces. See *Report of the Defense Science Board Task Force on Future Strategic Strike Forces*, pp. 4–10.

[44] See General Accounting Office, *Military Space Operations: Common Problems and Their Effects on Satellite and Related Acquisitions* GAO-03-825R (Washington, DC: General Accounting Office, June 2003), and General Accounting Office, *Improvements Needed in Space Systems Acquisition Management Policy* GAO-03-1073 (Washington, DC: General Accounting Office, September 2003). The Space Radar (formerly Space-based Radar) program is not covered in either report, but basic information about shortcomings in its architecture and acquisition schedule is available from *Senate Report 108-46*, pp. 243–244.

Given the long timelines associated with Chinese strategic programs such as the CSS-X-10 missile, some planners in Beijing must be concerned about the evolutionary nature of the U.S. missile defense architecture, which could improve the ability of the United States to deal with larger salvos of warheads and more sophisticated countermeasures. The 200 interceptors in the proposed U.S. C3 architecture would be "enough to knock out several dozen warheads accompanied by advanced defense penetration aids."[45] General Ronald Kadish confidently predicted in his Congressional testimony that "we're going to be very good at" dealing with countermeasures.[46]

Moreover, the 2001 *Nuclear Posture Review* called for enhanced capability to target mobile ballistic missiles, upon which the Chinese deterrent may depend. The document speculates that "a demonstration of the linkage between long-range precision strike weapons and real-time intelligence systems may dissuade a potential adversary from investing heavily in mobile ballistic missiles."[47] The Defense Science Board was optimistic about the ability to achieve the "extraordinarily responsive and adaptive planning" necessary to target mobile and elusive targets.[48] The DSB concluded that this capability "can be achieved through the recommended C2 and communications developments."[49]

Even if U.S. strategic forces continue to have significant limitations, the Chinese leadership must worry that U.S. policymakers will develop a false sense of confidence in the system. In October 2004, Undersecretary of Defense E. C. "Pete" Aldridge expressed confidence that the Ground-Based Midcourse Defense system in Alaska would have a 90 percent chance of intercepting a ballistic missile in flight. Aldridge affirmed that he would advise the president during a crisis that the United States had a 90 percent chance of intercepting a North Korean ballistic missile fired at Los Angeles or San Francisco—a statement that Senator Carl Levin (D-

---

[45] *Talking Points for Ambassador John Holum* (January 20, 2000). Copy available from the Bulletin of Atomic Scientists website: http://www.thebulletin.org/.

[46] Ronald Kadish in "Hearing of the Defense Subcommittee of the Senate Appropriations Committee," FDCH *Political Transcripts* (April 21, 2004), np.

[47] *Nuclear Posture Review* (2001), p. 12, available at: http://www.globalsecurity.org/wmd/library/policy/dod/npr.htm.

[48] *Report of the Defense Science Board Task Force on Future Strategic Strike Forces*, pp. 4–10.

[49] Ibid., pp. 4–10.

Mich.) implied contradicted classified analysis.[50] Similarly, the DSB concluded that achieving 54 percent of the "objective" capability against "near-peer WMD capabilities" was a "significant" improvement and would "give future Presidents realistic, high confidence strategic strike options to reassure friends, change the behavior of enemies, and protect American interests."[51]

Absent a resolution of the status of Taiwan, China is not likely to ignore indefinitely substantial U.S. preparations to conduct preventive interference against Chinese strategic forces. Sun Xiangli, deputy director of the Arms Control Research Division at the Institute of Applied Physics and Computational Mathematics, has argued that China's quest for the minimum means of reprisal "does not mean the number of weapons that make up a limited nuclear force is immutably fixed. In fact, the required size for such a capability is a dynamic quantity relating to the nuclear arsenal's survivability. For instance, one guide to the size required of China's nuclear force is to be able to mount a nuclear strike that can penetrate an enemy's missile defense system after surviving a first strike."[52]

In the event of a dramatic collapse of confidence among China's leaders in the county's nuclear deterrent, emulation of more extensive U.S. or Russian force deployments does not appear to be a likely outcome. Instead, Chinese leaders might prefer asymmetric approaches if the current modernization program is judged inadequate. This tactic would be consistent with Chinese preferences for an arsenal that incurs few costs in terms of political control, economic expenditure, and the like. Within China, of course, voices for much larger deployments do exist, but these voices seem unlikely to exert much influence over the next decade given the nature of the Chinese political system.

The Soviet leadership seems to have seriously considered "asymmetric responses" to President Reagan's Strategic Defense Initiative (SDI).[53]

---

[50] See http://www.armscontrol.org/act/2003_04/missiledefense_apr03.asp.

[51] *Report of the Defense Science Board Task Force on Future Strategic Strike Forces*, p. iv.

[52] Sun Xiangli, "Analysis of China's Nuclear Strategy," in *China Security*, Issue No. 1 (Autumn 2005), p. 28.

[53] In open publications, A.A. Kokoshin suggests, that official thinking was fairly reflected in E. P. Velikhov, A. A. Kokoshin, and R. Z. Sagdeev, *Kosmicheskoe oruzhie: dilemma bezopasnosti [Space Weapons: A Security Dilemma]* (Moscow: Mir, 1986), pp. 117–127 [pp. 98–105 in the English translation published by Mir press], and A. A. Vasil'ev, M. I. Gerasev, and A. A. Kokoshin, "Asimmet

At the time, several Russian observers predicted that the Soviet Union would respond to future SDI deployments with "active and passive counter-measures. The former would be based on the development of means for neutralizing and destroying the various components of a multilayererd BMD, and the latter on the buildup, modification, and diversification of strategic offensive nuclear forces."[54] Senior Chinese diplomats and military specialists reportedly told one visiting American that they would mirror the asymmetric response—which they called the "Andropov Solution"—planned, though never executed, by the Soviet Union.[55] In an interview with the *New York Times*, Sha Zukang expressed his conviction that China "will do whatever possible to ensure that our security will not be compromised, and we are confident that we can succeed without an arms race. We believe defense itself needs defense. It is a defense system. It has many, many parts and most of them are vulnerable to an attack."[56]

One possible response includes anti-satellite weapons. Two Chinese scientists, including one from the IAPCM, noted over a decade ago that space-based missile defenses "would pose a threat to the retaliatory capability of the Soviet Union" and suggested a variety of countermeasures including "an anti-satellite weapon system to penetrate this defensive net."[57] Although Chinese officials are circumspect in detailing specific responses to U.S. missile defense deployments, one Chinese academic admitted that among the countermeasures that China might consider, anti-satellite weapons "might…be tempting."[58]

---

richnyi otvet (vozmozhnye mery protivodeistviya SOI)" ["Asymmetric Response (Possible Methods of Countering SDI),"] *SShA: ékonomika, politika, ideologiya* no. 2 (1987), pp. 27–32.

[54] Velikhov et al., p. 98.

[55] Rose Gottemoeller, "If China Builds More Warheads," *The Washington Post,* (September 6, 2001), p. A23.

[56] Michael R. Gordon, "China, Fearing a Bolder U.S., Takes Aim on Proposed National Missile Shield," *New York Times* (April 29, 2001), p. A1.

[57] Cheng Dongquan and Huang Zhen, "Banning ASAT Weapons" in Carlo Schaerf, Giuseppe Longo, and David Carleton, eds., *Space and Nuclear Weaponry in the 1990s* (New York: Macmillan, 1992), p. 41.

[58] Shen Dingli, "A Chinese Perspective on National Missile Defence," in Paolo Cotta-Ramusino and Maurizio Martellini, eds., *Missile Threats and Ballistic Missile Defense: Technology, Strategic Stability, and Impact on Global Security* (Rome: Landau Network-Centro Volta and Italian Ministry of Foreign Affairs, January 18–19, 2001), p. 223. Available at: http://lxmi.mi.infn.it/~land-net/NMD/volume.pdf.

China can detect and track most satellites with sufficient accuracy for targeting purposes.[59] The extent of Chinese reliance on foreign tracking facilities, however, is unclear. Although China has some domestic telemetry facilities, China also has one overseas facility and international agreements for telemetry, tracking, and control, including stations operated by France, Brazil, and Sweden. The United States, for instance, provided collision avoidance analysis for China's Shenzhou manned spaceflight missions.[60] The political problems with overseas tracking stations are evident from a recent event when China dismantled its second overseas tracking site, in Kiribati, after Kiribati recognized Taiwan.[61]

Compared to penetration aids, however, anti-satellite countermeasures would be far more complicated. A 1995 BMDO countermeasure study, which considered several possible Chinese anti-satellite systems to suppress space-based early warning systems, concluded that such measures "are too complex, are too costly, or pose too many unacceptable trade-offs to warrant serious consideration by China."[62] China currently has no dedicated anti-satellite weapons; its only means of destroying or disabling a satellite, according to the U.S. intelligence community, would be to launch a ballistic missile or space launch vehicle armed with a nuclear weapon.[63]

China's scientific and educational centers conduct basic research on technologies with anti-satellite implications. During the 1970s, China examined missile defense and anti-satellite systems under its Project 640, until Deng Xiaoping canceled the program. Current activities, inferred from press reports, scientific publications, and technology imports all suggest that China's current research on anti-satellites remains investiga-

[59] Department of Defense, *The Security Situation in the Taiwan Strait* (Washington, DC: Department of Defense, February 1999), p. 14.

[60] Richard Boucher, *State Department Daily Press Briefing* (October 15, 2003), p. 16. Available at: http://www.state.gov/r/pa/prs/dpb/2003/25203.htm.

[61] Robert Keith-Reid, "China Scraps Kiribati Satellite Tracking Station," Associated Press (November 16, 2003).

[62] Ballistic Missile Defense Organization Countermeasure Integration Program, *Country Profiles: China*, p. 16.

[63] Department of Defense, *Annual Report on the Military Power of the People's Republic of China* (Department of Defense, June 2004). Unless otherwise noted, the claims regarding Chinese counterspace systems are drawn from this report.

tory in nature.[64] There are, broadly speaking, three types of anti-satellite weapons that China is sometimes said to be developing:

- *Laser programs:* Specific Chinese programs for laser anti-satellites have not been identified. Intelligence reports are based on press articles and publications in scholarly journals.[65] During the mid-1990s, China may have acquired high-energy laser equipment and technical assistance, which could be used in the development of ground-based anti-satellite weapons.[66] Beijing may possess the capability under specific conditions to damage optical sensors on satellites that are very vulnerable to damage by lasers. But China is more than a decade away from developing "lasers that are capable of disabling the sensors on U.S. satellites."[67]

- *Space-based parasitic satellites:* Claims that China is working on a parasitic microsatellite are unconfirmed and most likely false.[68] Qinghua University in Beijing has built and launched two small satellites in cooperation with the British firm Surrey Satellite Technology Ltd. (SSTL). The first satellite, launched in 2000, contained a multi-spectral camera with forty-meter resolution to contribute to a constellation of

---

[64] The degree of Chinese development can be inferred from the 1998–2004 editions of *Chinese Military Power*, which contain little direct evidence of Chinese research on counterspace programs and couches most claims in the most tentative language. Claims are made in the 1998–2004 editions of *Chinese Military Power* without citation or much detail; this section attempts to examine each claim in light of the available knowledge about Chinese space programs.

[65] My best guess is that the articles in question are: Zhang Hongqi, "High Power Microwaves and Weaponry," *Xiandi Fangyu Jishu* (April 1994), pp. 38–46 in *China Aeronautics and Missilery Abstracts*, and "Beam Energy Weaponry as Powerful as Thunder and Lightening," *Jiefangjun Bao* (December 25, 1995), FBIS-CHI-96-039.

[66] "Chinese Military Power," (1998), p. 9.

[67] Mike Doubleday *DoD News Briefing* (November 3, 1998), http://www.fas.org/news/china/1998/t11031998_t103asd_3.html.

[68] The Department of Defense claims that it is "still investigating" a 2002 Hong Kong press report that China is working on a "parasitic micro-satellite." However, Gregory Kulacki and David Wright at the Union of Concerned Scientists found that the report, as well as more than seventy other references, could be traced to a single website in China maintained by a self-described "space enthusiast" named Hong Chaofei. See Gregory Kulacki and David Wright, *A Military Intelligence Failure? The Case of the Parasite Satellite* (Cambridge, MA: Union of Concerned Scientists, August 16, 2004). See also Bradley Graham, "Some Question Report on Chinese Space Arms," *Washington Post* (August 14, 2004), p. A14.

SSTL remote sensing micro-satellites for natural disaster monitoring and mitigation.[69] A second satellite, Naxing 1, was launched in April 2004. Naxing 1 is an experimental vehicle with mass under 25 kilograms. It is designed to test small satellite technology.[70]

- *Co-orbital or direct-ascent weapons:* China is said to be conducting research and development on a direct-ascent anti-satellite system that "could be fielded in the 2005–2010 timeframe."[71] The congressional investigation that produced the 1999 Cox Report claimed that China could use existing ballistic missiles, such as the CSS-2, to develop what the Cox committee called a "direct ascent" system—although the system would operate like the Soviet co-orbital interceptor.

The activities described in open literature for all three of these programs fall within the first phase of the Chinese weapons development process, theoretical evaluation (See Table 6-3).[72] It is not unusual for Chinese weapons development programs to remain in the first phase for many years; Project 640 appears to have remained in the first phase for more than a decade. There are some reports that anti-satellite work was moved

---

[69] You Zheng and M. Sweeting, "Initial Mission Status Analysis of 3-axis Stable Tsinghua-1 Microsatellite," The 14th Annual AIAA/Utah State University Conference on Small Satellites, Logan, UT, (August 21–24, 2000), and Xiong Jianping et al., "On board Computer Subsystem Design for the Tsinghua Nanosatellite," 20th AIAA International Communication Satellite Systems Conference, Montreal, Canada (May 12–15, 2002).

[70] *Jonathan's Space Report* 524 (April 23, 2004), http://www.planet4589.org/space/jsr/back/news.524.

[71] Wang Jian, "US Pursuing Vigorous Development of Space Weapons," *Renmin Ribao, Guangzhou South China News Supplement* (August 19, 2002), FBIS-CHI-2002-0819, and Fang Fenghui, "Preparations for Military Struggle Assume New Importance in the Age of High-Tech Local Warfare," *Jiefangjun Bao* (August 27, 2002), p. 6, FBIS-CHI-2002-0819.

[72] Although DIA presents these steps as indicative of the entire Chinese research and development process, the information appears to reflect aircraft programs. Some variation may exist for ballistic missiles, missiles defenses, anti-satellites, and other special weapons programs. See Defense Intelligence Agency, *Technological Base Resources—China: An Overview of the Military Products Research & Development System*, DST-18308-407-92 (Washington, DC: Defense Intelligence Agency and Department of the Air Force, February 10, 1992), pp. 9–12, and Defense Intelligence Agency, *People's Republic of China People's Liberation Army Air Force* DIC-1300-445-91 (Washington, DC: Defense Intelligence Agency, May 1991), 23-2-23-5.

to the national-level "863 Program for High Technology Development."[73] If true, this would support the hypothesis that Chinese anti-satellite work remains in the early stages of research and development.[74]

Table 6-3: General Procedures for Weapons Development

1. Theoretical Evaluation (*Lunzheng*)
2. Program Phase (*Fangan*)
3. Engineering Development (*Gongchang Yanzhi*)
4. Design Finalization (*Sher Dingxing*)
5. Product Finalization (*Shengchang Dingxing*)

Adapted from *Technological Base Resources—China: An Overview of the Military Products Research & Development System*, DST-18308-407-92 (Defense Intelligence Agency and Department of the Air Force, February 10, 1992), pp. 9–12 and *People's Republic of China People's Liberation Army Air Force* DIC-1300-445-91 (Defense Intelligence Agency, May 1991), pp. 23–25.

The one exception may be the direct ascent anti-satellite—although all available evidence suggests that China's research into this technology also remains exploratory in nature. The relatively strong claim that a Chinese direct ascent anti-satellite "could be fielded in the 2005–2010 timeframe" is belied by the lack of similar statements in other additions of *Chinese Military Power* and in the Congressional testimony by U.S. Secretary of Defense Rumsfeld, who made no mention of the threat from co-orbital or direct ascent anti-satellites. Instead, Rumsfeld emphasized that "Adversaries are likely to develop ground-based lasers, space jamming and 'killer' micro-satellites to attack U.S. space assets."[75]

The lack of specific programs at this time suggests that China is serious about its willingness to forgo anti-satellite weapons and that substan-

[73] Mark A. Stokes, *China's Strategic Modernization: Implications for the United States*, (Carlisle, PA: Strategic Studies Institute, U.S. Army War College, 1999), p. 118.

[74] For a review of the 863 program, see Kathleen Walsh, *Foreign High-Tech R&D In China: Risks, Rewards, and Implications for U.S.-China Relations* (Washington, DC: Henry L. Stimson Center, 2003), pp. 44–46.

[75] Donald H. Rumsfeld, *Prepared Testimony before House Appropriations Defense Subcommittee* (February 14, 2002), http://www.defenselink.mil/speeches/2002/s20020214-secdef.html.

tial investment in counterspace systems would require a major change in Chinese threat perceptions. Such changes could result from concerns about the survivability of Chinese strategic forces. In lieu of well-defined architectures for emerging missile defense and non-nuclear strike capabilities, China will continue to keep its counterspace options open and will not commit to specific programs.

CRISIS STABILITY CONCERNS

How would the U.S. strategic forces such as those outlined by the 2001 *Nuclear Posture Review* interact with Chinese strategic forces equipped with a variety of countermeasures? Would the resulting balance be more or less stable? These questions are difficult to answer with certainty, but there is reason to be concerned.

Table 6-4: Cold War Alerts to DEFCON 3 or Above

1. The "Unintended" DEFCON Alert	May 26,1960
2. The 1962 Cuban Missile Crisis	October 22–November 20, 1962
3. The "Madman Alert"	October 10, 1969
4. The October 1973 Middle East War	October 24, 1973

See Scott D. Sagan, "Nuclear Alerts and Crisis Management," *International Security,* vol. 9, no. 4 (Spring 1985), pp. 99–139 and Scott D. Sagan and Jermi Suri, "The Madman Alert: Secrecy, Signaling and Safety in October 1969," *International Security,* vol. 27, no. 4 (Spring 2003), pp. 150–183.

One potential source of instability would be if China were to conduct an "alert operation" to reduce the vulnerability of strategic forces to attack and to prepare them for potential use. Alert operations may be used to signal resolve in crisis, a potentially important function for Chinese leaders concerned about the sense of confidence that U.S. missile defense systems might create among U.S. policymakers during a crisis.

Alert operations are largely indistinguishable from actual preparations to launch an attack. Moreover, the principal benefit to the state placing its strategic forces on alert—increasing its ability to use nuclear weapons—presents a strong and urgent incentive for its adversary to interfere with the operation. Given the increasing U.S. focus on preemption implicit in the 2001 *Nuclear Posture Review*, concern about an accidental launch or unnecessary and dangerous crisis escalation is far from hypothetical. China's mobile ballistic missiles would presumably be dispersed in a crisis, creating an incentive for the United States to attempt to catch CSS-X-10s in their garrisons and CSS-4s in their silos—particularly if the penetration packages associated with each missile were very effective against a U.S. missile defense system. These incentives would be greater if U.S. offensive and defensive capabilities were highly dependent on space-based assets vulnerable to Chinese anti-satellite weapons.

The potential for escalatory dynamics was also present in U.S.–Soviet strategic force interactions during the Cold War. Fortunately, alert operations have been exceptionally rare, occurring far less frequently than serious crises. Since the inception of the [U.S.] Defense Condition (DEFCON) system, U.S. forces were placed on increased readiness, DEFCON 3 or above, only four times and never after 1973—until after the September 11, 2001 attacks (See Table 6-4).

Of the four different Cold War–era alerts, the first one in 1960 is considered unintentional, and the last two in 1969 and 1973 were attempted by the Nixon administration to signal resolve to the Soviet Union. Only the alert during the Cuban Missile Crisis, during which the then–Strategic Air Command became the only command ever placed on DEFCON 2, occurred during a serious crisis. All of the Cold War alerts occurred more than thirty years ago, when the United States enjoyed substantial nuclear superiority that would overwhelm any Soviet incentive to initiate nuclear use.[76] Whether and to what extent the Soviet Union alerted its forces in response to U.S. alerts and on other occasions remains unclear.[77]

There is no evidence that the China's strategic rocket force, the Second Artillery, has ever been placed on alert. Although there are reports that Second Artillery units maintain what Xue Litai refers to as "round the clock" alerts, the overall readiness of the Second Artillery to conduct nuclear operations remains very low—with ballistic missiles kept unfueled

---

[76] Although this author is skeptical of the concept of nuclear superiority, even opponents of SALT II, who deeply believed both in the importance of nuclear superiority and that the Soviet Union had achieved it, argued that the United States did not begin to lose such superiority until after 1973. For example, see Nitze, Paul H. Nitze, "Assuring Strategic Stability in an Era of Détente," *Foreign Affairs*, vol. 54, no. 2 (January 1976), pp. 224–226.

[77] For a review of Soviet nuclear alerts, see Bruce G. Blair, *The Logic of Accidental Nuclear War* (Washington, DC: Brookings Institution, 1993), pp. 23–26.

and stored separately from warheads.[78] The reluctance of the Chinese leadership to place its nuclear forces on alert may reflect concerns, outlined in the introduction of this book, that alert operations may risk unexpected and dangerous interactions during a crisis. One passage in *Operational Studies,* a text book used at China's National Defense University, reflects this concern, stressing that units must "strictly follow" orders issued by the national command during alert operations.[79]

Chinese strategic forces have not been structured in a way that would make alert operations meaningful. There is, consequently, the possibility that during a significant crisis in the future, alert Chinese forces might interact unexpectedly with U.S. strategic forces. Without any actual Chinese alert operations as an historical reference, analysts must speculate about the impact that changes in the composition of Chinese forces, such as the introduction of mobile ballistic missiles and the improvement of command-and-control networks, will have for the Chinese alerting process and for its interaction with its U.S. counterpart.[80] At some point in a severe crisis, Chinese leaders probably plan to raise the Second Artillery forces' alert level to demonstrate their resolve and capability to retaliate in the event of an attempted nuclear first strike. *Operational Studies* calls such alert operations "anti-nuclear deterrence combat...the military operation that shows our nuclear power and will."[81] It also instructs commanders to "have the troops fully prepared for nuclear retaliation. Comprehensive and firm combat readiness is itself an important means and firm backing to show a strong resolve and will."

The purpose an alert operation would be to increase the readiness of Chinese nuclear forces to conduct retaliatory strikes. Based on press

---

[78] Xue Litai, "Evolution of China's Nuclear Strategy," in John C. Hopkins and Weixing Hu, eds., *Strategic Views from the Second Tier: The Nuclear Weapons Policies of France, Britain, and China,* (Transaction Publishers: New Brunswick, 1995), p. 178.

[79] *Operational Studies (Zhanyi xue)* (Beijing: National Defense University, 2000), ch. 14, p. 6.

[80] This point was made by Blair in reference to U.S.–Soviet strategic interactions, prior to his discovery of Soviet alert operations. See Bruce Blair, "Alerting in Crisis and Conventional War," in *Managing Nuclear Operations,* Ashton Carter, John Steinbruner, and Charles Zraket, eds. (Washington DC: Brookings Institution Press, 1987), p. 77.

[81] All quotes are from chapter 14 of *Operational Studies (Zhanyi xue)* (Beijing: National Defense University, 2000), unless otherwise noted.

reports of Second Artillery exercises, alert operations would involve the dispersal of CSS-2 (DF-3) and CSS-5 (DF-21) mobile ballistic missiles. In 1984, DIA reported that mobile Chinese missile units "practice quick reaction alert responses to sudden alert notification by withdrawing from their normal garrisons. Secretly deploying over a period of several hours or days to new launch positions that are unknown to the enemy, they may move hundreds of kilometers away from their home bases."[82] A 2001 press report describes an exercise in which Second Artillery "units hidden in various assembly areas rapidly moved to the launching position" after receiving orders issued by "the party Central Committee and the Central Military Commission." According to the press report, the missiles "stood upright, fully prepared for any eventuality" for several hours while the unit received orders to "deal with various situations in a timely manner" before eventually being ordered to launch the missiles.[83] Large CSS-3 (DF-4) and CSS-4 (DF-5) ballistic missiles are not mobile and could not conduct such "guerilla tactics." Raising alert rates for the silo-based CSS-4 (DF-5) probably entails fueling the missile, since the designers of this weapon deliberately chose storable liquid propellants that "offer the advantage of high readiness for the DF-5 and could be maintained in a launch mode for prolonged periods."[84]

How changes in China's strategic posture would affect Beijing's alert operations is uncertain. China will probably keep CSS-X-10 mobile ballistic missiles in shelters during peacetime operations, dispersing them at some point in a crisis to conduct "anti-nuclear deterrence combat." This is reportedly the practice maintained by Russia. Chinese operating practices have historically been extremely conservative. China's interest in permissive action link technology may suggest a desire to maintain control over its nuclear weapons during alert operations, given the onus *Operational Studies* places on the Second Artillery units conducting alert operations "to strictly follow the intention and order of the supreme

---

[82] *Handbook of the Chinese People's Liberation Army*, DDB-2680-32-84 (Washington, DC: Defense Intelligence Agency, 1984), p. 72.

[83] Dong Jushan and Wu Xudong, "Build New China's Shield of Peace," *Beijing Zhongguo Qingnian Bao* (July 1, 2001) FBIS-CPP-2001-0703-000119. The report does not indicate how long the missiles remained on alert, but the launch order did not come until "late at night" suggesting the missiles were on alert for several hours.

[84] John W. Lewis and Xue Litai, "Strategic Weapons and Chinese Power: The Formative Years," *The China Quarterly*, no. 112 (December 1987), p. 550.

command and to comply with the need of political and diplomatic struggle." If accounts suggesting that China has had difficulty developing PALs are accurate, Beijing would be less likely to maintain continuous patrols and more reluctant to order alert operations.

In addition to increasing the readiness of China's ballistic missile units, Chinese leaders would also increase the readiness of all other units that would participate in a strategic retaliatory strike, including command elements and any units that would target U.S. command-and-control assets. This would include preparations for use of any anti-satellite weapons, such as a decision to fuel co-orbital interceptors or prepare ground-based lasers.

The history of U.S. alert operations suggests that alert operations have an inherent escalatory potential. In a study of the four U.S. DEF-CON-3 or higher alerts, Scott Sagan found that orders were frequently misunderstood and that ambiguous events were misinterpreted to confirm the sense of crisis. Recognizing that the potential for escalation provides some deterrent benefit, Sagan nonetheless concluded that policy-makers must remain aware that "keeping the alert at the desired level will be extremely difficult, and the degree of further grave escalation uncertain."[85] The inherent risk in alert operations is captured by John F. Kennedy's sardonic remark, upon learning that a U2 had strayed over Soviet airspace during the Cuban Missile Crisis: "There's always some son-of-a-bitch who doesn't get the message."[86]

A Naval War College exercise, held from August 14 to August 25, 2000, suggests one possible cataclysmic result from alert operations during a crisis, particularly in the presence of anti-satellite weapons. According to press accounts, "Red"—a large Asian nation with over a billion people—was conducting large-scale military exercises that "Blue" believed were a prelude to an attack on "Brown," an island neighbor to Red and a U.S. ally.[87]

---

[85] Scott D. Sagan, "Nuclear Alerts and Crisis Management," *International Security*, vol. 9, no. 4 (Spring 1985), p. 136.

[86] Scott D. Sagan, *Limits of Safety: Organizations, Accidents, and Nuclear Weapons* (Princeton, NJ: Princeton University Press, 1995), p. 117–118.

[87] Accounts of this war game are available in Kenneth Watman, "Global 2000," *Naval War College Review*, vol. 54, no. 2 (Spring 2001), pp. 75–88 and William B. Scott, "Wargames Zero In On Knotty Milspace Issues," *Aviation Week & Space Technology*, vol. 154, no. 5 (January 29, 2001), p. 52.

Red strategic forces were configured to rely on ground-based lasers to target extensive Blue space assets that are necessary for coercive, strategic strikes. During these exercises, the commander of the Blue Forces became concerned that Red was readying its ground-based lasers for use against Blue satellites. Although press reports do not indicate whether Red had also dispersed mobile ballistic missiles in this scenario, dispersal might be seen as equally hostile. Fearing the loss of important space assets, the Blue commander ordered a *limited* preemptive strike—using a fleet of Common Aero Vehicles deployed in space—against suspected ground-based laser sites inside Red territory. At the same time, he refrained from striking other targets, "rationalizing that the preemptive strike was only protecting high-value space assets, not initiating hostilities."[88] Limited strikes such as this have been discussed as one possible option for U.S. strategic forces in a crisis. The Defense Science Board, for example, rejected a full-scale effort to disarm either Russia or China in a crisis, but concluded that "the United States might seek to eliminate a portion of the WMD capability most threatening to a particular regional operation or ally." These targets could include not just anti-satellite weapons, but perhaps mobile ballistic missile shelters or selected command-and-control facilities.

The Blue Team was stunned when Red viewed the strike on targets deep inside its territory as an act of war and retaliated—causing a general war. One flabbergasted Blue participant, sounding not completely convinced of what had just happened, reportedly explained: "We thought these preemptive strikes might very well have stopped the crisis situation. But there were some who had a different point of view—that the strikes may have been provocative."[89] It is important to note that China's ability to disperse mobile ballistic missiles or conduct counterspace operations need not be effective to be destabilizing. The natural tendency of defense planners is to assume the worst. Although Blue claimed after the game that it had acted on an "unambiguous warning" of a threat to space assets, even a relatively small risk of anti-nuclear deterrence operations undermining U.S. freedom of action might create a strong incentive to use U.S. space-based systems before they are lost.

---

[88] Scott, p. 52.
[89] Simon "Pete" Worden quoted in Scott, p. 52.

CONCLUSION

Of course, this one exercise does not prove that future deployments will be destabilizing. But *elements* in the U.S. strategic forces modernization may create adverse incentives. Given the risks inherent in the proposed remedies, the burden of proof ought to rest with the advocates of the 2001 *Nuclear Posture Review* to demonstrate that their proposed modernization are enhancing, rather than detracting from, crisis stability and the common interest in avoiding nuclear war.

Advocates of enhancing U.S. preemptive strike capabilities must reconcile their depiction of Chinese intentions and capabilities with the evidence marshaled in this book. If China maintains strategic forces off alert, at levels in the tens, and in support of an operational doctrine that rejects the initiation of nuclear war under any circumstances, then China's nuclear weapons only deter the first use of U.S. nuclear weapons. If this is the case, the only plausible rationale for strategic forces outlined in the 2001 *Nuclear Posture Review* is to support a doctrine for U.S. strategic forces that includes options for the first use of nuclear weapons, either for coercion or a preventive strike against China's strategic forces. This could be the conclusion drawn by Chinese officials, who may eventually choose to respond by altering the Chinese arsenal in ways that would reduce U.S. security. There is no evidence, yet, that China is doing so; in fact, the response of the Chinese government appears limited to a diplomatic initiative in Geneva, which is considered in the next chapter.

CHAPTER 7

A Legal Undertaking to Prevent an Arms Race in Outer Space

We believe that at present the priority issue is that of securing a common understanding by means of a legal undertaking or instrument on the need to prevent the weaponization of and an arms race in outer space.

> —Hu Xiaodi, Statement at the Informal Plenary of the Conference on Disarmament, May 27, 2004[1]

In March 1999, the Chinese delegation to the Conference on Disarmament announced that it would not support a work program for the CD that did not include an *ad hoc* committee with a mandate to negotiate a "legal instrument on the prevention of an arms race in outer space." This sudden obstruction was a change for the Chinese delegation, which prior to 1999 had played a largely constructive role in efforts to develop a CD program of work.

Explaining China's recent arms control diplomacy is, admittedly, a speculative enterprise. Participants are, for obvious reasons, reluctant to share information about internal discussions as they relate to ongoing negotiations. Understanding recent developments requires a more inductive approach and produces less definitive conclusions.

In the preceding chapters, I have suggested that China's strategic force deployments and arms control policies were complementary efforts to construct and then preserve what Marshal Nie called "the minimum means of reprisal." The delegation's March 1999 statement seems very much like the culmination of a growing concern about the potential of

---

[1] Hu Xiaodi, *Statement at the Informal Plenary of the Conference on Disarmament on Item3 "Preventing an Arms Race in Outer Space"* (Geneva: May 27, 2004). Available at: http://www.china-un.ch/eng/65284.html.

U.S. missile defense systems to someday threaten those means. Chinese leaders have yet to alter their strategic force deployments in response to U.S. missile defenses and other modernization programs. Chinese arms control policies, however, have changed—China's new position in Geneva closely followed a January 1999 announcement by U.S. Secretary of Defense William Cohen regarding significant changes to U.S. missile defense programs, which was itself a response to growing political pressure in the United States.

Until March 1999, China's post-CTBT arms control policies focused on bilateral proposals regarding the mutual no-first use of nuclear weapons and securing China's adherence to the ABM Treaty.[2] China's shift in strategy toward the non-weaponization of outer space was lost on the United States—perhaps in the strain on Sino–American relations during the run-up to Operation Allied Force, the NATO military action to stop ethnic cleansing in Kosovo.[3] Although China has since softened its demand for an explicit mandate to negotiate a legal instrument concerning the prevention of an arms race in outer space, China continues to

---

[2] In January 1994, China formally submitted a draft "Treaty on the Mutual No-First Use of Nuclear Weapons" to the United States, Russia, France and Britain. The presidents of China and the Russian Federation undertook, in September 1994, not to be the first to use nuclear weapons against each other or to target each other with their nuclear weapons. China pressed again, in 1998, for an agreement, which led to the June 1998 "de-targeting" agreement. See "China, U.S. Should Sign No-first-use Pact" (Washington, DC: Embassy of the People's Republic of China, June 18, 1998), http://www.china-embassy.org/eng/7063.html. On Chinese views of no-first use, see Li Bin, "Visible Evidences of No-First-Use Nuclear Strategies," *INESAP Information Bulletin*, no. 17 (August 1999), pp. 44–45; Wu Jun, "On No-First-Use Treaty" (Shanghai: The Sixth ISODARCO Beijing Seminar on Arms Control, October 1998); Pan, "On China's No First Use of Nuclear Weapons," Pugwash Meeting no. 279: No First Use of Nuclear Weapons, London, UK (November 15–17, 2002), np; and a pair of essays, published electronically by the Stimson Center but regrettably no longer available online: *No-First-Use and China's Security* by Liu Huaqiu and *China's Negative Security Assurances* by Shen Dingli (no date; about 1998).

[3] The Council on Foreign Relations, for example, published a study entitled *China: Nuclear Weapons and Arms Control* that did not refer to Chinese proposals in Geneva or China's position regarding the non-weaponization of outer space. Robert A. Manning, Ronald Montaperto, and Brad Roberts, *China, Nuclear Weapons, and Arms Control: A Preliminary Assessment* (New York: Council on Foreign Relations, 2000).

maintain the substantive position that a new, legally binding instrument is necessary to prevent an arms race in outer space.

This chapter draws largely on official Chinese government working papers submitted to the Conference on Disarmament, as well as other official statements and a series of interviews conducted in Beijing and Geneva, to describe and analyze China's position on the weaponization of outer space. The basic outline of the Chinese position in Geneva can be found in five working papers submitted to the Conference on Disarmament:

- CD/579: *China's Basic Position on the Prevention of an Arms Race in Outer Space* (March 15, 1985)

- CD/1606: *China's Position on and Suggestions for Ways to Address the Issue of Prevention of an Arms Race in Outer Space at the Conference on Disarmament* (February 9, 2000)

- CD/1645: *Possible Elements of the Future International Legal Instrument on the Prevention of the Weaponization of Outer Space* (June 7, 2001)

- CD/1679: *Possible Elements for a Future International Legal Agreement on the Prevention of the Deployment of Weapons in Outer Space, the Threat or Use of Force against Outer Space Objects* (June 23, 2002)[4]

- *Unofficial Annex: Compilation of Comments and Suggestions to the* CD *Working Paper CD/1679* (July 31, 2003)[5]

- Three "non-papers" circulated at the Conference on Disarmament: *Existing International Legal Instruments and Prevention of the Weaponization of Outer Space* (August 26, 2004), *Verification Aspects of PAROS* (August 28, 2004), and *Definition Issues Regarding Legal Instruments on the Prevention of Weaponization of Outer Space* (June 9, 2005)

These documents are reproduced in the appendix. On the whole, they present a reasonably coherent view of the threats to China's deterrent from space-based systems. These working papers suggest that the proce-

---

[4] Working Paper Presented by the Delegations of China, The Russian Federation, Vietnam, Indonesia, Belarus, Zimbabwe, and Syria. Reproduced in the appendix.

[5] This annex was compiled by the delegations of China and the Russian Federation.

dural obstruction in Geneva regarding the weaponization of outer space reflected Beijing's continuing concern about the viability of its deterrent and was designed to induce a dialogue on strategic issues that is otherwise absent from U.S.–China relations.[6]

CHINA'S POSITION ON THE WEAPONIZATION OF SPACE

China's working papers on outer space have been issued episodically. The first working paper (CD/579) was submitted in 1985, following President Ronald Reagan's "Star Wars" speech. Fifteen years later, in 2000 and 2001, China issued a pair of working papers (CD/1606 and CD/1645), followed by a joint working paper (CD/1679) issued with the Russian Federation and five other delegations in 2002. The Chinese working papers span almost two decades, but reflect a consistent concern that space-based systems might be used to achieve nuclear superiority that would subject China's leaders to what they view as the "nuclear blackmail" that Beijing experienced during the 1950s.

1985: CD/579

President Reagan's announcement of the Strategic Defense Initiative (SDI) in 1983 appears to have unnerved many Chinese analysts. Interviews at the time with Chinese officials and academics revealed that the Chinese elite saw SDI as an "attempt to achieve clear nuclear superiority over the Soviet Union and understand such superiority to mean a first strike capability"—a view consistent with long-standing Chinese concerns about so-called nuclear blackmail.[7] Chinese concerns about SDI were probably related both to the objective threat SDI posed to China's deter-

---

[6] Following a May 2001 consultation regarding U.S. missile defense plans with Assistant Secretary of State for East Asian and Pacific Affairs James Kelly, the Chinese government expressed a desire to make such consultations more frequent in the future. See Wade Boese, "Missile Defense Consultations abroad Yield Little Progress," *Arms Control Today* (June 2001), p. 19, and "Missile Meeting Ends in Stalemate," *BBC News* (May 15, 2001), http://news.bbc.co.uk/1/hi/world/asia-pacific/1331585.stm.

[7] Bonnie S. Glaser and Banning N. Garrett, "Chinese Perspectives on the Strategic Defense Initiative," *Problems of Communism*, vol. 35, no. 2 (March/April 1986), pp. 28–44, and John Garver, "China's Response to the Strategic Defense Initiative," *Asian Survey*, vol. 26, no. 11 (November 1986), pp. 1220–1239.

rent as well as the legacy of the Johnson administration's decision to openly rely on a notional ICBM threat from China as the principal rationale for the Sentinel missile defense system.[8]

In March 1985, China submitted a working paper to the Conference on Disarmament, CD/579: *China's Basic Position on the Prevention of an Arms Race in Outer Space*, outlining the emerging threat from anti-ballistic missile and anti-satellite systems.[9] This document contains most of the essential features of the current Chinese position on the weaponization of outer space, focusing heavily on the development of technologies to intercept ballistic missiles and satellites in outer space.

CD/579 expressed Chinese support for "the exclusive use of outer space for peaceful purposes." Although this broad interpretation would require the limitation of "military satellites of all types," the Chinese proposal accepted that the "complexities" of doing so would permit that question to be deferred indefinitely. Instead, CD/579 focused on a single, core obligation—"banning the development, testing, production, deployment and use of any space weapons and the thorough destruction of all space weapons." Space weapons were defined as:

> ...all devices or installations either space-, land-, sea-, or atmosphere-based, which are designed to attack or damage spacecraft in outer space, or disrupt their normal functioning, or change their orbits; and all devices or installations based in space (including those based on the moon and other celestial bodies) which are designed to attack or damage objects in the atmosphere, or on land, or at sea, or disrupt their normal functioning.

CD/579 set out the requirement for a new agreement, established the CD as the appropriate forum, and called on the United States and the Soviet Union to honor "special responsibilities" for the prevention of an arms race in outer space. All countries were called on to "refrain from developing, testing and deploying space weapons."

---

[8] On announcing the Johnson Administration's intention to deploy the Safeguard anti-ballistic missile (ABM) system, then-Secretary of Defense referred to it as "an ABM deployment designed against a possible Chinese attack..." See "Remarks by Robert S. McNamara Before UPI Editors and Publishers," San Francisco, CA, September 18, 1967. An actual Chinese ICBM threat would not emerge until after the system, by then reconfigured as Safeguard, had been shut down.

[9] Reproduced in the appendix.

As SDI evolved into less ambitious missile defense concepts, Chinese diplomatic efforts shifted during the 1990s toward more general efforts to manage the threat from offensive systems. China pressed to include negative security assurances in the text of the Comprehensive Test Ban Treaty and, in 1994, submitted draft "no-first use" treaties to the other NPT nuclear-weapons states. China again pressed the United States for a bilateral no-first-use agreement, before settling in 1998 for a mutual "non-targeting" agreement.[10] At the same time, China continued to object to the development of various successor systems to SDI. In 1992, for example, China expressed concern that the Global Protection against Limited Strikes (GPALS) system "would not be totally defensive, and that its development would inevitably give rise to mutual suspicion among states."[11]

2000–2001: CD/1606 and CD/1645

During the late 1990s, China's concern about missile defense and anti-satellite technologies re-emerged in response to the growing political pressure in the United States for a national missile defense system. That pressure culminated in 1999. In January, U.S. Secretary of Defense William Cohen announced that the administration would seek $6.6 billion from 2000 to 2005 for the *deployment* of a national missile defense (previous funding had been restricted to research and development) and would explore the "nature and scope" of modifications to the ABM Treaty.[12] In July, President Bill Clinton signed the National Missile Defense Act of 1999 (Public Law 106-38), which made it "the policy of the United States to deploy as soon as is technologically possible" a missile defense system.[13] In May, following Cohen's announcement and during the debate over the Missile Defense Act of 1999, the Chinese delegation to the CD announced that China would withhold its consent from

---

[10] On earlier Chinese refusals to accept a non-targeting agreement in place of a no-first-use pledge, see Howard Diamond, "Sino-U.S. Summit Yields Modest Advances in Arms Control Agenda," *Arms Control Today* (June/July 1998), p. 23.

[11] *The United Nations Disarmament Yearbook*, vol. 17 (New York: United Nations Department of Political Affairs 1992), p. 198.

[12] Craig Cerniello, "Cohen Announces NMD Restructuring, Funding Boost," *Arms Control Today* (January/February 1999), p. 20.

[13] Public Law 106-38, National Missile Defense Act of 1999. Available at: http://thomas.loc.gov/cgi-bin/query/z?c106:S.269.PCS:.

any work plan in the CD that did not include negotiations on an agenda item to "prevent an arms race in outer space." In early 2000, the Chinese government submitted a new working paper, CD/1606: *China's Position on and Suggestions for Ways to Address the Issue of Prevention of an Arms Race in Outer Space at the Conference on Disarmament*, which updated the 1985 working paper. CD/1606 was itself modified the next year with CD/1645: *Possible Elements of the Future International Legal Instrument on the Prevention of the Weaponization of Outer Space.*

CD/1606 and CD/1645 largely repeated the spirit and emphasis of the 1985 document, with three significant elaborations that suggest that China's focus was, initially, to induce a dialogue about restricting missile defense deployments. CD/1606 proposes a ban on the testing, deployment, and use of space "weapons, weapon systems or their components"—a specific choice of wording that also appears in the 1972 ABM Treaty's obligation "not to deploy ABM systems or their components." To the extent that a missile defense interceptor is a weapon, China's draft proposal would prohibit the United States from basing a missile defense system or any of its components—including sensors—in space. Both Space Based Infrared System-High and -Low (now the Space Tracking and Surveillance System) would have been considered "components" of a weapon system under the Chinese definition, especially in light of the fact that the latter was considered a prohibited component under the 1972 ABM Treaty.[14]

CD/1645 also included an obligation "not to use any objects launched into orbit to directly participate in combatant activities." Chinese Ambassador to the CD Hu Xiaodi explained that from the Chinese perspective, "laser, particle beam, kinetic weapons, high precision targeting and guidance, remote sensing and detecting, etc., all are space weapons and weapon systems" [sic].[15] At the same time, CD/1645 also reiterated China's willingness to defer discussions about other military uses of outer space and contained a new proposal for an article on "per-

---

[14] See John B. Rhinelander, *Statement before the International Security, Proliferation and Federal Services Subcommittee of the Senate Committee on Governmental Affairs* (April 28, 1999), http://www.senate.gov/~gov_affairs/042899_rhinelander_testimony.htm.

[15] A transcript of Hu's remarks before the NGO Committee on Peace and Disarmament panel *A Treaty to Prohibit Weapons and War in Space?* (October 11, 2001) can be found at the NGO Committee on Disarmament website, http://www.igc.org/disarm/T101101os3.html.

missible activities" that would "distinguish between activities that are prohibited and those that are not" in the military arena.

Finally, the documents proposed confidence-building measures, but deferred the discussion of verification provisions to a future date. The confidence-building measures in the 2000 and 2001 working papers—which permitted state parties to publish information about their space programs, declare the locations of space launch sites, and provide notification and basic information about objects launched into outer space—are almost identical to those provided for by the International Code of Conduct against Ballistic Missile Proliferation (Hague Code) (See Table 7-1).

The Chinese government rejected the Hague Code on the grounds that its transparency measures were obligatory.[16] This is an interesting development that perhaps points to the internal bureaucratic obstacles to transparency. The Hague Code bears noting because its proponents initially advanced the idea of a code of conduct as a multilateral diplomatic alternative to missile defense systems. When the successful negotiation of the code produced no change in U.S. missile defense policy, support for the code within the Chinese government may have dwindled.[17]

2002–2003: CD/1679 and the Unofficial Annex

In 2002, China, along with the Russian Federation and five other delegations, issued CD/1679: *Possible Elements for a Future International Legal Agreement on the Prevention of the Deployment of Weapons in Outer Space, the Threat or Use of Force against Outer Space Objects*.[18] CD/1679 represented an amalgam of Russian and Chinese positions, which often differ in wording and approach—although not in substance. The two delegations later issued an unofficial annex to the document that compiled comments of other states, *Compilation of Comments and Suggestions to*

---

[16] Liu Jieyi, Remarks at the Carnegie International Nonproliferation Conference (Washington, DC: Carnegie Endowment, November 14, 2002). Available at: http://www.ceip.org/files/projects/npp/pdf/conference/lui.pdf.

[17] Undersecretary of State John Bolton made clear that although the International Code of Conduct was "an important addition" to nonproliferation efforts, an equally "important element is missile defense." John R. Bolton, *Remarks at the Launching Conference for the International Code of Conduct against Ballistic Missile Proliferation*, The Hague, Netherlands: November 25, 2002. Available at: http://www.uspolicy.be/Issues/ND/bolton.112502.htm.

[18] Joining China and the Russian Federation on CD/1679 were Vietnam, Indonesia, Belarus, Zimbabwe, and Syria.

Table 7-1: Confidence-building Measures in the Hague Code

"Transparency measures as follows, with an appropriate and sufficient degree of detail to increase confidence and to promote non-proliferation of Ballistic Missiles capable of delivering weapons of mass destruction:

i) With respect to Ballistic Missile programmes to:

   • make an annual declaration providing an outline of their Ballistic Missile policies. Examples of openness in such declarations might be relevant information on Ballistic Missile systems and land (test-) launch sites;

   • provide annual information on the number and generic class of Ballistic Missiles launched during the preceding year, as declared in conformity with the pre-launch notification mechanism referred to hereunder, in tiret iii);

ii) With respect to expendable Space Launch Vehicle programmes, and consistent with commercial and economic confidentiality principles, to:

   • make an annual declaration providing an outline of their Space Launch Vehicle policies and land (test-) launch sites;

   • provide annual information on the number and generic class of Space Launch Vehicles launched during the preceding year, as declared in conformity with the pre-launch notification mechanism referred to hereunder, in tiret iii);

   • consider, on a voluntary basis (including on the degree of access permitted), inviting international observers to their land (test-) launch sites;

iii) With respect to their Ballistic Missile and Space Launch Vehicle programmes to:

   • exchange pre-launch notifications on their Ballistic Missile and Space Launch Vehicle launches and test flights. These notifications should include such information as the generic class of the Ballistic Missile or Space Launch Vehicle, the planned launch notification window, the launch area and the planned direction."

Note: CD/1645 calls for confidence-building measures "to enhance mutual trust," stating "each State Party shall promulgate its space programme, declare the locations and scopes of its space launch sites, the property and parameters of objects to be launched into outer space, and notify the launching activities [sic]." See CD/1645: *Possible Elements of the Future International Legal Instrument on the Prevention of the Weaponization of Outer Space* (June 7, 2001).

---

the CD Working Paper CD/1679. CD/1679 contains some suggestions that reference wording from previous Chinese documents. Overall, the working paper reaffirms the positions outlined in previous working papers issued to the CD by the Chinese delegation, although it also draws on language from Soviet draft treaties submitted to the United Nations General Assembly in the early 1980s.[19]

The obligations regarding the non-weaponization of outer space are themselves framed somewhat differently, probably to reconcile different approaches taken in prior Russian and Chinese drafts (See Table 7-2).[20] Under CD/1679, states parties undertake:

- Not to place in orbit around the Earth any objects carrying any kinds of weapons, not to install such weapons on celestial bodies, or not to station such weapons in outer space in any other manner.

- Not to resort to the threat or use of force against outer space objects.

- Not to assist or encourage other States, groups of States, [or] international organizations to participate in activities prohibited by this Treaty.

These obligations are somewhat less comprehensive in scope, restricting only deployment. Research, testing, and development of space-based weapons and anti-satellite weapons would be permitted, as would the deployment of ground-based anti-ballistic missile systems.[21]

The unofficial annex contains suggestions for strengthening the obligations articulated in CD/1679. It suggests restrictions on testing, production, deployment, transfer, and use "to elaborate the intended prohibitions" on the deployment of weapons in outer space. The annex also suggests that the second obligation could be strengthened to preclude "temporary operational disruption, displacement or other non-damaging interference with a space object by another space object" and to "include the testing of any weapons against space objects" or "for anti-satellite purposes."

---

[19] See *Soviet Draft Treaty on the Prohibition of the Use of Force in Outer Space and from Space against the Earth*, U.N. General Assembly document A/38/194 (August 22, 1983).

[20] On Soviet drafts, see *Anti-Satellite Weapons, Countermeasures, and Arms Control* (Washington, DC: Office of Technology Assessment, September 1985), pp. 96–99, and *Arms Control in Space* (Washington, DC: Office of Technology Assessment, May 1984), pp. 25–27.

[21] While early Chinese drafts would have restricted theater missile defenses, the Soviet-era submissions permitted ground-based missile defenses. The current draft is probably compatible with Russian Federation efforts to promote a regional theater missile defense for Europe. On Chinese restrictions on TMD, see Li Changhe, "Statement at the Conference on Disarmament," in *Final Record of the 803rd Plenary Meeting of Conference on Disarmament* CD/PV.803

Table 7-2: Obligations and Definitions in Selected Chinese Working Papers Submitted to the CD

CD/579 (March 15, 1985)	CD/1645 (June 7, 2001)	CD/1679 (June 23, 2002)
At the present stage, the primary objective in the efforts to prevent an arms race in outer space should be "the de-weaponization of outer space," i.e. banning the development, testing, production, deployment and use of any space weapons and the thorough destruction of all space weapons.	Not to test, deploy or use in outer space any weapons, weapon systems or their components. Not to test, deploy or use on land, in sea or atmosphere any weapons, weapon systems or their components that can be used for war-fighting in outer space. Not to use any objects launched into orbit to directly participate in combatant activities. Not to assist or encourage other countries, regions, international organizations or entities to participate in activities prohibited by this legal instrument.	Not to place in orbit around the Earth any objects carrying any kinds of weapons, not to install such weapons on celestial bodies, or not to station such weapons in outer space in any other manner. Not to resort to the threat or use of force against outer space objects. Not to assist or encourage other States, groups of States, international organizations to participate in activities prohibited by this Treaty.
The aforesaid space weapons should include all devices or installations either space-, land-, sea-, or atmosphere-based, which are designed to attack or damage spacecraft in outer space, or disrupt their normal functioning, or change their orbits; and all devices or installations based in space (including those based on the moon and other celestial bodies) which are designed to attack or damage objects in the atmosphere, or on land, or at sea, or disrupt their normal functioning.	Outer space is the space above the Earth's atmosphere, i.e. space 100km above the sea level of the Earth. Weapons are devices or facilities that strike, destroy or disrupt directly the normal functions of a target by various destructive ways. Weapon systems are the collective of weapons and their indispensably linked parts that jointly accomplish battle missions. Components of weapon systems are subsystems that directly and indispensably involved in accomplishing battle missions.	

Documents are reproduced in the appendix.

The substantive equivalence of the two pairs of documents—the Chinese documents issued in 2000–2001 and the Sino–Russian documents issued in 2002–2003—is evident in how they each treat permissible military activities in outer space. Although the Sino–Russian working paper is, *prima facie*, more permissive by permitting all military uses "not prohibited by this Treaty," the Russian statement accompanying CD/1679 articulated the same test for permissible activities as CD/1606, which stipulated that permissible activities should require affirmative approval. Although this difference is not trivial in a negotiating context, the more restrictive language does not appear designed to exclude military missions in outer space beyond anti-ballistic missile and anti-satellite missions. Just as CD/1606 recognized that "military satellites involve rather complex issues and their role should not be all together negated," the Russian delegate to the CD endorsed "auxiliary" military uses that are "applied to maintain strategic stability in the world" such as arms control. The Russian representative added, however, that his endorsement did "not mean, not at all, that military activities in outer space should be used to obtain the superiority in force."[22]

The Sino–Russian working paper does not contain any discussion of verification measures. The annex merely notes the suggestion by some countries that verification would be an important element, but indicates that specific verification measures would depend upon the "the obligations to be verified and the level of confidence to be required."

(Geneva: August 13, 1998), pp. 2–5; For a review of Russian proposals for a "European Theater Ballistic Missile Defense (EuroPro) system," see Nikolai Sokov, *Russian Missile Defense For Europe: The February 20 Proposal is More Serious than It Seems* (Monterrey, CA: Center for Nonproliferation Studies, March 14, 2001), and Victor Mizin, *Russian Cooperative Proposals for Missile Defenses with NATO, European BMD: 'EuroPro'—Any 'Contra'?* (Southampton, UK: Mountbatten Centre for International Studies, 2000). For Chinese commentary on these proposals, see Sha Zukang, *Transcript Briefing on Missile Defense Issue* (Beijing: March 23, 2001).

22 Leonid Skotnikov, "Statement at the Conference on Disarmament" in *Final Record of the 907th Plenary Meeting of Conference on Disarmament* CD/PV.907 (Geneva: June 27 2002), pp. 19–21. Available at: http://www.ln.mid.ru/Bl.nsf/arh/FDC3CF91FADC6EC443256BE600374C1F?OpenDocument. See also Hu Xiaodi, "Statement at the Conference on Disarmament," in *Final Record of the 907th Plenary Meeting of Conference on Disarmament* CD/PV.907 (Geneva: June 27, 2002), pp. 17–19.

ASSESSING CHINA'S PROPOSALS ON PREVENTING
THE WEAPONIZATION OF SPACE

China's position on arms control is best viewed as a mechanism to
address Chinese concerns about the U.S. strategic forces modernization
begun under the Clinton administration and codified in the Bush administration's 2001 *Nuclear Posture Review*. Although some observers dis-
miss China's proposals as "a delaying tactic aimed at hampering American
progress on ballistic-missile defense," a plausible case can be made that
China's proposals are designed to induce a dialogue about strategic stability.[23] United States missile defense deployments are important to
China, but only as part of a broader concern about the security of
China's deterrent. This concern extends to other elements of the 2001
Nuclear Posture Review's "New Triad."

Appropriate Forum and Agenda

Perhaps the most important conclusion that can be drawn from the Chinese working papers is that the Chinese government *did react* to the possibility of U.S. missile defense deployments—although perhaps not in the
manner many U.S. observers expected. While Bush administration officials have denied that Chinese actions are linked to U.S. missile defense
developments including U.S. withdrawal from the ABM Treaty, the working papers submitted to the CD by the Chinese government, and the subtle changes in strategy those working papers represent, suggest that Chinese leaders are reacting in the forum they consider to be appropriate,
under the agenda item they consider relevant.[24]

Since 1999, China has sought a multilateral treaty regarding the military use of outer space. This change in China's position followed a major
foreign policy address by Jiang Zemin, then the Chinese head of state,
before the Conference on Disarmament. During his remarks, Jiang issued
a very strong warning that:

---

[23] Larry Wortzel, *China Waging War on Space-Based Weapons* (August 11,
    2003). Available at: http://www.heritage.org/Press/Commentary/ed
    081103b.cfm?RenderforPrint=1.
[24] See Paul D. Wolfowitz, "Remarks to the Frontiers of Freedom," Dirksen Sen-
    ate Office Building, Washington, DC, Thursday (October 24 , 2002), and
    Donald H. Rumsfeld, *Secretary Rumsfeld Interview with Group of Reporters*,
    Washington, DC (July 11, 2001).

The research, development, deployment and proliferation of sophisticated anti-missile systems and the revision of, or even withdrawal from, the existing disarmament treaties on which global strategic equilibrium hinges will inevitably exert an extensive negative impact on international security and stability and trigger off a new round of arms race in new areas, thereby seriously obstructing or neutralizing international efforts of nuclear disarmament and nuclear non-proliferation.[25]

In hindsight, the subsequent change in China's negotiating position at the CD in Geneva suggests Jiang's choice of venue was not a coincidence. China had abandoned its unsuccessful effort, conducted from 1994 to 1998, to extract a pledge from the United States to refrain from the first use of nuclear weapons.

China's shift from a bilateral strategy to a multilateral one may have reflected the state of relations between the United States and China. Relations experienced a difficult period in the late 1990s, ostensibly related to concerns about alleged export control violations and Chinese espionage at nuclear laboratories. Whatever motive or merit the charges had, these allegations resulted in a Congressional investigation that produced the *Final Report of The United States House of Representatives Select Committee on U.S. National Security and Military/Commercial Concerns with the People's Republic of China* (The Cox Report) and a lengthy rebuttal by the Chinese government entitled *Facts Speak Louder Than Words and Lies Will Collapse by Themselves.*[26]

As multilateral forums go, the Conference on Disarmament—which the director-general of China's Department of Arms Control and Disarmament at the Chinese Ministry of Foreign Affairs described as "the sole multilateral arms control negotiating forum"—offers a number of advan-

---

[25] Jiang Zemin, "Promote Disarmament Process and Safeguard World Security, Address at the Conference on Disarmament," in *Final Record of the 822nd Plenary Meeting of Conference on Disarmament* CD/PV.822 (Geneva: March 26, 1999), pp. 2–5.

[26] See *Final Report of The United States House of Representatives Select Committee on U.S. National Security and Military/Commercial Concerns with the People's Republic of China*, House Report 105–851 (Washington, DC: Government Printing Office, January 1999), http://www.access.gpo.gov/congress/house/hr105851/, and *Facts Speak Louder than Words and Lies Will Collapse by Themselves—Further Refutation of the Cox Report* (Beijing: Information Office of the State Council, July 15, 1999), http://www1.china.org.cn/Beijing-Review/Beijing/BeijingReview/99Jul/bjr99-30e-11.html.

tages.[27] The CD operates with rules that require consensus, which gives China comparative leverage to hold at risk agenda items that the United States presumably values. It also has a broad membership that includes Russia as well as some U.S. allies that are sympathetic to China's concerns.

The timing of the Sino–Russian working paper is instructive. It followed the 2002 *Moscow Treaty*. China may have been attempting to shore up a "common front" with Russia, in the wake of a treaty some in the Bush administration treated as a *de facto* Russian acceptance of U.S. missile defense deployments. Finally, Chinese leaders might have expected that negotiations in the CD would create a venue for informal P5 consultations like the ones that were common in the CTBT negotiations.

"Preventing an arms race in outer space" is a plausible agenda item under which to address the question of strategic force modernization. Space-based systems play an important role in enabling both anti-ballistic missile and long-range precision strike missions.[28] SDI was historically associated with its space-based assets because of the prompt global coverage conferred by space-basing. Even the current ground-based midcourse missile defense depends heavily on space-based sensors. Current Missile Defense Agency plans include space-based interceptor options, beginning with a constellation of three to six space-based interceptors that are scheduled to be in orbit by 2011–2012.[29] Similarly, long-range precision strike capabilities will require space-based platforms for intelligence and communications, even if space-based strike platforms remain many years from deployment.

China's decision to pursue a dialogue about strategic stability through negotiations may also reflect the historical organization of Chinese research efforts, which confined anti-ballistic missile and anti-satellite research to the work under Program 640, which ended in the 1980s.[30] In fact, the

---

[27] Liu Jieyi, "Interview: Director Liu Jieyi on Disarmament and Arms Control Conducted by Phillip Saunders," *The Nonproliferation Review,* vol. 11, no. 1 (Spring 2004), p. 8.

[28] For a U.S. expression of this idea, see Simon P. Worden and Martin E. B. France, "Towards an Evolving Deterrence Strategy: Space and Information Dominance," *Comparative Strategy,* vol. 20, no. 5 (October–December 2001), pp. 453–466.

[29] FY 2005 MDA R-2, PE 0603886C, Ballistic Missile Defense System (BMDS) Interceptor (February 2004), p. 2.

[30] For basic information about the "640 program," see Lewis and Xue, *China's Strategic Seapower,* p. 182, and Mark A. Stokes, *China's Strategic Moderniza-*

technologies for intercepting satellites and ballistic missiles are quite similar.[31]

The United States has tended to treat missile defense and outer space as separate issues.[32] This tendency appears to some Chinese observers to be deceptive. Chinese officials and academics often express skepticism about the stated rationale for both missile defense and space control programs. In the case of outer space, the Chinese ambassador to the CD questioned Bush administration officials who warned of a "space Pearl Harbor": "If any country is really worried about possible menace to its space interests, this could certainly be alleviated through the negotiation and conclusion of a treaty on the prevention of space weaponization, as suggested by China." He went on to say, however, that "the [United States] real motivation towards outer space is to defy the obligations of international legal instruments and seek unilateral and absolute military and strategic superiority based on the political, economic and military strength..."[33]

Scope of Obligations

The weaponization of outer space is a plausible agenda item under which to address strategic force modernization and the CD is a suitable forum.

---

tion: Implications for the United States (Carlisle, PA: Strategic Studies Institute, U.S. Army War College, 1999), p. 118.

[31] David Wright and Laura Grego, "Anti-Satellite Capabilities of Planned US Missile Defence Systems," *Disarmament Diplomacy*, vol. 68 (December 2002–January 2003), pp. 7–10.

[32] For example, Donald Rumsfeld told KNBC-TV reporter Conan Nolan:

The report that is the foundation for the ballistic missile defense issue is the Ballistic Missile Threat Commission, and it pointed out that a number of countries will be getting weapons of mass destruction and ballistic missiles to deliver them within the coming period of years.

The Space Commission report that I chaired had nothing to do with anything other than how the United States government and the Pentagon are organized to deal with space issues. It did not change U.S. space policy at all. Indeed, the space policy today is identical to what it was during the prior administration.

See Donald H. Rumsfeld, *Secretary Rumsfeld Interview with KNBC-TV Los Angeles* (August 14, 2001).

[33] Hu Xiaodi, "Statement at the Conference on Disarmament," in *Final Record of the 876th Plenary Meeting of Conference on Disarmament* CD/PV.876 (Geneva: June 7, 2001), pp. 2–5.

A similarly plausible case can be made that China's support for outer space negotiations reflects a straightforward arms control rationale. China's previous nuclear weapons deployments and negotiating behavior at the CD both suggest Chinese policymakers strive to preserve a small retaliatory force capable of providing a sufficient measure of deterrence against nuclear attack. An upper bound on the capability of U.S. anti-ballistic missile and precision strike systems would reassure Chinese leaders that the United States is not seeking the capability to deny these deterrent means to the Chinese. A political commitment along the lines of a no-first-use agreement might usefully build on the 1998 "non-targeting" agreement signed by presidents Jiang and Clinton.[34]

If China's leaders view deterrence as relatively insensitive to changes in the balance of force size, configuration, and readiness, they should prefer an arms control solution. The alternative, an outcome where Chinese strategic forces were drawn into day-to-day operational confrontation with U.S. strategic forces, would require a large investment in and greater sacrifice of control over China's strategic forces. Beijing's preference for arms control has been an enduring feature of Chinese strategic policy and China's strategy in Geneva seems to suggest that it remains influential among China's leaders.

China's preference for arms control is also evident in the relatively limited nature of Chinese missile defense and anti-satellite research, which remains largely compatible with obligations outlined in the Chinese CD working papers. Although China has a small number of surface-to-air missiles for air and missile defense missions, the U.S. intelligence community assesses that China "lacks a coherent, national, strategic-level integrated air defense system (IADS)."[35] Similarly, China has limited anti-satellite capabilities (see chapter 6), with current research reportedly car-

---

[34] See The White House Office of the Press Secretary, *Fact Sheet: Achievements of U.S.-China Summit*, June 27, 1998.

[35] Department of Defense, *Annual Report On The Military Power Of The People's Republic Of China*, Report To Congress Pursuant To The FY2000 National Defense Authorization Act (July 2003), p. 29. Some reports suggest this may include an unknown number of Russian SA-300 surface-to-air missiles. For example, see Richard D. Fisher, Jr. *The Impact of Foreign Weapons and Technology on the Modernization of China's People's Liberation Army: A Report for the U.S.-China Economic and Security Review Commission* (January 2004), http://www.uscc.gov/researchreports/2004/04fisher_report/04_01_01fisherreport.htm.

ried out under the 863 Program, a national-level science and technology research and development effort.

Verification

Judging by the working papers submitted by China to the CD, verification provisions may be the most difficult element to negotiate. If the United States insists on stringent verification mechanisms, China is likely to raise a series of objections, including concerns about compromising national security information, technical challenges, and the cost of verification measures. Hu Xiaodi, the Chinese ambassador to the CD, addressed the topic of verification during a United Nations Institute for Disarmament Research (UNIDIR) workshop in May 2004, concluding, "It may be advisable to put the verification issue aside for the time being," and "the most important thing to do at present is to reach a political consensus on the prevention of an arms race of and their weaponization in outer space."[36] This viewpoint is reiterated in the non-paper concerning verification.[37]

For a variety of security, bureaucratic, and political reasons, transparency is a high cost concession for the Chinese government.[38] The technology, personnel, and facilities in China's space launch and ballistic missile programs are essentially coextensive. Most of China's space launch vehicles are derived from Chinese ballistic missiles and are manufactured in the same factories. All Chinese ballistic missiles undergo final assembly at the China Academy of Launch Technology plant in Wanyuan.[39] The United States Defense Intelligence Agency was able to estimate that China produced ten DF-5-type airframes a year from 1978–1982, but could not be sure how many were space launch vehicles.[40]

---

[36] Hu Xiaodi, Remarks to the Seminar on Safeguarding Space for All: Security and Peaceful Uses, Geneva, March 26, 2004.

[37] This document is reproduced in the appendix.

[38] Li Bin, "China and Nuclear Transparency," in Nicholas Zarimpas, ed., *Transparency in Nuclear Warheads and Materials: The Political and Technical Dimensions,* (Oxford: Oxford University Press, 2003), pp. 50–57.

[39] Craig Covault, "Chinese Facility Combines Capabilities to Produce Long March Boosters, ICBMs," *Aviation Week & Space Technology* (July 27, 1987), p. 50.

[40] Robert S. Norris, Andrew S. Burrows, and Richard W. Fieldhouse, *Nuclear Weapons Databook: British, French, and Chinese Nuclear Weapons* (Boulder, CO: Westview Press, 1994), p. 364.

Chinese leaders may require political commitments from the United States to refrain from using verification and confidence-building measures for espionage. The decision by the Chinese government to reject the Hague Code on the grounds that transparency measures were obligatory suggests that transparency issues may divide Chinese policymakers. According to one Chinese participant, a decisive signal of reassurance during the CTBT negotiations was "a commitment to China regarding possible abuse of verification [in a letter from Secretary of State Warren Christopher to Minister of Foreign Affairs Qian Qichen expressing that] the United States understood China's concern on NTM and was committed to compliance by all parties to the CTBT with these CTBT provisions against possible abuse."[41]

China—as well as a number of other states—may also require assurances that verification assets would not also be used to circumvent agreements. A United Nations *Study On The Application Of Confidence-building Measures in Outer Space*, in which three Chinese delegates participated, expressed concern that radars that "can track satellites and other objects in space and observe missile defense tests to obtain information for monitoring purposes are also an essential component of present generation missile defense systems, providing early warning of an attack and battle management support, distinguishing reentry vehicles from decoys, and guiding interceptors to their targets."[42] Similarly, a study by RAND concluded, "X-band radars designed for debris monitoring could provide a ballistic missile mid-course tracking capability that would be useful in a National Missile Defense system."[43]

Space-based verification technologies produce the same set of challenges. The UN study suggests:

---

[41] Zou Yunhua, *China and the CTBT Negotiations* (Stanford, CA: Stanford University Center for International Security and Cooperation, 1998), p. 24.

[42] The primary Chinese delegate accepted the study's conclusions without reservation and the Chinese Representative to the UN voted to commend the study to member states. See *Report of the Secretary-General, Study on the Application of Confidence-building Measures in Outer Space* (New York: United Nations, 1994), quotation on p. 36. The Chinese Ministry of Foreign Affairs sent Yu Mengjia to the first two sessions, Sha Zukang to the third and Wu Chengjiang to the fourth. See also Du Shuhua, "The Outer Space and Moon Treaties," in Serge Sur, ed., *Verification of Current Disarmament and Arms Limitation: Ways, Means, and Practices* (New York: United Nations, 1992), pp. 123–148.

[43] Daniel Gonzales, *The Changing Role of the U.S. Military in Space* (Washington, DC: RAND, 1999), p. 4.

...technical collection systems should not be so powerful that they reproduce the...systems that they intend to limit. Verification schemes that require inspection satellites to rendezvous with other satellites in order to determine the presence or absence of prohibited activities may be difficult to distinguish from prohibited anti-satellite systems. Similarly, large space-based infrared telescope sensors used for verification may be difficult to distinguish from sensors that would form the basis for [a] missile defense battle management system.[44]

The similarity between space-based verification technologies and offensive counterspace capabilities is evident in the relevant U.S. programs. The space-based sensor currently used by the United States for space surveillance is a re-tasked Ballistic Missile Defense Organization satellite, the U.S. Midcourse Space Experiment (MSX) Satellite. The U.S. Air Force considers space object identification (SOI)—roughly analogous to on-orbit inspections—as part of the "space control" mission that also includes anti-satellite intercepts. The Air Force also intends to conduct both inspections and intercepts with the same platform, based on the Experimental Spacecraft System (XSS), a prototype series of micro-satellites. The first satellite in the series, the XSS-10, was launched in 2003. That satellite maneuvered to within 35 meters of an expended Delta II rocket body, transmitting digital images to Earth, and conducted a number of other on-orbit maneuvers for twenty-four hours before completing its mission. The Air Force launched the second satellite in the series, the XSS-11, in 2005. Unlike the XSS-10, the XSS-11 was expected to remain in orbit for a year and conduct close-proximity operations to multiple targets of opportunity.[45] The source and nature of these missions are understandably suspicious to other space users, China included.

A political commitment to refrain from abusing verification protocols may be enhanced by arrangements among parties to share data. A cooperative approach, drawing from experience with the CTBT's International Monitoring system, would be for parties to share space situational awareness data and certain space technologies. At this time, the world relies exclusively on the United States for the provision of orbital data neces-

[44] *Report of the Secretary-General*, p. 36.
[45] Russ Partch, *XSS-11 (AFRL-0003) DoD Space Experiments Review Board*, Program Briefing, November 2002.

sary to avoid collisions.[46] The United States is currently exploring mechanisms to disseminate satellite tracking data and analytic services to other space-faring states. The United States, for instance, provided collision avoidance analysis for China's Shenzhou manned space missions. Sharing space situational awareness data with China might be an important method of reassurance.

Other forms of civil space cooperation may also be essential. Some observers have suggested, for instance, encouraging China's participation in the International Space Station. Microsatellite technology might offer another area for cooperation. A Chinese university has launched a pair of small satellites built in cooperation with a British University firm, Surrey Satellite Technology Ltd (SSTL). SSTL built and launched a satellite, SNAP-1, that maneuvered to within nine meters of a Surrey-Qinghua University satellite in 2000. The Chinese satellite contained a multi-spectral camera with forty-meter resolution to demonstrate a constellation of remote-sensing micro-satellites for natural disaster monitoring and mitigation.[47] Qinghua University launched a second satellite with SSTL, the twenty-five-kilogram Naxing 1 (a contraction of *Nami Weixing*, or "Nanosatellite"), in 2004.

Although China would, in principle, be interested in expanded civil space cooperation, any enthusiasm will be tempered by lingering wariness and animosity over accusations in the late 1990s that the Chinese military obtained "dual use" technology by launching U.S.-made satellites. For this reason, European initiatives may in fact be more helpful.[48]

---

[46] General Accounting Office, *Space Surveillance Network: New Way Proposed to Support Commercial and Foreign Entities*, GAO-02-403R Space Surveillance Network (Washington, DC: General Accounting Office, June 7, 2002), p. 1.

[47] You Zheng and M. Sweeting, "Initial Mission Status Analysis of 3-axis Stable Tsinghua-1 Microsatellite," The 14th Annual AIAA/Utah State University Conference on Small Satellites, Logan, UT (August 21–24, 2000), and Xiong Jianping et al., "On board Computer Subsystem Design for the Tsinghua Nanosatellite," 20th AIAA International Communication Satellite Systems Conference, Montreal, Canada (May 12–15, 2002). Despite the innocuous mission of the Chinese satellite and its relatively limited capabilities, the Department of Defense identified TsinghuaSat-1 as evidence that China is developing "parasitic microsatellites" for use as anti-satellite weapons. See Chinese Military Power (July 2003), p. 36.

[48] Wei Long, "ESA to Help China Join ISS," Space.com (July 29, 2001), http:// www.spacedaily.com/news/china-01zr.html.

CONCLUSION

The deadlock at the Conference on Disarmament after March 1999 is perhaps the most visible result of U.S. missile defense policy during the 1990s. The timing, choice of venue and choice of agenda items all suggest a real concern about the modernization of U.S. strategic forces. A legal instrument for the prevention of an arms race in outer space would provide the same sort of political assurance as a no-first-use pledge from the United States, trading some clarity of political commitment for more observable restrictions on U.S. behavior. This sort of compromise would require more intrusive verification measures, which are a high-cost concession for the Chinese. Resolving Chinese concerns may require additional political commitments, as well as confidence-building measures centered on cooperation in the peaceful use of outer space.

CHAPTER 8

China's Search for Security in the Nuclear Age

Senator, you have raised a range of very interesting questions. One that is particularly important to address is this notion that we have a relationship of mutual assured destruction with China, which is implied in your question. It is not the case, and I think it is important that we do not import that into our thinking about U.S.-China relations, and in particular the nuclear issues in that relationship. We should not import into our thinking about China the cold war concepts of mutual assured destruction that applied between the United States and the Soviet Union.

> —Douglas Feith, U.S. Undersecretary of Defense for Policy, 2001[1]

Over the years, the international situation has undergone drastic changes, but the basic international strategic configuration has remained relatively unchanged in one important aspect, i.e., the strategic balance and mutual deterrence between major powers.... No matter if the U.S. like[s] it or not... it is precisely because of this global strategic balance that the major powers have felt compelled to address global and regional security issues through peaceful means and avoid direct confrontation with each other.

> —Sha Zukang, PRC Ambassador at Large for Disarmament Affairs, 1999[2]

---

[1] *Administration's Missile Defense Program and the ABM Treaty*, Hearing before the Committee on Foreign Relations, United States Senate, S. Hrg. 107–110 (July 24, 2001), p. 32.

[2] Sha Zukang, *Speech at the NMD Briefing*, Beijing, March 14, 2001. Available at: http://www.chinaembassy.se/eng/9186.html.

W hen he signed the Comprehensive Nuclear Test Ban Treaty in 1996, President Clinton chose the same pen that John F. Kennedy used to sign the Limited Test Ban Treaty (LTBT) more than thirty years before. The symbolism was obvious: The CTBT completed a decades-long effort to ban the testing of nuclear weapons. How China, which had dismissed the 1963 LTBT as a "big fraud to fool the people of the world," came to share in this goal is part of the much broader story of China's search for security in the nuclear age.[3]

This search is poorly understood within the United States, yet it has important implications for international security. A small risk of an unlikely but very destructive event like a nuclear exchange, even one limited to a few weapons, must be taken seriously. A crisis over the status of Taiwan is among a small number of scenarios in which the deliberate use of nuclear weapons against the United States is plausible.

The deliberations of China's leaders are not, of course, directly visible, nor are the documents that record their decisions likely to be available in the near future. But Chinese statements, deployments, and arms control behavior suggest that China's search for security in the nuclear age has consistently been a search for what Marshal Nie described as "the minimum means of reprisal."[4] Beijing's decisions about force configuration and arms control suggest a planning system that treats deterrence as easily maintained, even by very low force levels that are kept off alert. The overall Chinese force configuration, then, reflects a distinctive calculus of risk—in effect trading offensive capability for other virtues, including better control over nuclear forces and economic savings.

This judgment explains the unusual configuration and operational doctrine of China's nuclear forces. U.S. intelligence estimates suggest that China deploys about eighty land-based ballistic missiles that are kept unfueled and stored separately from their warheads. China maintains a no-first-use policy and an operational doctrine restricted to the retaliatory use of nuclear weapons.

---

[3] The "big fraud..." quote comes from *Statement of the Government of the People's Republic of China*, October 16, 1964 in John W. Lewis and Xue Litai, *China Builds the Bomb* (Stanford, CA: Stanford University Press, 1988), p. 241.

[4] Nie Rongzhen, *Inside the Red Star: The Memoirs of Marshal Nie Rongzhen*, trans. Zhong Rongyi (Beijing: New World Press, 1988), p. 702.

ASSESSING CHINA'S STRATEGIC DECISIONS

The historical record indicates that China's current posture is, above all, a deliberate choice that reflects certain attitudes about nuclear weapons. Although most analysts focus their attention on the January 1955 decision that began China's efforts to develop ballistic missiles and nuclear weapons, the 1961 decision to continue the program after the withdrawal of Soviet assistance is more important. While Chinese leaders in 1955 expected significant Soviet support, by 1961 they could not avoid recognizing the significant costs of "going it alone." The decision to proceed, despite the high costs, would create the organizational structure and bureaucratic rationale that would sustain the program over the coming decades.

The Chinese leadership in the 1950s and 1960s expressed skepticism that nuclear weapons had much use on a battlefield—perhaps a result of the experience of the Korean War. Advocates of the nuclear weapons program rebutted arguments in favor of devoting money to "aircraft and conventional equipment" by emphasizing the role that nuclear weapons could play in deterring coercion and putting an end to being "bullied, humiliated and oppressed" by nuclear-weapons states.[5]

The Chinese leadership believed this goal was achieved with the very first deployments of nuclear weapons. This attitude was most evident in China's deployment posture throughout the 1969 Sino–Soviet crisis, but it was also apparent in the internal report for the Central Committee prepared by Marshal Nie and three colleagues.[6] The posture and report were remarkable expressions of confidence in the deterrent effect of China's extremely small arsenal.

During the depths of the Sino-Soviet crisis, Chinese leaders appear to have eschewed survivability measures—such as dispersing the available stockpile of nuclear gravity bombs to airbases for prompt delivery—that would compromise control over strategic forces.[7] This is a very different

---

[5] Ibid.

[6] Nie et al., *Report to the Central Committee: A Preliminary Evaluation of the War Situation*, in Chen Jian and David L. Wilson, "All under the Heaven is Great Chaos: Beijing, the Sino-Soviet Border Clashes, and the Turn toward Sino-American Rapprochement, 1968–69," *Cold War International History Project Bulletin*, vol. 11 (1996), p. 167.

[7] According to a 1972 DIA report, "operational storage sites for nuclear bombs at airfields have not been identified in China" although "it is not possible at this time to rule out the possibility that some nuclear weapons may already be dis-

calculus of risk than that which prevailed in the United States. It remains evident today in both in the configuration of Chinese forces, which emphasizes keeping ballistic missiles and nuclear warheads under extremely tight control, and in statements by Chinese leaders to the Second Artillery.[8]

A rationale for the Chinese strategic weapons program within the Chinese bureaucracy was also articulated in the 1961 decision to continue the program after the withdrawal of Soviet assistance, with proponents emphasizing the program's potential to "advance [China] in many other branches of modern science and technology."[9] The Chinese leadership has since emphasized development over deployment. China has spent vast sums to develop the technical competence to build the most sophisticated weapons, but only small amounts of funds were made available for procurement of these weapons and training. China's operationally deployed force peaked around 150 ballistic missiles in the mid-1980s—a figure well below U.S. estimates of what China's resources, material, manpower, and industrial capacity would have allowed.[10] In addition, China has built only one ballistic missile submarine, which never became operational. It also conducted a number of low-yield nuclear tests, including an enhanced radiation warhead, but has not deployed tactical nuclear weapons.

The first phase of China's search for security in the nuclear age came to an end in the 1980s, as deployments reached their peak and Chinese leaders detected a relaxation of international tension.[11] The deterrent role of

---

persed to temporary, non-identifiable storage facilities at TU-16 capable airfields around China." *Soviet and People's Republic of China Nuclear Weapons Employment Strategy* (Washington, DC: Defense Intelligence Agency, 1972).

[8] "Forging the Republic's Shield of Peace," *People's Daily* (March 21, 2002), FBIS-CPP-2002-03210-00103, and "Chinese Military Leader Outlines Goals for Army Missile Unit," *Xinhua News Agency* (June 7, 2002).

[9] Nie, p. 702.

[10] According to the Defense Intelligence Agency in 1984, at the peak of China's nuclear deployments, China maintained the capability to "produce more delivery systems than are currently estimated." See Defense Intelligence Agency, *Defense Estimative Brief: Nuclear Weapons Systems in China*, DEB-49-84 (April 24, 1984), p. 3.

[11] For example, in 1984 the Defense Intelligence Agency reported that a "high-level Chinese defense official" expressed confidence that "the Soviet Union no longer had a first strike capability against China...." Jack Anderson, "China Shows Confidence in Its Missiles," *Washington Post*, December 19, 1984, p. F11.

nuclear weapons continued, but like other military programs, the government reduced the number of forces and subjected the strategic weapons complex to defense conversion.[12] Between the mid-1980s and mid-1990s, China reduced the number of ballistic missiles in its arsenal by half. Near-term modernization plans for a follow-on, liquid-fueled ICBM and a new ballistic missile submarine were canceled in favor of longer-term efforts to develop the CSS-X-10 family of solid-fueled ballistic missiles.[13]

During this new phase, China was increasingly acting as a nuclear "have" as opposed to a nuclear "have-not." Arms control agreements were an increasingly viable mechanism to reinforce China's deterrent posture. The costs associated with formal arms control were declining as Chinese technical competence improved, rendering the nonproliferation benefits a more decisive factor in Chinese thinking, both in terms of halting the emergence of new nuclear states and limiting the development of the superpowers' arsenals. In March 1986, China announced that it would no longer conduct atmospheric nuclear testing and that it would participate in an *ad hoc* group on the Comprehensive Test Ban Treaty if one were convened in 1986.[14] This announcement was more than politi-

---

[12] For a summary of Chinese defense conversion, see Evan A. Feigenbaum, *China's Techno-Warriors: National Security and Strategic Competition from the Nuclear to the Information Age* (Stanford, CA: Stanford University Press, 2003); John Frankenstein, "China's Defense Industries: A New Course?" in James C. Mulvenon and Richard H. Yang, eds., *The People's Liberation Army in the Information Age* (Santa Monica: CA: RAND, 1999); Jorn Brommelhorster and John Frankenstein, eds., *Mixed Motives, Uncertain Outcomes: Defense Conversion in China* (Boulder, CO: Lynne Rienner Publishers, 1997); John Frankenstein and Bates Gill, "Current and Future Challenges Facing Chinese Defense Industries," *China Quarterly*, no. 146 (June 1996), pp. 394–427; and Yitzhak Shichor, "Peaceful Fallout: The Conversion of China's Military–Nuclear Complex to Civilian Use," BICC Brief 10 (November 1997).

[13] John W. Lewis and Xue Litai, *China's Strategic Seapower: The Politics of Force Modernization in the Nuclear Age* (Stanford, CA: Stanford University Press, 1994), pp. 211–214.

[14] On the commitment to cease atmospheric nuclear testing, see Zhao Ziyang's speech at the Chinese People's Rally for World Peace, quoted in "China Urges Superpowers to End Nuclear Testing," *United Press International* (March 21, 1986); Qian Jiadong, "Statement at the Conference on Disarmament," in *Final Record of the 339th Plenary Meeting of Conference on Disarmament*, CD/PV.339 (Geneva: February 13, 1986), p. 32; and Qian Jiadong, "Statement at the Conference on Disarmament," in *Final Record of the 292nd*

cal theater—the timing overlapped with a Central Committee decision to approve a series of nuclear tests that would allow China to agree to a test ban. Although China's nuclear weapons designers still described a test ban as a superpower effort to "restrict other countries from developing nuclear weapons," they also realized that China had increasingly less in common with "other countries."

With its signature on the CTBT, and its newfound support for the Nuclear Nonproliferation Treaty, in the mid-1990s China's search for security in the nuclear age was coming to an end.[15] China would continue the strategic forces modernization program it established in the mid-1980s, emphasizing work on solid-fueled ballistic missiles and countermeasures.[16]

Yet just as China arrived at something like mutual deterrence, some in the United States were contemplating a very different future. During the mid-1990s, proponents of missile defenses began to articulate a new vision for U.S. strategic forces that included missile defenses and a denigration of the Cold War concept of mutual vulnerability. Support for missile defenses, in particular, was an element of the 1994 "Contract with America." The Republican Party successfully campaigned on this platform, taking control of both houses of Congress for the first time since

---

Plenary Meeting of Conference on Disarmament, CD/PV.292 (Geneva: February 19, 1985), pp. 32–33.

[15] On China's changing attitude toward nuclear nonproliferation, see Shen Dingli, *The Current Status of Chinese Nuclear Forces and Nuclear Policies*, Center for Energy and Environmental Studies Report no. 247 (Princeton, NJ: Princeton University, February 1990), p. 2, and Zhu Mingquan, "The Evolution of China's Nuclear Nonproliferation Policy," *The Nonproliferation Review* (Winter 1997), pp. 40–48.

[16] Lewis and Xue, pp. 211–214, and John Lewis and Hua Di, "China's Ballistic Missile Program: Technologies, Strategies, Goals," *International Security*, vol. 17, no. 2 (Fall 1992), pp. 26–31. When asked about the relationship between the U.S. withdrawal from the ABM Treaty and Chinese actions, Robert Walpole, the national intelligence officer for strategic and nuclear programs, responded that "the [Chinese] modernization program to develop the two mobile ICBMs and the one SLBM that I talked about date clear back to the 1980's." CIA *National Intelligence Estimate of Foreign Missile Developments and The Ballistic Missile Threat through 2015*, Hearing before the International Security, Proliferation, and Federal Services Subcommittee of the Committee on Governmental Affairs, United States Senate, S. Hrg. 107–467 (March 11, 2002), p. 27.

1954. The political pressure behind missile defense generated by the Republican Congress was evident by 1999. That year opened with Secretary of Defense William Cohen's January announcement that the Clinton administration would seek funds for the *deployment* of a national missile defense system and modifications to the ABM Treaty.[17] In July, President Clinton would sign into law a bill committing the United States "to deploy as soon as is technologically possible" a missile defense system.[18]

These decisions had profound effects on the agenda for the Conference on Disarmament, which by consensus was moving slowly toward a program of work that would include negotiations on a treaty to ban the production of fissile material for nuclear weapons. The growing support for missile defense within the United States generated increasing expressions of concern among Chinese leaders. In early 1999, following Cohen's announcement and the progress of the National Missile Defense Act of 1999 in both houses of Congress, China announced that it would not support a program of work at the Conference on Disarmament that did not include negotiations on a legal undertaking to prevent an arms race in outer space—an undertaking that would directly address U.S. missile defense plans. China called for a "balanced and comprehensive plan of work"—a program including negotiations on both preventing an arms race in outer space and fissile material stockpiles. China's willingness to agree to a constraint on the size of its arsenal required a corresponding constraint on the prospects for U.S. strategic forces modernization. The nature of this linkage is largely symbolic: the current U.S. modernization program, when matched to its Chinese counterpart, is unlikely to result in a substantial change in the strategic situation. Yet the Chinese leadership must worry that U.S. policymakers might one day believe that the United States could build strategic forces that would alter this balance. China's refusal to enter FMCT negotiations underscores the point that a much larger Chinese arsenal remains an option.

Whether or not the United States will accept China's possession of the minimum means of reprisal is now the central issue for the future of both countries' nuclear forces.

---

[17] Craig Cerniello, "Cohen Announces NMD Restructuring, Funding Boost," *Arms Control Today* (January/February 1999), p. 20.

[18] Public Law 106-38, National Missile Defense Act of 1999. Available at: http://thomas.loc.gov/cgi-bin/query/z?c106:S.269.PCS:.

IMPLICATIONS FOR U.S. POLICY

If China's forces are, in fact, configured to achieve the most basic deterrent effect, then the United States derives several security benefits:

• China's nuclear weapons deter the first use of U.S. nuclear weapons, but do not otherwise constrain U.S. freedom of action, including intervention in defense of Taiwan. The United States faces no risk of nuclear retaliation if it does not use its own nuclear weapons first.

• The Chinese arsenal is likely to remain small enough to permit substantial reductions in U.S. and Russian force levels. One major constraint on reductions below the 1,700 to 2,200 range outlined in the Moscow Treaty is the possibility that China would attempt to "sprint up" to numerical parity with the United States. China's evident lack of interest in numerical parity suggests that the United States need not be concerned about such a scenario. In any event, the size of the current Chinese arsenal and the possibility of new fissile material constraints suggest that the United States could safely reduce its forces to several hundred warheads while enjoying years of warning before China could achieve numerical parity.

• Chinese operational practices emphasize the safety and security of nuclear warheads at the expense of pre-launch vulnerability. The risk of theft, accidental launch, or uncontrollable escalation involving Chinese nuclear weapons is negligible. Given concerns about a terrorist theft of a nuclear device, China's practice of keeping warheads within secure stockpiles provides a particularly substantial benefit to U.S. security.

• The small and relatively static size of the Chinese arsenal, as well as China's no-first-use pledge and other negative security assurances, minimize incentives for other states in the region to develop nuclear weapons or expand existing arsenals.

China does not appear to be moving away from its current nuclear posture. Beijing will probably continue to modernize its delivery vehicles and develop the CSS-X-10 (DF-31) family of mobile, solid-fueled ballistic missiles. It will also likely persist in testing ballistic missiles with penetration aids. China has undertaken periodic upgrades on the CSS-4, perhaps in order to extend the missile's service life beyond its anticipated 2010 withdrawal.[19] It also began replacing older CSS-2 MRBMs with the newer CSS-5 MRBM.

It is difficult to place much confidence in the U.S. intelligence community's prediction that China's introduction of new ballistic missiles will result in a large increase in the size of the Chinese arsenal. Past intelligence community estimates have exaggerated future Chinese deployments, in some cases egregiously. For example, the Defense Intelligence Agency in 1984 predicted that China would add about 100 ballistic missiles over the next decade, resulting in a force of approximately 250 nuclear warheads deployed on ballistic missiles and another 250 nuclear weapons in the form of nuclear gravity bombs and tactical nuclear weapons; instead the size of China's arsenal fell to below seventy warheads deployed exclusively on ballistic missiles. Although China is no longer reducing its nuclear arsenal, the size of China's operationally deployed nuclear force has remained stable since the introduction of ten new ICBMs between 1994 and 1997.

China's current modernization programs, set in place during the 1980s, will probably maintain China's deterrent even with the deployment of the U.S. Ballistic Missile Defense System. That system will have limited operational capability, particularly against the kind of countermeasures that China most likely deploys on its ballistic missiles. The U.S. Department of Defense remains many years away from deploying weapon systems capable of holding at risk China's hard and deeply buried targets and mobile ballistic missiles in a preventive attack. Shortcomings in U.S. command, control, and intelligence systems in particular will continue to leave a U.S. president short of the confidence necessary to conduct a disarming first strike against Chinese forces.

The possibility remains, however, that Chinese leaders will eventually lose confidence in their deterrent. A loss of confidence would likely result from many factors not related to quantitative measures of capability such as capability of a U.S. missile defense system to intercept Chinese ballistic missiles. Internal Chinese politics, rather than external pressure, is likely to be decisive. Yet, the actions of the United States are important. An

---

[19] Continuing CSS-4 upgrades are noted in *Annual Report on The Military Power of the People's Republic of China, Report to Congress Pursuant to The FY2000 National Defense Authorization Act* (Washington, DC: Department of Defense, July 2003), p. 31.

implicit goal of the 2001 *Nuclear Posture Review* is a crisis in confidence among Chinese leaders. The nuclear posture outlined in this document creates adverse incentives for China to change its nuclear posture. More important, should the confidence of China's leaders in their deterrent begin to fail, the United States could do many things to reassure China's leadership. Washington will not, of course, do so if a collapse in Chinese confidence is a policy goal.

Although a catastrophic loss of confidence in its deterrent would, in theory, open China up to nuclear coercion by the United States, this is unlikely to be the only result or an enduring relationship. Many options are available to China, including increasing the size of its arsenal, rushing mobile ballistic missiles into "operational training," keeping forces on alert, and developing asymmetric responses (anti-satellite weapons to target U.S. command, control, and intelligence assets). If the Chinese leadership operates under the calculation of risk described in this book, Beijing will not pursue these options in the near term except under duress. Each option improves China's deterrent effect only marginally, at the risk of weakening national control over the country's nuclear forces and initiating an action-reaction cycle with the United States. China's efforts at the CD suggest that the Chinese leadership recognizes the mutual interest it shares with the United States and is seeking to avoid this outcome. China's substantive support for a legal undertaking on preventing an arms race in outer space is a response to the impending modernization of U.S. strategic forces, including missile defense deployments. This position follows Chinese efforts in the 1990s to win a no-first-use pledge from the United States. This effort ended somewhat unsatisfactorily, from a Chinese perspective, in the 1998 mutual "non-targeting" agreement.[20] Further negotiations would induce a dialogue on strategic stability that is otherwise lacking in the Sino–U.S. relationship and would implicitly endorse a mutual deterrent relationship between the two countries. A formal agreement would enshrine mutual deterrence, much as the 1972 ABM Treaty did for the United States and the Soviet Union.

Although China appears to recognize the mutual interests at stake, the same cannot be said of the United States. Inaccurate predictions

---

[20] On earlier Chinese refusals to accept a non-targeting agreement in place of a no-first-use pledge, see Howard Diamond, "Sino-U.S. Summit Yields Modest Advances in Arms Control Agenda," *Arms Control Today* (June/July 1998), p. 23.

about the future size, configuration, and operational doctrine of Chinese strategic forces suggest that American analysts and policymakers have been operating with a poor understanding of Chinese attitudes toward nuclear weapons and arms control. Many in the U.S. intelligence community have consistently, and incorrectly, predicted that China would deploy a larger, more diverse force and abandon its restrictive operational doctrine of no-first use. These incorrect predictions included the particularly egregious failure to anticipate the impending reduction in Chinese strategic forces between 1984 and 1994.

China's relatively stable force deployments since the late 1990s and its more assertive arms control diplomacy in Geneva may represent an opportunity to build a more stable nuclear relationship between the two countries. Whether or not this occurs will depend, in part, on whether the United States will accept a deterrent relationship with China. Vulnerability is a fact—Chinese technical capabilities and Beijing's commitment to its nuclear posture are sufficient to preserve a small deterrent. Whether the U.S. political system recognizes this fact is another question.

Changes in the U.S. force posture will probably not be the decisive factor affecting the future direction of China's nuclear forces. This does not mean, however, that the United States does not have the opportunity to play a significant role. The United States has a considerable number of options to reinforce the commitment among China's leaders to Marshal Nie's "minimum means of reprisal."

Perhaps the most basic suggestion is to resume the dialogue on strategic issues that began in the context of deliberations among the nuclear power states during the negotiation of the Comprehensive Test Ban Treaty. Such deliberations have been shuttered in recent years owing to the lack of progress at the Conference on Disarmament in Geneva and bilateral disputes between the United States and China over allegations of nuclear espionage. A welcome respite in this regard was Secretary of Defense Donald Rumsfeld's October 2005 visit to the headquarters of China's Second Artillery, where he reportedly received a briefing on the organization and mission of China's strategic forces. Rusmfeld also spoke with the commander of the Second Artillery, who reiterated China's position on no-first use.[21] The Bush administration should seek more regular

---

[21] Paul Eckert, "China Allows Rumsfeld Peek at Secretive Military," Reuters (October 19, 2005), np.

exchanges of this kind at less senior levels. The Second Artillery, however, is merely one—and not necessarily the main—voice regarding China's strategic posture and arms control diplomacy. Historically, the Chinese military appears to have played a relatively minor role in the discussion of policy questions regarding China's strategic forces, although this may change with the increasing professionalization of the People's Liberation Army. The process by which China's policymakers decide nuclear weapons policy remains somewhat unclear, although weapons laboratories within China appear to play an important role. Contact between these laboratories and their U.S. counterparts under the U.S.–China Lab-to-Lab Technical Exchange Program was suspended in the wake of the congressional espionage investigation that produced the Cox Report and has not resumed.[22] A resumption of such contacts would provide the United States a greater opportunity to influence the future direction of China's strategic forces.

These contacts could include discussions on a number of policies that would presumably make clear to China's leaders that their minimum means of reprisal provide a substantial measure of deterrence against a resumption of the "nuclear blackmail" of the 1950s—something no future U.S. Administration is likely to revive anyway.

A first step is simply to resume work on the arms control agenda agreed to during the 1995 NPT Review Conference, including ratification of the Comprehensive Test Ban Treaty and the negotiation of a verifiable Fissile Material Cut-off Treaty in the Conference on Disarmament. These are feasible steps that would provide not only a forum for strategic dialogue, but directly address U.S. and Chinese concerns about the development of new nuclear weapons and the number of nuclear weapons worldwide. Both treaties impose significant technical burdens that could usefully be the subject of dialogue between the two countries.

The United States might also reconsider China's proposal for a bilateral no-first-use pledge to follow the non-targeting agreement that Presi-

---

[22] On "lab-to-lab" cooperation, see Nancy Prindle, "The US-China Lab-to-Lab Technical Exchange Program," *Nonproliferation Review,* vol. 5 (Spring–Summer 1998), pp. 111–118; Shirley A. Kan, *China: Suspected Acquisition of U.S. Nuclear Weapon Secrets,* RL30143 (Washington, DC: Congressional Research Service, February 1, 2006), pp. 61–63; and Li Bin, "Appendix 3A. China and Nuclear Transparency," in Nicholas Zarimpas, ed., *Transparency in Nuclear Warheads and Materials: The Political and Technical Dimensions* (Oxford: Oxford University Press, 2003), pp. 50–57.

dents Clinton and Jiang Zemin signed in 1998. China's no-first-use pledge is not merely a constraint that China accepts for its own forces, but it is rather an aspect of the nation's deterrent strategy. In stating that China would "not be the first to use nuclear weapons at any time or under any circumstances," China also reiterated the dictum that "atom bombs are a paper tiger" and denied the "omnipotence" of nuclear weapons.[23] China's early leaders were advancing a general proposition about the purposes for which any nation's nuclear weapons could—and could not—be used. If Washington were to accept a bilateral no-first-use pledge, two conclusions would logically follow. First, it would mean that the United States accepted the fundamental adequacy of China's nuclear forces within their current, limited role. Second, as a corollary to the first principle, the United States would not be coerced by Chinese efforts to increase the number or capability of its nuclear weapons.

A bilateral no-first-use pledge reflects a very different philosophical approach to meeting the challenge posed by China's nuclear forces than does the 2001 *Nuclear Posture Review*, which implicitly recommends at least the option of the first use of U.S. strategic, including nuclear, forces in a conflict with China. The *Nuclear Posture Review* implies that China's future force modernization could produce two challenges to the United States: a "sprint" to numerical parity with a declining number of U.S. strategic forces and the coercive use of China's nuclear forces in a crisis over Taiwan. Such scenarios are possible, but—in light of the preceding arguments—extremely unlikely given China's current force posture and past decision-making. The argument advanced in this book suggests that if U.S. policymakers are truly interested in discouraging a Chinese sprint to parity or the development of a Chinese ballistic missile force that could undertake coercive operations, a bilateral no-first-use pledge is a policy choice far superior to the vision for nuclear forces outlined in the *Nuclear Posture Review*. The Chinese leadership chose its arsenal in part on the belief that the United States would not be foolish enough to use nuclear weapons against China in a conflict. By asserting that Washington *may be* that foolish and by attempting to exploit the weaknesses inherent in China's decision to rely on a small and vulnerable force, the recent shifts in U.S. nuclear policy create incentives for Beijing to increase the

---

[23] On the current role of China's no-first-use pledge, see Pan Zhenqiang, "China Insistence on No-First-Use of Nuclear Weapons," *China Security*, no. 1 (Autumn 2005), pp. 5–9.

size, readiness, and usability of its nuclear forces. The direction of strategic policy is, therefore, fundamentally incompatible with proposals to reassure China that its current nuclear forces are adequate.

Larger, more ready Chinese nuclear forces are not in the best interest of the United States. In the midst of a crisis, any attempt by Beijing to ready its ballistic missiles for a first strike against the United States, let alone to actually fire one, would be suicide. The only risk that China's current nuclear arsenal poses to the United States is an unauthorized nuclear launch—something the U.S. intelligence community concludes "is highly unlikely" under China's current operational practices. That might change, however, if China were to keep its nuclear forces on alert, as the United States and Russia do even today to demonstrate the credibility of their nuclear deterrents. China might also increase its strategic forces or deploy theater nuclear forces that could be used early in a conflict; these developments might alarm India and have predictable secondary effects on Pakistan.

So far, none of the U.S. intelligence community's dire predictions about China's nuclear forces have come to pass. Chinese nuclear forces today look remarkably like they have for decades. The picture of China's nuclear arsenal that emerges from this study suggests a country that—at least in the nuclear field—deploys smaller, less ready forces than are within its capabilities. That reflects a choice to seek the "minimum means of reprisal"—a nuclear deterrent that sacrifices offensive capability in exchange for maximizing political control and minimizing economic cost. This decision, in retrospect, seems eminently sensible. The great mystery is not that Beijing chose such an arsenal, but why anyone would be eager to do anything that might change it.

Selected Documents Submitted by the Chinese Delegation to the Conference on Disarmament, 1985–2006

APPENDIX A

CONFERENCE ON DISARMAMENT

CD/579
19 March 1985

ENGLISH
Original: CHINESE

China

Working Paper

China's Basic Position on the Prevention of an Arms
Race in Outer Space

1. With the intensification of the development of anti-satellite and anti-ballistic missile weapons, the question of preventing an arms race in outer space is becoming ever more urgent. Resolution A/39/59 adopted at the thirty-ninth session of the United Nations General Assembly by an overwhelming majority with only one abstention fully reflects the grave concern and anxiety of the international community about an arms race in outer space.

2. Consistent with its stand against any arms race, China is opposed to an arms race in outer space. It holds that the exploration and use of outer space should in the interest of mankind serve to promote the economic, scientific and cultural development of all countries. China fully subscribes to the objective of "the non-militarization of outer space" and "the exclusive use of outer space for peaceful purposes."

3. In principle, "the non-militarization of outer space" requires both space weapons with actual lethal or destructive power and military satellites of all types be limited and prohibited.

4. In view of their complexities, the limitation and prohibition of military satellites may be left to be considered and resolved at an appropriate time in future.

5. At the present stage, the primary objective in the efforts to prevent an arms race in outer space should be "the de-weaponization of outer space", i.e. banning the development, testing, production, deployment and use of any space weapons and the thorough destruction of all space weapons.

6. The aforesaid space weapons should include all devices or installations either space-, land-, sea-, or atmosphere-based, which are designed to attack or damage spacecraft in outer space, or disrupt their normal functioning, or change their orbits; and all devices or installations based in space (including those based on the moon and other celestial bodies) which are designed to attack or damage objects in the atmosphere, or on land, or at sea, or disrupt their normal functioning.

GE.85-60812

7. While certain restrictions on the military activities in outer space have been provided by the existing international legal instruments regarding outer space, especially the 1967 Treaty on Principles Governing the Activities of States in the Exploration and Use of Outer Space, Including the Moon and Other Celestial Bodies, these documents, however, because of their limited scope, are far from being adequate for the total prevention of an arms race in outer space. It is, therefore, necessary to undertake an analysis and examination of the major existing instruments, and to formulate new provisions and conclude new agreements.

8. The two Powers which possess the greatest space capabilities and are right now intensifying their efforts in the development and testing of space weapons bear special responsibilities for the prevention of an arms race in outer space. They should demonstrate genuine political will, conduct their bilateral negotiations in good faith and keep the Conference on Disarmament appropriately informed of the progress of the negotiations.

9. The prevention of an arms race in outer space is a priority agenda item of the Conference on Disarmament. As the single multilateral negotiating forum on disarmament, the Conference on Disarmament should establish a subsidiary body and undertake negotiations on this subject. The mandate of the subsidiary body should have a clear ultimate objective, i.e. the conclusion of an agreement or agreements and at the same time, may include an exploratory stage to identify issues.

10. In order to create conditions and an atmosphere favourable for negotiations, all countries with space capabilities should refrain from developing, testing and deploying space weapons.

CONFERENCE ON DISARMAMENT

CD/1606
9 February 2000
ENGLISH
Original: CHINESE

LETTER DATED 9 FEBRUARY 2000 FROM THE PERMANENT
REPRESENTATIVE OF CHINA TO THE CONFERENCE ON DISARMAMENT
ADDRESSED TO THE SECRETARY-GENERAL OF THE CONFERENCE
TRANSMITTING A WORKING PAPER ENTITLED "CHINA'S POSITION ON
AND SUGGESTIONS FOR WAYS TO ADDRESS THE ISSUE OF PREVENTION
OF AN ARMS RACE IN OUTER SPACE AT THE CONFERENCE ON
DISARMAMENT"

On instructions from the Chinese Government, I have the honour to attach herewith a working paper entitled "China's position on and Suggestions for Ways to Address the Issue of Prevention of an Arms Race in Outer Space at the Conference on Disarmament".

I would be grateful if this document could be issued and circulated as an official document of the Conference on Disarmament.

(Signed)   Hu Xiaodi
Ambassador for Disarmament Affairs
Head of the Delegation of China to
the Conference on Disarmament

GE.00-60481 (E)

CD/1606
page 2

China

Working Paper

CHINA'S POSITION ON AND SUGGESTIONS FOR WAYS TO ADDRESS
THE ISSUE OF PREVENTION OF AN ARMS RACE IN OUTER SPACE
AT THE CONFERENCE ON DISARMAMENT

Outer space belongs to all mankind. All countries have equal rights in the exploration and use of outer space for peaceful purposes although their levels of economic and scientific development may differ. It is the shared desire of all mankind to forestall the spread of weapons and an arms race in outer space.

Some people believe that since currently there is no arms race in outer space, the CD has no need to discuss its prevention or negotiate the conclusion of international legal instruments in this regard. However, history and reality have both shown not only that there are indeed attempts, programmes and moves unilaterally to seek military and strategic superiority in or control over outer space but that there have been new developments in this respect. Such development, if unchecked, may lead to the weaponization of outer space in the near future or even to a multilateral arms race in outer space. Therefore, it is a present and pressing necessity for the international community to take effective measures to stop such negative developments.

I. OUR VIEWS ON HOW TO ADDRESS THE ISSUE OF PAROS
AT THE CONFERENCE ON DISARMAMENT

As the single multilateral disarmament negotiating forum, the Conference on Disarmament (Conference) should concentrate on the most pressing and prominent issues in international arms control and disarmament, the ones that have the greatest bearing on global peace and security in the twenty-first century. PAROS is one such important issue, and should therefore be a top priority at the Conference. The Conference should play a primary role in the negotiations to prevent any form of arms race in outer space.

At its fifty-fourth session the United Nations General Assembly once again adopted, by an overwhelming majority, a resolution on PAROS. It was reaffirmed that negotiating an international agreement or agreements to prevent an arms race in outer space remains a priority task of the CD's Ad Hoc Committee. The fact that the resolution was adopted without opposition reflects the common aspiration and insistent demand of the international community to prevent an arms race in outer space.

The General Assembly also adopted at its fifty-fourth session, and also by an overwhelming majority, a resolution on preservation of and compliance with the Anti-Ballistic Missile Treaty, an issue that is related to the prevention of an arms race in outer space. In the resolution the General Assembly recognizes the historical role of the 1972 Treaty as a cornerstone for maintaining global peace and security and strategic stability, reaffirms its continued validity and relevance in the current international situation and supports further efforts

CD/1606
page 3

by the international community in the light of emerging developments with the goal of safeguarding the inviolability and integrity of the ABM Treaty in which the international community bears strong interest.

Since PAROS was put on the CD agenda in 1982, the Conference has, through the establishment of the Ad Hoc Committee and other means, held discussions on definitions, principles, existing treaties and confidence-building measures, and accumulated experience in this field, preparing the ground for future work in this area. With the accelerated development of outer space weapons, anti-ballistic missiles and other weapon systems, individual countries have stepped up efforts to secure military superiority in outer space and have mapped out and are pursuing plans to secure military superiority on the ground from space. In these circumstances, preventing outer space from becoming a new venue for an arms race without prejudice to its peaceful uses has obviously become the most important and pressing task of the Conference.

To accomplish this, the Conference must first re-establish the Ad Hoc Committee under agenda item 3 to negotiate and conclude an international legal instrument prohibiting the testing, deployment and use of weapons, weapon systems and components in outer space so as to prevent the weaponization of, and an arms race in, outer space.

In carrying out its mandate, the Ad Hoc Committee must take into account all relevant developments and specific proposals, present and future. As a preliminary step towards the negotiation of an international legal instrument, it might discuss and review all pertinent issues, including current military activities in outer space and related developments, their influence on the prevention of an arms race in outer space; shortcomings in the existing international instruments; and the basic elements of the future international legal instrument.

The Chinese delegation has taken note of the various ideas and suggestions on PAROS put forward in the CD. China believes that the re-established Ad Hoc Committee should be an open-ended, all-embracing mechanism where all participants may air and discuss different views. It should set as its ultimate goal and clear mandate the negotiation and conclusion of one or several international legal instruments to prevent the weaponization of and an arms race in outer space.

II. OUR VIEWS ON THE EXISTING INTERNATIONAL LEGAL INSTRUMENTS CONCERNING PAROS

A number of international legal instruments on the peaceful uses of outer space and the prevention of an arms race in outer space have been concluded.

The 1963 Treaty Banning Nuclear Weapon Tests in the Atmosphere, in Outer Space and Under Water prohibits any nuclear weapon test explosion in outer space. The 1996 Comprehensive Nuclear Test Ban Treaty prohibits any nuclear weapon test explosion in any circumstances.

According to the 1967 Treaty on Principles Governing the Activities of States in the Exploration and Use of Outer Space, including the Moon and other Celestial Bodies, outer space, including the moon and other celestial bodies, is not subject to national appropriation by claim of

CD/1606
page 4

sovereignty, by means of use or occupation, or by any other means. States Parties to the Treaty undertake not to place in orbit around the Earth any objects carrying nuclear weapons or any other kinds of weapons of mass destruction, install such weapons on celestial bodies, or station such weapons in outer space in any other manner. The establishment of military bases, installations and fortifications, the testing of any type of weapons and the conduct of military manoeuvres on celestial bodies is forbidden.

The 1972 Treaty between the United States and the Union of Soviet Socialist Republics on the Limitation of Anti-Ballistic Missile Systems prohibits the development, testing and deployment of space-based ABM systems or components.

Besides these, the 1972 Convention on International Liability for Damage Caused by Space Objects, the 1975 Convention on Registration of Objects Launched into Outer Space and the 1979 Agreement Governing the Activities of States on the Moon and other Celestial Bodies all contain provisions on outer space activities which have helped to constrain some aspects of military activities in outer space to some extent.

However, these instruments have been ineffective in preventing the weaponization of and an arms race in outer space. Some have imposed limited prohibitions and contained many loopholes and ambiguities. Some have not been fully complied with or are in danger of being violated, amended or even abrogated. Most crucially, as they have failed to reflect the latest developments in aerospace technology they cannot prevent the potential weaponization of outer space or an arms race in outer space in the twenty-first century.

The Chinese delegation believes that the most direct and effective way to prevent the weaponization of and an arms race in outer space is to negotiate and conclude new international legal instruments while strictly observing the existing bilateral and multilateral agreements.

III. CHINA'S BASIC POSITION ON PAROS

China has always opposed arms races, in outer space and elsewhere. It maintains that the exploration and use of outer space should only serve to promote countries' economic, scientific and cultural development and benefit all mankind.

With the use of military satellites, outer space has already been militarized to some extent. Military satellites involve rather complex issues and their role should not be all together negated. Therefore, the primary goal at present in our efforts to prevent the weaponization of and an arms race in outer space is to ban the testing, deployment and use of weapons, weapon systems and components in outer space.

What should be particularly emphasized is that the Powers with the greatest space capabilities bear a special responsibility for preventing the weaponization of and an arms race in outer space and ensuring the use of space for peaceful purposes. Pending the conclusion of a new multilateral legal instrument on the prevention of an arms race in outer space, all countries concerned should undertake not to test, deploy or use any weapons, weapon systems or components in outer space.

IV. TENTATIVE IDEAS ON NEW INTERNATIONAL LEGAL INSTRUMENTS

The Chinese delegation tentatively suggests that the new international legal instruments to prevent the weaponization of and an arms race in outer space, in whatever form or by whatever name, might contain the following basic elements:

(i)   Purposes: to prevent the weaponization of and an arms race in outer space, and to use outer space for peaceful purposes.

(ii) Basic obligations: not to test, deploy or use weapons, weapon systems or components. Consideration could also be given to an article on "permissible activities" thus helping to distinguish between activities that are prohibited and those that are not, and thereby safeguarding States Parties' lawful right to utilize outer space for peaceful purposes.

(iii) An article on definitions, providing clear definitions of the concepts mentioned, e.g. "outer space", "space weapons", "weapon systems" and "components of weapon systems".

(iv) Provision for appropriate national implementation measures and the designation or establishment of organizations to ensure that States Parties implement the instruments consistently and effectively.

(v)   An article on international cooperation in the peaceful use of outer space promoting international exchanges, technical assistance and cooperation for peaceful purposes so that all countries can share in the economic and technological benefits of scientific advances in outer space, and outer space truly serves all mankind.

(vi) Verification: we must first consider fully how technically feasible it is, and on that basis determine whether to use inspections or alternative means to prevent treaty violations.

(vii) Establishment of an appropriate mechanism for consultations, clarifications and resolution of possible disputes in order to appropriately address such suspicions and disputes as might arise among States Parties.

(viii) Appropriate, rational and workable confidence-building measures to enhance mutual trust among States Parties and forestall unnecessary suspicion about particular activities.

(ix) The procedural articles commonly found in international legal instruments dealing with amendment, length of validity, signature, ratification, entry into force, depository and authentic texts. These may of course also have to resolve some sensitive and key issues.

CD/1606
page 6

The Chinese delegation wishes to emphasize that these are only tentative ideas that need to be developed. Our aim in putting them forward is to give all participants food for thought, pool our collective wisdom and encourage a fuller, more detailed examination of the relevant issues at the Conference. We will participate in such discussions and negotiations with an open mind, listening to and accepting good ideas and proposals from all parties and striving unremittingly to prevent the weaponization of and an arms race in outer space and to ensure the continued peaceful use of outer space for the benefit of all mankind.

- - - - -

CONFERENCE ON DISARMAMENT

CD/1645
6 June 2001

ENGLISH
Original: CHINESE and
ENGLISH

LETTER DATED 5 JUNE 2001 FROM THE PERMANENT REPRESENTATIVE OF CHINA
ADDRESSED TO THE SECRETARY-GENERAL OF THE CONFERENCE ON DISARMAMENT
TRANSMITTING A WORKING PAPER ENTITLED "POSSIBLE ELEMENTS OF THE FUTURE
INTERNATIONAL LEGAL INSTRUMENT ON THE PREVENTION OF THE WEAPONIZATION
OF OUTER SPACE"

Upon the instruction from the Chinese government, I have the honor to attach herewith the Chinese and English text of a working paper entitled *"Possible Elements of the Future International Legal Instrument on the Prevention of the Weaponization of Outer Space"*.

I would be grateful if this document could be issued and circulated as an official document of the Conference on Disarmament.

(Signed):   Hu Xiaodi
Ambassador for Disarmament Affairs
Head of Delegation of China to
The Conference on Disarmament

GE.01-62244

CD/1645
Page 2

Delegation of China

Possible Elements of the Future International Legal Instrument
on the Prevention of the Weaponization of Outer Space

China is dedicated to promoting the international community to negotiate and conclude an international legal instrument on the prevention of the weaponization of and an arms race in outer space. In February 2000, the Chinese delegation submitted to the Conference on Disarmament a working paper (CD/1606, 9 February 2000) entitled *"China's Position on and Suggestions for Ways to Address the Issue of Prevention of an Arms Race in Outer Space at the Conference on Disarmament"*, which outlined China's tentative ideas on the above mentioned international legal instrument. China has further substantiated and developed these ideas. In our view, the future legal instrument may include, *inter alia*, the following elements:

• • •

I. Possible Name of the Instrument

-Treaty on the Prevention of the Weaponization of Outer Space.

II. Preamble

-Outer space is the common heritage of mankind. It is the common aspiration of mankind to use outer space for peaceful purposes.

-Outer space is playing an ever-increasing role in future development of mankind.

-There is a potential danger of armament development and combatant activities being extended to outer space.

-Prevention of the weaponization of and an arms race in outer space becomes a realistic and pressing task facing the international community.

-The United Nations General Assembly has adopted a series of resolutions on peaceful uses of outer space and prevention of an arms race in outer space, which have provided a prerequisite for and a basis of the prevention of the weaponization of and an arms race in outer space.

-The existing arms limitation and disarmament agreements relevant to outer space, including those bilateral ones, and the existing legal regime concerning the use of outer space, have played a positive role in the peaceful use of outer space and the regulating of activities in outer space. These agreements and regime should be strictly complied with. However, these agreements and legal regime are unable to effectively prevent the weaponization of and an arms race in outer space.

-For the benefits of mankind, outer space shall always be used for peaceful purposes, and shall never be allowed to become a battlefield.

-Only strict prevention of the weaponization of outer space can eliminate the emerging danger of an arms race in outer space and fully safeguard the security of outer space properties of all countries, which is indispensable for maintaining global strategic balance, world peace and security of all countries.

III. Basic Obligations

- Not to test, deploy or use in outer space any weapons, weapon systems or their components.

- Not to test, deploy or use on land, in sea or atmosphere any weapons, weapon systems or their components that can be used for war-fighting in outer space.

- Not to use any objects launched into orbit to directly participate in combatant activities.

- Not to assist or encourage other countries, regions, international organizations or entities to participate in activities prohibited by this legal instrument.

IV. Definitions

- *Outer space* is the space above the earth's atmosphere, i.e. space 100km above the sea level of the earth.

- *Weapons* are devices or facilities that strike, destroy or disrupt directly the normal functions of a target by various destructive ways.

- *Weapon systems* are the collective of weapons and their indispensably linked parts that jointly accomplish battle missions.

- *Components of weapon systems* are subsystems that directly and indispensably involved in accomplishing battle missions.

V. National Measures for Implementation

-Each country shall, in accordance with its constitutional process, take any

CD/1645
Page 4

necessary measures to prohibit or prevent any activities in violation of this legal instrument on its territory or in any other place under its jurisdiction or control.

VI. Peaceful Use of Outer Space

-This legal instrument shall not be construed as impeding scientific exploration in outer space by all its States Parties or other military uses not prohibited by this legal instrument.

-Each country shall abide by general principles of international laws in conducting outer space activities, and shall not undermine the sovereignty, security and interests of other countries.

VII. Confidence Building Measures

- To enhance mutual trust, each State Party shall promulgate its space programme, declare the locations and scopes of its space launch sites, the property and parameters of objects to be launched into outer space, and notify the launching activities.

VIII. Verification Measures

(Needs further consideration and development)

IX. Settlement of Disputes

- If a State Party suspects treaty violation by another State Party, States Parties concerned shall undertake to consult and cooperate to resolve the issue. Each State Party shall have the right to request clarification from the suspected State Party. The suspected State Party is obliged to provide relevant information to clarify the matter.

- If consultation and clarification fail to produce satisfactory results for the States Parties concerned, the suspecting State Party can file charges to the executive organization of this legal instrument. The charges shall include the supporting evidence as well as the request for the organization to review the matter.

- Each State Party undertakes to cooperate in the investigation by the executive organization of this legal instrument in accordance with the request it has received.

X. Executive Organization of this Legal Instrument

In order to achieve the purposes and objectives of this legal instrument, and

CD/1645
Page 5

ensure compliance with the obligations of this instrument, the States Parties hereby establish an executive organization of this legal instrument, whose duties are, inter alia, as follows:

- To receive charges of non-compliance by States Parties.

- To investigate whether there are non-compliant activities.

- To organize consultations on non-compliance concerns between States Parties concerned.

- To urge States Parties that have violated this legal instrument to take measures to stop non-compliant activities and make up for the consequences arising therefrom.

XI. Amendments

- Any State Party may propose amendments to this legal instrument. The text of any proposed amendment shall be submitted to the depositary who shall circulate it to all the State Parties. Thereupon, if requested to do so by one-third or more of the States Parties, the depositary shall convene a conference, to which he shall invite all the States Parties, to consider such an amendment.

- Any amendment to this legal instrument must be approved by a majority of vote of all its States Parties. The amendment shall enter into force for all the States Parties upon the deposit of such instruments of ratification by a majority of all the States Parties.

XII. Duration and Withdrawal

- This legal instrument shall be of unlimited duration.

- Each State Party to this legal instrument shall, in exercising its national sovereignty, have the right to withdraw from this legal instrument if it decides that extraordinary events, related to the subject matter of this legal instrument, have jeopardized the supreme interests of its country. It shall give notice of such withdrawal to the depositary of this legal instrument six months in advance. Such notice shall include a statement of the extraordinary events it regards as having jeopardized its supreme interests.

XIII. Signature and Ratification

-This legal instrument shall be open for signature by all States at United Nations headquarters in New York. Any State which does not sign this legal instrument before its entry into force may accede to it at any time.

CD/1645
Page 6

-This legal instrument shall be subject to ratification by signatory states. Instruments of ratification or accession shall be deposited with the Secretary-General of the United Nations.

XIV. Entry into Force

- This legal instrument shall enter into force upon the deposit of instruments of ratification by XX States, including the Permanent Member States of the United Nations Security Council.

- For those States whose instruments of ratification or accession are deposited after the entry into force of this legal instrument, it shall enter into force on the date of the deposit of their instruments of ratification or accession.

XV. Authentic Texts

-This legal instrument, of which the Arabic, Chinese, English, French, Russian and Spanish texts are equally authentic, shall be deposited with the Secretary-General of the United Nations, who shall send certified copies thereof to all signatory and acceding States.

*   *   *

The Chinese delegation would like to reiterate that the above-mentioned elements are still very tentative. Further revision, amendment, improvement and perfection are needed. We are ready, in an open attitude, to work with other delegations, to conclude at an early date a legal instrument aimed at preventing the weaponization of and an arms race in outer space, through hard work and serious negotiations.

CONFERENCE ON DISARMAMENT

CD/1679

28 June 2002

ENGLISH
Original: CHINESE, ENGLISH
And RUSSIAN

LETTER DATED 27 JUNE 2002 FROM THE PERMANENT REPRESENTATIVE OF THE
PEOPLE'S REPUBLIC OF CHINA AND THE PERMANENT REPRESENTATIVE OF THE
RUSSIAN FEDERATION TO THE CONFERENCE ON DISARMAMENT ADDRESSED TO
THE SECRETARY-GENERAL OF THE CONFERENCE TRANSMITTING THE CHINESE,
ENGLISH AND RUSSIAN TEXTS OF A WORKING PAPER ENTITLED "POSSIBLE
ELEMENTS FOR A FUTURE INTERNATIONAL LEGAL AGREEMENT ON THE
PREVENTION OF THE DEPLOYMENT OF WEAPONS IN OUTER SPACE, THE THREAT
OR USE OF FORCE AGAINST OUTER SPACE OBJECTS"

We have the honour to transmit the Chinese, Russian and English texts of a working paper
entitled "Possible Elements for a Future International Legal Agreement on the Prevention of the
Deployment of Weapons in Outer Space, The Threat or Use of Force Against Outer Space Objects".

We would be grateful if this document could be issued and circulated as an official document of
the Conference on Disarmament.

(Signed:)   HU Xiaodi   Leonid A. SKOTNIKOV
                     Ambassador   Ambassador
                     Head of Delegation of the   Permanent Representative of the
                     People's Republic of China to the   Russian Federation to the
                     Conference on Disarmament   Conference on Disarmament

GE.02-42978

WORKING PAPER

PRESENTED BY THE DELEGATIONS OF CHINA, THE RUSSIAN FEDERATION,
VIETNAM, INDONESIA, BELARUS, ZIMBABWE AND SYRIAN ARAB REPUBLIC

**Possible Elements for a Future International Legal Agreement
on the Prevention of the Deployment of Weapons in Outer Space,
the Threat or Use of Force Against Outer Space Objects**

I. Possible Name of Such Agreement

Treaty on the Prevention of the Deployment of Weapons in Outer Space, the threat
or Use of Force Against Outer Space Objects

II. Preamble

Outer space is the common heritage of mankind and plays an ever-increasing role
in its future development.

There exists a potential danger of an armed confrontation and combatant activities
being extended to outer space.

The prevention of the deployment of weapons and an arms race in outer space
becomes a pressing task facing the international community.

The United Nations General Assembly has adopted a series of resolutions on
peaceful use of outer space and prevention of an arms race in outer space, which have
provided a prerequisite and basis for the prevention of the deployment of weapons and
an arms race in outer space.

The existing agreements on arms control and disarmament relevant to outer space,
including those bilateral ones, and the existing legal regimes concerning outer space have
played a positive role in the peaceful use of outer space and in regulating outer space
activities. These agreements and legal regimes should be strictly complied with.
However, they are unable to effectively prevent the deployment of weapons and an arms
race in outer space.

For the benefit of mankind, outer space shall be used for peaceful purposes, and it
shall never be allowed to become a sphere of military confrontation.

Only a treaty-based prohibition of the deployment of weapons in outer space and
the prevention of the threat or use of force against outer space objects can eliminate the
emerging threat of an arms race in outer space and ensure the security for outer space
assets of all countries which is an essential condition for the maintenance of world peace.

CD/1679
Page 3

III. Basic Obligations

Not to place in orbit around the Earth any objects carrying any kinds of weapons, not to install such weapons on celestial bodies, or not to station such weapons in outer space in any other manner.

Not to resort to the threat or use of force against outer space objects.

Not to assist or encourage other States, groups of States, international organizations to participate in activities prohibited by this Treaty.

IV. National Measures for the Implementation of the Treaty

Each State Party to the Treaty shall, in accordance with its constitutional process, take any measures necessary to prevent or prohibit any activity contrary to this Treaty on its territory, or in any other place under its jurisdiction or control.

V. The Use of Outer Space for Peaceful and Other Military Purposes

This Treaty shall not be construed as impeding the research and use of outer space for peaceful purposes or other military uses not prohibited by this Treaty.

Each State Party to the Treaty shall carry out activities in outer space in accordance with the general principles of international law and shall not violate the sovereignty and security of other States.

VI. Confidence Building Measures

To enhance mutual trust, each State Party to the Treaty shall promulgate its space programme, declare the locations and scopes of its space launch sites, the property and parameters of objects being launched into outer space, and notify the launching activities.

VII. Settlement of Disputes

If a suspicion arises against any State Party to the Treaty that it is violating the Treaty, the suspecting State Party, or a group of the suspecting State Parties to this Treaty shall conduct consultations and cooperate with the suspected State Party to this Treaty in order to settle down the aroused suspicion. Each suspecting State Party to this Treaty shall have the right to request clarification from the suspected State Party to this Treaty, whereas the suspected State Party to this Treaty shall undertake to provide requested clarifications.

CD/1679
Page 4

If consultations or clarification fail to settle down the dispute, the suspicion that has aroused shall be referred to the executive organization of the Treaty for consideration together with relevant arguments.

Each State Party to this Treaty shall undertake to cooperate in the settlement of the suspicion that has aroused by the executive organization of the Treaty.

VIII. The Executive Organization of the Treaty

To promote the objectives and implementation of the provisions of this Treaty, the States Parties to the Treaty shall hereby establish the executive organization of the Treaty, which shall:

(a) receive for consideration inquires by any State Party or a group of States Parties to the Treaty related to the suspicion, which has aroused by the violation of this Treaty by any State Party to the Treaty;

(b) consider matters concerning the compliance with the obligations taken by the States Parties to this Treaty;

(c) organize and conduct consultations with the States Parties to the Treaty with a view to settling down the suspicion that has aroused against any State Party to the Treaty concerning its violation of this Treaty;

(d) take necessary measures to end violation of this Treaty by any State Party to the Treaty.

IX. Amendments to the Treaty

Any State Party to this Treaty may propose amendments to the Treaty. The text of any proposed amendment to this Treaty shall be submitted to the Depositary Governments who shall promptly circulate it to all the States Parties to the Treaty. Upon the request of at least one third of the States Parties to the Treaty, the Depositary Governments shall convene a conference to which all the States Parties shall be invited to consider the proposed amendment.

Any amendment to this Treaty must be approved by a majority of the votes of all the States Parties to the Treaty. The amendment shall enter into force for all the States Parties to the Treaty in accordance with the procedures governing the entry into force of this Treaty.

X. Duration of the Treaty and Withdrawal from the Treaty

The Treaty shall be of unlimited duration.

Each State Party to the Treaty shall, in exercising its state sovereignty, have the right to withdraw from this Treaty if it decides that extraordinary events, related to the subject matter of this Treaty, have jeopardized its supreme interests. It shall give notice to the Depository Governments of the decision adopted six months in advance of the withdrawal from the Treaty. Such a notification shall include a statement of the extraordinary events, which the notifying State Party to the Treaty regards as having jeopardized its supreme interests.

XI. Signature and Ratification of the Treaty

This Treaty shall be open for signature by all States at United Nations Headquarters in New York. Any State, which does not sign this Treaty before its entry into force, may accede to it at any time.

The Treaty shall be subject to ratification by signatory States in accordance with their constitutional process. Instruments of ratification or accession shall be deposited with the Depositary Governments.

This Treaty shall be registered by the Depositary Governments pursuant to Article 102 of the Charter of the United Nations.

XII. Entry into Force of the Treaty

This Treaty shall enter into force upon the deposit of instruments of ratification by twenty States, including all Permanent Member States of the United Nations Security Council.

For States whose instruments of ratification or accession are deposited after the entry into force of this Treaty, it shall enter into force on the date of the deposit of their instruments of ratification or accession.

XIII. Authentic texts of the Treaty

This Treaty, of which the Arabic, Chinese, English, French, Russian and Spanish texts are equally authentic, shall be deposited in the archives of the Depositary Governments, who shall send duly certified copies thereof to all the signatory and acceding States.

CONFERENCE ON DISARMAMENT

CD/1769
14 February 2006

ENGLISH
Original: CHINESE, ENGLISH
and RUSSIAN

LETTER DATED 14 FEBRUARY 2006 FROM THE PERMANENT REPRESENTATIVE
OF THE RUSSIAN FEDERATION AND THE PERMANENT REPRESENTATIVE OF
CHINA TO THE CONFERENCE ON DISARMAMENT ADDRESSED TO THE
SECRETARY-GENERAL OF THE CONFERENCE TRANSMITTING A
COMPILATION OF COMMENTS AND SUGGESTION TO THE WORKING PAPER
ON PAROS CONTAINED IN DOCUMENT CD/1679 DATED 28 JUNE 2002

We have the honour to transmit the Chinese, Russian and English texts of the working paper "Compilation of Comments and Suggestions to the CD PAROS Working Paper CD/1679)", prepared by the Russian and Chinese delegations to the CD.

We would be grateful if this letter and the attached working paper could be issued and circulated as official documents of the Conference on Disarmament.

(Signed:)   Valery Loshchinin
Ambassador
Permanent Representative of the
Russian Federation to the
Conference on Disarmament

(Signed:)   Cheng Jingye
Ambassador for Disarmament Affairs
Head of Delegation of the
People's Republic of China
to the Conference on Disarmament

GE.06-60310

Compilation of Comments and Suggestions to the CD
PAROS Working Paper (CD/1679)[1]

(Second, revised and amended version as of February 13, 2006)

I. General Comments

Some delegations believed the joint Chinese and Russian initiative is a timely one with a view to cover the loopholes of the current legal system with regard to the peaceful use of outer space. They commended the Russian and Chinese delegations for the Working Paper CD/1679 of June 2002 on draft elements for a PAROS agreement and the three subsequent thematic non-papers, which were useful in helping to identify and consider possible elements of a PAROS treaty.

They also noted the contributions of the three conferences on space security, involving governmental, NGO and academic experts, which were held in Geneva in November 2002, March 2004 and March 2005. These meetings had served to illustrate the wide interest in an agreement on the non-weaponization of outer space. These meetings urged the CD to start substantive work on PAROS issues at an early date so as to enable full-fledged discussion and negotiation on this matter.

One delegation preferred to negotiate as a first step an instrument best regarded as a space-based weapon ban. One delegation suggested working on building norms in the area of space asset safety, rather than negotiating a treaty in the first place. Some delegations suggested starting with CBMs, such as pre-notification of ballistic missile launches.

One delegation suggested giving consideration to putting forward in-depth papers on specific topics, such as "definitions", "the use of outer space for civilian and military purposes", etc, to explore possible legal methods for ensuring the maintenance of a weapons-free outer space. A new title of CD/1679, i.e., "Elements for Dealing with Outer Space Issues" was proposed. A suggestion of avoiding duplicating the work of the Committee on the Peaceful Uses of Outer Space (UNCOPUOS) at Vienna was also made.

As regards working out an international instrument on outer space, it was suggested that the most efficient legal approach would be to incrementally secure international instruments in the areas where consensus may exist.

It was repeatedly noted that the Conference on Disarmament was the designated forum to carry out the relevant negotiations. Negotiation efforts should be coordinated within and between

---

[1] Prepared by the delegations of Russia and China to the CD on the basis of comments and suggestions made by members and observers of the CD and the UNIDIR in their notes, non-papers, addresses and consultations, as well as statements and interventions at the open-ended meetings on PAROS, including on August 16, 2005.

the different forums dealing with specific aspects of outer space: the CD, the UNCOPUOS, the UNGA First Committee, the NPT review process.

In addition to discussing comprehensive legal norms for a ban on space based weapons it also makes sense to include measures for space security that are easier to obtain because they more or less serve the interests of all states, such as space monitoring, confidence building, debris reduction, space cooperation, and rules of the road.

II. Definitions

Some countries are suggesting definitions should be included in the proposed treaty. It was suggested that the thematic non-paper on definitions issues of PAROS would form the basis of focused discussions in a working group or in the CD. One delegation reiterated that a technical examination of these definitions would be necessary

It was also recommended that the number of definitions included in an international legal instrument on PAROS should be kept to a minimum. It was recalled in this context that the Outer Space Treaty had no definitions. Even with a shortened list, one will have to guard against becoming stuck on any definition. For example, a definition to delimit "outer space" has been discussed by the COPUOS Legal Subcommittee since 1959 without agreement.

A section containing definitions of the major key terms or expressions would help to clarify the intended scope of the treaty.

The definition of a "space object" would be useful. It might therefore be best to coin a term or phrase other than "space object" to clarify the intent of the instrument.

This paragraph would benefit from definitions for "objects" and "weapons" to enunciate clearly the scope of the intended obligation and help establish clarity of purpose.

More clarity might also be gained if a "weapon" were defined in terms of a component of a system, its intended effects and the means it employs to achieve its intended effects.

"Peaceful purposes" includes "non-aggressive" military use of outer space. The term "peaceful purposes" could be explicitly defined.

"Peaceful purposes" includes "other military purposes". "Other military purposes" should be clearly defined.

The term "trajectory" should be clarified, because objects like intercontinental missiles are not outer space weapons, although they partly pass through outer space.

The notion of "peaceful use" should be defined to exclude different interpretations of the proposed Agreement's provisions aimed to prevent the deployment of weapons, the threat or use of force in outer space.

CD/1769
Page 4

Some definitions that deal with physical issues should not be seen as irresolvable. With "space objects" being ruled by orbital mechanics, it is not necessary to set a precise line where outer space begins.

Banning weapons in space should focus on those systems that are "specially designed" to destroy space objects (including ASAT on the ground, in the sea or air) and space objects themselves specially designed to destroy any other target. While the clause "specially designed" does not resolve the dual-use issue, it would include a large class of the most threatening systems and activities.

Another issue is the difference between a generic weapon system and a system that might be used as a weapon (an ASAT vs. the space shuttle). A related issue is a weapon intended for one purpose (ABM) but which has a residual capability in another field (ASAT). These points are not captured. The text defining weapons does not include terrestrially based ASAT weapons.

The language on location of launchers technically would not cover sea launch activities or any other launch activities that are not undertaken "in the territory of a state."

Missing here is any discussion of weapons used to support aggressive military activities - targeting and cueing satellites, for example, or even GPS. A third paragraph should be devoted to uses that go beyond non-aggressive use.

The line about "self-protection" for cosmonauts opens cracks that might be abused; that measure does not seem necessary. This item should not be included as it defeats the purpose, as some states may demand other weapons for "self-defense." Various agreements already pledge all states to help astronauts in distress.

There is a need to provide definitions for "space debris" and "launching state". The latter is fundamental for all space activities. As a starting point of reference, the Liability and Registration Conventions can be used, as they provide a definition for "launching state", although not perfect one.

One delegation suggested that the treaty must ban only offensive weapons in space. There should be an exception for weapon-like systems for satellite protection against debris.

It was also suggested to define "non-destructive" space weapons and "legitimate military activities".

III. Basic Obligations

Para. 1: a) The words "testing", "production", "deployment", "transfer" and "use" could be used to elaborate the intended prohibitions; b) Include new sub-para: "prohibition on the deployment of weapons on orbital trajectories to and from celestial bodies including the Moon, or in orbit around the Moon or any other celestial body".

Para. 2: a) The reference to "general principles of international law" in Article V of CD/1679 could perhaps cover the issue of "threat or use of force" curbing the need for definitions; b) The concept of a temporary operational disruption, displacement or other non-damaging interference with a space object by another space object may also need to be addressed; c) Frame the inherent use ban of this obligation to include the testing of any weapons against space objects or "for anti-satellite purposes".

Para. 3: International trade in dual-use space hardware, software and technical data is enormous, thus this obligation could be hard to fulfill. Suggestions: a) Consider controls or limitations on launches of weapons into outer space on behalf of other states; or b) Focus on the use of the hardware, software and technical data, which have to be consistent with the obligations set out in the instrument.

Should include prohibition of objects not only in orbit, but also in a trajectory status taking the spirit of Article 3 (3) of the Agreement Governing the activities of States on the Moon and other Celestial Bodies.

It was proposed that such an instrument need not be a blanket prohibition on all weapons in space. A gradation of measures could be envisaged: from prohibitive measures, through restrictive measures and to permissive measures. For example, measures relating to lasers would therefore not be prohibitive but rather restrictive (allowing the use of only certain categories of lasers while banning other uses).

A treaty should not only focus on deployment restraints but also on the whole process from research to use. A test ban for space weapons is the key issue in this process as it limits capabilities before they emerge and is the most visible part to be monitored. In addition, there should be a monitoring system also focusing on the production process and production facilities.

A concern was voiced that it could be counter-productive to seek to include measures to prevent temporary and reversible disruption of normal functioning of outer space objects. Jamming technology is already widely available, as are other types of electronic warfare.

IV. The Use of Outer Space for Peaceful and Other Military Purposes

In Para. 2, a variation of the OST could be considered in this context: "States Parties shall carry on activities [...] in outer space [,including the Moon and other celestial bodies]in accordance with the general principles of international law, including the Charter of the United Nations, in the interest of maintaining international peace and security and promoting international cooperation and understanding".

Some concrete steps towards securing the peaceful use of outer space were accentuated. It was suggested that the UNGA: pass a resolution defining the "peaceful uses of outer space" (prohibiting weapons in space but allowing military uses of space); seek an advisory opinion of the International Court of Justice on the definition of the "peaceful uses" clause; and convene an open-ended working group or establish an Ad-Hoc Committee within the CD to discuss a treaty on cooperative security in outer space.

V. CBMs

Consider moving from CBMs to actual verification measures, of a sort sufficient to generate the evidence upon which objective compliance determinations could be made, and to feed into the dispute resolution mechanism.

Since the International Code of Conduct on Prevention of Proliferation of Ballistic Missiles (ICOC) aims to increase confidence by such transparency measures as pre-launch notification, its relevant wording can be incorporated into CD/1679 to win the support of ICOC subscribing states.

The wording of CBMs for a future outer space treaty should refer to multilaterally negotiated and internationally accepted languages rather than copying non-negotiated text. In this context, the experience gained in civil space activities could be used for elaborating Codes of Conduct.

Establish a regime of prior notification of launches of space launchers and ballistic missiles which could be supplemented by the setting-up of an international center responsible for the centralization and redistribution of collected data, so as to increase the transparency of space activity.

The States parties should transmit in writing to an international center notification of launches of space launchers (carrying satellites or other space objects) and ballistic missiles which they have planned. Such notification could take place one month before the planned date of launch (launch windows in terms of weeks or days, and time of each launch) and would be confirmed 24 hours before the actual launch.

As for space launchers, apart from the planned date of launch, the launching state should communicate the geographic impact area.

Regarding space objects, the owning State or State of registry should communicate the following information:

Name of owning State or State of registry; Orbital parameters (perigee, apogee, nodal period, inclination); General function of the space object; Reference to its unarmed character; Indication of maneuverability; Physical characteristics (mass, planned lifetime).

With respect to missiles with a ballistic trajectory having a range of 300 km or more, the launching State should communicate:

Date of launch; Launching area; Impact area.

An international notification center should be set up. The center would essentially fulfill the following function:

CD/1769
Page 7

Receive notifications of launches of ballistic missiles and space launchers transmitted to it by States parties;

Receive the information transmitted by States parties on launches actually carried out. State-parties, possessing detection capabilities shall communicate to the international center, on a voluntary basis, data relating to launches detected by them;

Place through a data bank, the above-mentioned information at the disposal of the international community.

The view was expressed that other measures for space security ought to be also included, such as: space monitoring; debris reduction; space cooperation; "rules of the road", and further confidence building. It would also lay the necessary foundation for any future treaty.

Negotiating a treaty might take time and therefore immediate work on building norms in the area of space asset safety is essential. Improved space surveillance and data exchange would not only help to get a better handle on dangerous space debris and improve collision avoidance, but would also increase transparency of space operations that, in and of itself, would be a CBM.

A number of concrete CBMs was suggested that could be taken in parallel to negotiating a treaty on the prevention of weaponization of outer space and that would enhance security in outer space. Among other steps, nations could agree not to undertake weapon tests, including because they would create significant amounts of debris.

Establish "rules of the road", or a code of conduct, to regulate activities in outer space. A code of conduct in outer space, as proposed, would mean: no simulated attacks on space assets and satellites, no dangerous maneuvers, advance notice of maneuvers, no harmful laser use, mitigation of debris, advance notice of launch, regulation of access and launch, and no interference with national technical means. A code of conduct would require: cooperative monitoring, transparency, notification, traffic management and tracking, and verification.

It was suggested that states may seek inspiration from the Incidents at Sea Agreement, which defines good practice, in particular to avoid collisions and ambiguous situations.

Self-declared moratoria on tests and placement of weapons in space would also be an important political gesture of good will. Unilateral declarations by states not to be the first to place weapons in space could be very useful in promoting a "coalition of the willing" to prevent weaponization.

Space exploration is costly and is best served through international cooperation. A regime of international collaboration in space would prevent certain countries from the temptation of putting weapons in space by allaying their security concerns.

VI. Verification

It was suggested that as no weapons have yet been deployed in outer space, the verification measures under discussion are purely preventive in nature, and consensus must be achieved first on the prevention of deployment of weapons in outer space, rather than verification. Once a ban on the weaponization of outer space is realized, other issues, like verification, might be easier to approach.

Some countries suggested verification should be included in the proposed treaty.

Verification measures could include: open source information analysis; state declarations; terrestrial observation of space objects; space-based observation of space objects; sensors on board space objects for in situ sensing, and on on-site inspections. The negotiating parties of the treaty would first need to agree on the obligations to be verified and the level of confidence to be required.

CBMs could be included in this article.

As a further confidence building measure, there should be a moratorium on the testing of all kinds of weapons and development of weapons in outer space.

Verification is an essential element of the proposed treaty that could provide for the settlement of any concerns over other States parties' adherence to the treaty. It was suggested that verification issues could not be easily postponed.

Others argued that the technical challenges in ensuring effective verification of compliance with such an agreement, coupled with the political difficulties, meant that the development of a verification mechanism would have to be postponed and addressed within an additional protocol.

It was suggested that with current technology, and coupling in new reporting requirements for launchers and operators, an international system could be put together to carry out space surveillance with reasonable accuracy.

Verification of a treaty for outer space could adopt a layered approach of sufficient intrusiveness to discern weapon-related developments from non-weapon developments, even in an industry where military and civilian technologies are similar and missions frequently dual-use.

According to the 1975 Convention on Registration, launching states are required only to report the initial insertion orbit of a satellite, not its final destination. That is a critical loophole that needs to be plugged to ensure verification.

Space monitoring could be developed further. Some space-faring nations have a space tracking network that can be linked. With existing technical equipment and use of Internet, a lot of information can be gathered and exchanged, as is already being done to a degree.

CD/1769
Page 9

While understanding concerns about verification of any treaty that includes terrestrially based ASATs, testing of such weaponry could be banned and that ban could be verified.

A number of steps could be undertaken at an early stage, including better implementation of existing commitments, elaboration and adoption of CBMs.

Specific issues contained in the Russian-Chinese thematic paper on verification deserve a careful technical study. In this context one of the relevant issues is the cost of verification.

Verification is more than a purely technological issue and will require extensive discussion.

VII. Settlement of Disputes

Introduction of a third party mechanism might be useful. The entire section on Settlement of Disputes could be redrafted to mirror Paragraphs (2) and (3) of Article 15 of the Moon Treaty, along the following lines:

"A State Party which has reason to believe that another State Party is not fulfilling the obligations incumbent upon it pursuant to this Agreement or that another State Party is interfering with the rights which the former State has under this Agreement may request consultations with that State Party. A State Party receiving such a request shall enter into such consultations without delay. Any other State Party which requests to do so shall be entitled to take part in the consultations. Each State Party participating in such consultations shall seek a mutually acceptable resolution of any controversy and shall bear in mind the rights and interests of all States Parties. The Secretary-General of the United Nations shall be informed of the results of the consultations and shall transmit the information received to all States Parties concerned".

"If the Consultations do not lead to mutually acceptable settlement which has due regard for the rights and interests of all States Parties, the parties concerned shall take all measures to settle the dispute by other peaceful means of their choice appropriate to the circumstances and the nature of the dispute. If difficulties arise in connection with the opening of consultations or if consultations do not lead to a mutually acceptable settlement, any State Party may seek the assistance of the Secretary-General [in this context, the Executive Organization perhaps], without seeking the consent of any other State Party concerned, in order to resolve the controversy".

The joint working paper could also benefit from including provisions for the gathering and examination of agreed verification information as part of the operation of the dispute resolution mechanism.

A number of questions of detail will need to be settled. For example, which rules of procedure are to be applied? How will decisions be reached? Will the decisions be binding? If so, what would be the enforcement mechanism(s)?

CD/1769
Page 10

The relevant text of CD/1679 should be maintained since it is much better than the relevant part of the "Compilation of Comments and Suggestions to the CD PAROS Working Paper" of July 31, 2003.

The relevant content of CWC and BWC can be consulted in this article.

VIII. Executive Organization

This section needs significant expansion to address issues related to membership and authority of the Executive Organization, its exact mandate in relation to the settlement of disputes, and the case of whether an exiting organization could be pressed into service in lieu of creating a new body.

Para.1 a). Revise as: receive for consideration inquiries by any State Party or a group of States Parties to the Treaty related to a dispute aroused by a suspected violation of this Treaty by any State Party to the Treaty;

Para.1 d). This obligation could be read as an unbounded set of incentives or penalties. The treaty would need to set out clear provisions of objective criteria and verified evidence to ascertain non-compliance, and details of the decision-making mechanism.

The obligation of the executive organization and the mandate of meetings of State Parties should be clearly stipulated.

This Article should address issues related to membership and authority of the Executive Organization and its mandate to consider and resolve disputes. The CWC offers some useful food for thought in this regard, as does the IAEA Statute.

The role of the Executive Organization in registration - one of the fundamental verification means - should be explored.

IX. Amendments to the Treaty

The second half of Para. 2 shall spell out explicitly the amendment procedure of the OST: "Any State Party to the Treaty may propose amendments to this Treaty. Amendments shall enter into force for each State Party to the Treaty accepting the amendments upon their acceptance by the majority of the States Parties to the Treaty and thereafter for each remaining State Party to the Treaty on the date of acceptance by it".

This part should be consistent with the relevant content of the Vienna Convention on the law of the treaties.

X. Signature and Ratification of the Treaty

Instruments of ratification should be deposited with UN Secretary General.

XI. Entry-into-Force of the Treaty

Ratification of P5 should not be the precondition for treaty EIF, in order to avoid the fate of the CTBT. This is unduly restrictive and could act to condemn the entry-into-force to failure. It might be more effective to define a number of ratifications for EIF rather than to establish an explicit list of countries. It is better to avoid such a placement of P5 in an EIF formulation. One may consider two options:

Option 1: List all states with a space launch capability but indicate that the ratification of a specified number (i.e. not all) of them would trigger entry-into-force;

Option 2: Request ratification by a specific number of "states that can successfully launch objects into outer space" or something along those lines, rather than naming them.

It is the lack of political will rather than the EIF clause that obstructed CTBT from EIF. Conversely, the point was made that the future treaty should be ratified by all P5 states. Otherwise the effectiveness of the Treaty will be weakened.

A doubt was expressed over the relevance of ratification by 20 states as a precondition for the treaty EIF. It was underlined that the treaty would be effective only if ratified by all the states with capabilities in outer space.

XII. International Cooperation

The elements of cooperation and assistance of peaceful use of outer space should also be added to the proposed treaty.

"International cooperation" and "CBMs" are closely related, so they can be merged into one section. The proposed language is as follows: "Each State party shall endeavor to establish joint projects and programmes with other State parties to further promote peaceful uses of outer space for the benefit of all humankind".

"States shall follow the principle of mutual cooperation and assistance in the most adequate way, on an equitable and mutually acceptable basis, taking into account the particular needs of developing countries".

CD/1769
Page 12

XIII. Possible Additional Elements

Periodic review conferences.

An obligation not to enter into international obligations contrary to the obligations of the treaty.

Naming of the depository governments.

A requirement that a state party to the treaty may not make reservations.

A special provision banning anti-satellite weapons.

Specific technical measures to mitigate and prevent debris creation, as well as to track and to eliminate debris.

A specific language for issues of registration and liability.

———

About the Author

JEFFREY G. LEWIS is Executive Director of the Project on Managing the Atom at the Belfer Center for Science and International Affairs at the John F. Kennedy School of Government, Harvard University. He is also a member of the Editorial Advisory Board of the *Bulletin of the Atomic Scientists*. He founded and maintains the blog ArmsControlWonk.com.

Before going to the Belfer Center, he was a Research Fellow at the Center for International and Security Studies at the University of Maryland School of Public Policy (CISSM). He has previously held positions with the Association of Professional Schools of International Affairs, Center for Strategic and International Studies, and Office of the Undersecretary of Defense for Policy.

He received his Ph.D. in Policy Studies (International Security and Economic Policy) from the University of Maryland and his B.A. in Philosophy and Political Science from Augustana College in Rock Island, Illinois.

Index

THE AMERICAN ACADEMY OF ARTS AND SCIENCES

Founded in 1780, the American Academy of Arts and Sciences is an independent policy research center that conducts multidisciplinary studies of complex and emerging problems. The Academy's elected members are leaders in the academic disciplines, the arts, business and public affairs. With a current membership of 4,000 American Fellows and 600 Foreign Honorary Members, the Academy has four major goals:

- Promoting service and study through analysis of critical social and intellectual issues and the development of practical policy alternatives;

- Fostering public engagement and the exchange of ideas with meetings, conferences, and symposia bringing diverse perspectives to the examination of issues of common concern;

- Mentoring a new generation of scholars and thinkers through the Visiting Scholars Program;

- Honoring excellence by electing to membership men and women in a broad range of disciplines and professions.

The Academy's main headquarters are in Cambridge, Massachusetts.

THE COMMITTEE ON INTERNATIONAL SECURITY STUDIES

The Academy's Committee on International Security Studies (CISS), founded in 1982, plans and sponsors multi-disciplinary studies of current and emerging challenges to global peace and security. Recent and ongoing CISS projects examine: the governance of outer space, international security relationships in the region of the former Soviet Union, the costs and consequences of the war in Iraq, the global security implications of joint missile surveillance, and the implications of the International Criminal Court for U.S. national security. For more information on CISS, visit our website: http://www.amacad.org/projects/ciss.aspx.

CISS publications include:

Russian and Chinese Responses to U.S. Military Plans in Space, by Pavel Podvig and Hui Zhang (forthcoming).

United States Space Policy: Challenges and Opportunities, by George Abbey and Neal Lane (2005).

The Physics of Space Security: A Reference Manual, by David Wright, Laura Grego, and Lisbeth Gronlund (2005).

War with Iraq: Costs, Consequences, and Alternatives, by Carl Kaysen, Steven E. Miller, Martin B. Malin, William D. Nordhaus, and John D. Steinbruner (2002).

The Significance of Joint Missile Surveillance, by John D. Steinbruner (2001).

To order publications or for more information, please contact CISS at the American Academy of Arts & Sciences, 136 Irving Street, Cambridge, MA 02138.

Phone: 617-576-5024; email: ciss@amacad.org; Website: www.amacad.org.